SOCIAL WORK RECORDS

SECOND EDITION

SOCIAL WORK RECORDS

Jill Doner Kagle

Wadsworth Publishing Company
Belmont, California
A Division of Wadsworth, Inc.

1991

Social Work Editor: Peggy Adams
Editorial Assistant: Cathie Fields
Production Editor: Angela Mann
Managing Designer: Kaelin Chappell
Print Buyer: Barbara Britton
Designer: Leigh McLellan
Copy Editor: Robin Kelly
Compositor: DEKR Corp.
Cover: Nancy Brescia

Printed in the United States of America 49

1 2 3 4 5 6 7 8 9 10—95 94 93 92 91

Library of Congress Cataloging in Publication Data

Kagle, Jill Doner.
Social work records / Jill Doner Kagle.—2nd ed.
p. cm.
Previous ed.: Homewood, Ill. : Dorsey Press, 1984.
Includes bibliographical references.
ISBN 0-534-13986-8
1. Social service—Records and correspondence. 2. Social case work reporting. I. Title.
HV43.K27 1991
651.5—dc20 90-12350
CIP

Contents

Preface

Recording has always been an integral part of social work practice. Although the content and structure of records have changed through the years, social workers today, like those in the past, routinely document their services to clients. Records have many uses. Early in the history of the profession, Mary Richmond based her important study of practice, *Social Diagnosis*, on case records. Later, Gordon Hamilton showed that records were useful not just in the development of practice knowledge but also in enhancing services to clients. Today, records that document the purpose, plan, and progress of services promote case continuity, facilitate communication among professionals who are delivering services to the client, and serve as a basis for supervision, consultation, and peer review. They also may be used as a practice tool, supporting communication and providing feedback to the client and the worker.

Records also play an important part in the operation of educational, health, and human service organizations and departments. Records are the primary repository of information about clients and services and therefore are central to professional and organizational accountability. Records are used in claiming reimbursement for services that have been delivered and in seeking and maintaining funding for service programs. Records inform case management, caseload management, and agency management. Information culled from records demonstrates that the practitioner and the organization adhere to regulations, policies, and standards. Agencies may be asked to submit their records for accreditation review, utilization review, or court review. Managers use information in records in deciding how to allocate resources. Records are used to evaluate the quality of services as well as their efficiency and effectiveness.

The proliferation of uses for records, in an increasingly complex service environment, acts as a force toward keeping more detailed and inclusive records. There are other pressures in this direction as well. Social work practitioners and the organizations in which they work are being asked not just to describe what they do but to justify that it should be done, that they should do it, and that it should be funded at specified levels. Workers, then, are encouraged toward extensive documentation to show what was done, why it was done, and what effect it had on the client-situation. In addition, workers are asked to consider both current and potential future uses for information when they decide what to include in their records. If workers include more information than is clearly relevant at the time of recording, it may be because they believe the additional information may be important later. Finally, these records may be voluminous because they document the wide range of personal and social needs addressed in the course of service to a client. The complexity of social work records, then, mirrors the depth and breadth of social work practice.

At the same time, some opposing forces encourage social workers to simplify and limit the content of records. Of course, the most important of these forces is cost. Recordkeeping is time-consuming and therefore costly. Cutbacks in funding of the social services mean that agencies have fewer social workers managing larger caseloads supported by fewer clerical workers. Any time freed up from recordkeeping is available for other activities, notably providing services to clients. Moreover, the increasing potential for violations of the confidentiality of information in records also acts to discourage over-documentation. Although privacy legislation places limits on the flow of information into, within, and out of service organizations, a wide audience has access to records or to some of their contents. Records generally are accessible to professionals and nonprofessionals within the organization and may be available to clients and their families. Information culled from records is sent to pertinent insurance companies and may be accessible to employers or other interested parties. If there are breaches in security, others may gain access to confidential information in manual or computerized information systems. This diverse audience may not use personal information in ways that serve the best interests of the client, the worker, the organization, or the service transaction.

These conflicting forces characterize the environment in which social workers are asked to prepare their records. Practitioners today face increased demands for accountability, while they also must try to serve more clients with fewer resources. Social workers often have too little time to fulfill their responsibilities. With other more pressing demands on their time, it is not surprising that recordkeeping falls behind. Agencies cite three major record-keeping problems: (1) workers have insufficient time for recordkeeping, (2) recordkeeping takes too much time, and (3) records are not up-to-date. As a result of the overwhelming demand upon social workers' time, their records often do not reflect the quality of thought and action that has gone into the service transaction. Moreover, recordkeeping, never an easy task for most workers, has become more troublesome. Workers today seldom have the time to use the recording process as a time to reflect on continuing cases; indeed, they are often playing "catch-up" on cases that are completed. In many agencies, recording has become more of an administrative than a clinical activity. In some agencies, the demand for accountability appears even to have taken precedence over service delivery (Edwards & Reid, 1989). Unfortunately, when practitioners fail to keep up with their recordkeeping, they are sometimes called "resistant." Practitioners, in turn, often blame managers for unfair and unrealistic expectations and fault social work education for inadequately preparing them for the task. Although practitioners, managers, and social work educators have a role to play in improving social work records and recordkeeping practices, they are not responsible for the current problems in recording. Rather, these problems result from the increased demands placed on social work organizations and practitioners.

Yet, there is hope in this seemingly hopeless situation. The theory of recording in social work, which was formulated in a simpler age, is being revised. Hamilton's assumption about recording is no longer completely true. She wrote:

> "It is not the recording," as a wise case worker once said, "which is difficult; it is the thinking which precedes it." If we can think clearly about the client's needs, his circumstances, and the treatment proposed, the record will shape itself easily and simply. (1938, p. 207)

Certainly, clear thinking is essential, but it is not sufficient.

Practitioners, managers, and educators are beginning to rethink their assumptions about recordkeeping and to develop new policies and procedures that respond to the current practice environment. Recordkeeping today, like the practice it documents, involves many difficult decisions, ranging from choices about agencywide policies to the selection of information for a client's record. Many of these choices are not clear, but they involve weighing costs against benefits. Practitioners must balance one set of principles against another—notably, the value of accountability against the values of efficiency and confidentiality. Recording, then, is not just a practice skill; it involves critical professional judgment at all levels and in every case.

Social Work Records is an attempt to revise contemporary theory about recordkeeping. It is intended to aid social workers in developing their knowledge and skill in recordkeeping and to inform their critical policy and practice decisions. This book is the product of two grants, the Social Work Records Project, 1979–1983, and the Records II Project, 1987–1988, funded by the Lois and Samuel Silberman Fund. These projects have involved extensive reviews of social work literature; three surveys of agencies; interviews with agency-based and independent practitioners, supervisors, and managers; and a series of workshops conducted by the author.

Social Work Records presents an overview of the current status of recordkeeping in social work practice. It describes the process of recording but focuses on the product, the record. It delineates many of the issues facing practitioners at all levels of the organizational hierarchy and suggests alternative resolutions. It proposes guidelines for improving agencywide recordkeeping policies and procedures, and for selecting and organizing information in each case. It presents a number of forms and formats for recording, which may be adopted as is or may be adapted to suit particular needs. Finally, it proposes an approach to recordkeeping that is congruent with the current realities of practice and that can accommodate future change.

Chapter 1 defines and describes the contemporary social work record and introduces current issues in recordkeeping. It discusses the varied uses for records in direct practice, in the organization, in the service network, and in the profession. A brief historical review links recording to its current status and traces many of the dilemmas in recording to their roots.

Chapter 2 presents an overview of the content of social work records. It offers a model for selecting a record's content from the array of information about the client-situation and the service transaction available to the practitioner. It then outlines the elements of content in sequence, linking the record temporally to the phases of service: exploration, formulation, implementation, and evaluation. Finally, the chapter describes in some detail each element of content, including the social history, assessments of the client-situation, the plan of service, the closing summary, and follow-up information.

Chapters 3, 4, and 5 focus on the structure of the record, describing and analyzing a wide range of approaches, formats, and forms used in selecting and organizing information in the record. Each of these chapters also includes examples from social work records. Chapter 3 presents records used primarily in educating students; it also suggests ways for improving education for recording. These records are generally far more extensive than those used in day-to-day practice. Chapter 4 focuses on clinical records, including the narrative summary format as well as the problem-oriented record, time-series records, and goal attainment scaling. Chapter 5 presents a number of forms, using both fixed-choice and open-ended fields, that may be used in documentation of clinical or management information.

Chapter 6 presents issues in practice from both the direct-service and the administrative perspective. The author answers questions about improving the quality of records, using records to enhance practice, using records in private practice, client recordkeeping, reducing the costs of recording, retaining and destroying old records, and using records in research.

Chapter 7 describes privacy as an ethical as well as a legislative mandate. The discussion focuses on the principles of privacy—confidentiality, abridgment, access, and anonymity—and on the policies and procedures that support these principles. These policies and procedures include informed consent, authorization for release of information, and privileged communication. The author suggests general guidelines for evaluating records for adherence to these principles and for improving policies and procedures. This chapter presents a number of important issues facing social workers, including the limits of confidentiality, the handling of sensitive information, the social work role in advocating for client privacy, and the use of the record in court proceedings.

Chapter 8 discusses computerized recordkeeping. Most agencies today automate portions of their records. Social agencies use computers for word processing and management information processing. The chapter describes a number of approaches to automation available to social agencies and departments. Each approach is evaluated in terms of its special characteristics, uses, advantages, and disadvantages. The chapter highlights some of the problems that social agencies have encountered when automating their records. Among the most important aspects to consider here is the role of the practitioner in an agency that has acquired a computer. Although the computer is used to manage information, it leaves the practitioner's recordkeeping task largely unchanged and increases the demand for documentation.

Social Work Records is designed for a wide audience of students, practitioners, and managers. Although not specifically written as a textbook, it can be successfully integrated into courses on direct service and administration, and it should be particularly valuable in the field practicum and seminar. Practitioners at all levels of the service hierarchy will find the review of familiar concepts, new approaches to recordkeeping, and guidelines for evaluating and improving records especially helpful. For the profession as a whole, a critical reappraisal of recordkeeping policy and practice, of problems and alternative solutions, is long overdue. In an environment of scarcity and skepticism about the very existence of our clients' needs and about the relevance of our services, it is vitally important that our records, which we must rely upon in practice and in the organization, keep pace with the significant changes that have taken place in recent years.

Jill Doner Kagle

Acknowledgments

The support of a grant from the Lois and Samuel Silberman Fund made possible the breadth and depth of the research that forms the foundation of this book. I am grateful to the entire grant committee, and to Dr. Ellen Winston and Dr. Thomas Horton in particular, for their strong commitment to the project. I owe special thanks to Buddy Silberman for his genuine interest, his wide knowledge, and his unfailing good advice.

I am indebted to the direct-service workers, supervisors, and administrators who participated in surveys and workshops, and who let me observe their policies, procedures, and practices. They taught me much of what I know about records, and their probing questions impelled me to search for better answers.

In preparing both editions of this book, I received the advice and encouragement of many of my colleagues at the University of Illinois School of Social Work. In addition, I am grateful for the advice on computer applications that I received from Jonathan Kagle and for the help in design that I received from Matthew Kagle. Finally, I thank Steven Kagle, editor and cheerleader, whose wisdom and skill are exceeded only by his forebearance.

I wish to acknowledge and thank the following social work students, practitioners, managers, and educators who made a special contribution to *Social Work Records*:

Robert Barker, D.S.W., National Catholic University School of Social Service

William R. Benedict, A.C.S.W., Lutheran Social Services of Wisconsin and Upper Michigan

Philip Carey, M.S.W. student, research assistant on the Records I Project

Janice Hays Chadha, A.C.S.W., St. Louis University School of Social Service

Mary Darbes, M.S.W., research assistant on the Records II Project

Gerald Euster, Ph.D., University of South Carolina School of Social Work

Daniel Finnegan, Ph.D., State University of New York at Albany School of Social Welfare

Jannah J. Hurn, Ph.D., Florida State University School of Social Work

Mei-O Hsieh, Ph.D., research assistant on the Records II Project

Howard Hess, Ph.D., Indiana University School of Social Work

Cynthia Ozar, M.S.W. student, research assistant on the Records II Project

Ann Montz, M.S.W., research associate on the Records I Project

Lee Melhado, Ph.D. (chemistry), M.S.W. student, University of Illinois School of Social Work, Urbana-Champaign

Robert Mitchell, A.C.S.W., Seven Counties Services, Louisville, Kentucky

John Poertner, Ph.D., University of Kansas School of Social Welfare

Elaine Schott, M.S.W., C.S.W., Grand Valley College School of Social Work

Gary Shaffer, Ph.D., University of North Carolina School of Social Work

Judith C. Staley, Ph.D., Southern Illinois University School of Social Work

Merlin Taber, Ph.D., University of Illinois School of Social Work, Urbana-Champaign

Martin Tracy, Ph.D., University of Iowa School of Social Work

Leila Whiting, A.C.S.W., National Association of Social Workers, National Office, Washington, DC

Barbara Wichell, A.C.S.W., University of Illinois, Jane Addams College of Social Work, Chicago

Karl Zimmer, A.C.S.W., Our Lady of the Lake University of San Antonio, Worden School of Social Service

And the staff of 180 social work agencies and departments in 20 states who participated in the Records I and II survey

Reviewers Grafton H. Hull, University of Wisconsin-Eau Claire; Karen Kirst-Ashman, University of Wisconsin-Whitewater; and Paul A. Sundet, University of Missouri, all provided helpful suggestions for the second edition.

J.D.K.

1 Introduction

Recordkeeping is an important component of social work practice. Social workers keep records to document and retain information about their clients and about the process and progress of their services. Individual records are used in planning, implementing, and evaluating services to each client. Aggregated records are used in planning, monitoring, and evaluating services to groups of clients. Recording is a clinical as well as an administrative function. The record is a focal point for accountability to the client, to the organization, and to the profession.

Social work records vary widely. This diversity reflects the diversity of social work practice. Records are intended to highlight the special nature of each service transaction, and different styles of recording are appropriate for different service patterns, practice approaches, and organizational characteristics. Nonetheless, in general, social work records adhere to the following definition:

	Social Work Records
(Focus)	Individualize and typify the client, the need, the situation, and the service transaction
(Scope)	Link goals, plans, and activities to the assessment of the client-need-situation and to the resources available
(Purpose)	Facilitate the delivery of services to or on behalf of the client
(Functions)	Through the process of making the record, which involves reviewing, selecting, analyzing, and organizing

information; and through the product, the record itself, which becomes an important resource in communication about the case

The social work record has a number of uses. These uses are delineated in the following section.

Uses of Social Work Records

Identifying the Client and the Need

Records contain information that identifies the client-situation and the need for service. They contain descriptions and assessments of the client-situation and, in some cases, psychosocial diagnoses, as well as statements about reasons for initiating service and problems that are the focus of attention. This information, which is revised and updated throughout the service transaction, assists in case management and program management. Practitioners review this information to discover or recall basic details of the case. The information establishes the client's eligibility for service and is used in claiming third-party reimbursement for services rendered. When identifying information is pooled and analyzed, the organization can discern and monitor trends in service delivery.

Documenting Services

The record is a repository of information about activities performed with and on behalf of the client, from opening to closing the case. The record is used to document what takes place during each phase of the service process, linking decisions and actions to the client's need for service, and the service goal and plan. Workers describe meetings with the client, conferences with community agencies, and agency case reviews. They also report critical events that influence the client's situation or the service process. The purpose of these reports is to describe and to provide a rationale for the service process. Such information is used in claiming reimbursement, justifying funding, and demonstrating adherence to policy guidelines to outside agencies. It is used within the organization in supervision and consultation as well as in administrative and peer review. This material may also be useful in corroborating the worker's testimony in court proceedings.

Maintaining Case Continuity

One of the most important functions for records is to allow the worker, or others who are delivering services to the client in the worker's absence, to review the case to date. Information about the purpose, plan, process, and progress of service is particularly useful when another worker is asked to take over the case, when some time has elapsed since the previous contact with the client, or when the client-situation is complicated and the service extensive.

Interprofessional Communication

In interdisciplinary settings as well as settings in which services are delivered by a team of social workers, the record facilitates professional collaboration. Although the record can never substitute for team meetings and discussions among service providers, it provides team members with a resource that reinforces group decisions and actions, helps professionals to coordinate individual efforts, and makes new information available to all members of the team.

Sharing Information with the Client

The record may be used as a vehicle for communicating with the client. Some contemporary approaches to practice encourage the worker to share portions of the record or the recording process with the client. For example, a worker asks his client to document each time a specific target behavior occurs; these charts are reviewed during each meeting and become part of the case record. Another worker distributes copies of her summary of the previous group session to group members, who read and comment on the record at the beginning of the subsequent session. Most record sharing, however, is less direct. Privacy legislation and agency policies permit some clients, their families, and others acting on clients' behalf to have access to the record. Although the typical social work client does not read or receive copies of the record, some clients read their records while they are receiving services and others see the record after services have been terminated. In agencies where clients have access to records, workers should be aware that what they write may be read by their clients or by others who will share the contents of the record with the client. Whether or not workers intend them for this purpose, social work records are often a means of communication with the client.

Facilitating Supervision, Consultation, and Peer Review

The record is used by supervisors, consultants, peers, and others who act in an advisory capacity to learn about the client-situation and about the process and progress of service. Supervisors often read client records to gain an appreciation of a particular case or group of cases; they use this information in assisting the worker to plan and implement services. Supervisors also read records to assess the quality of a worker's performance and to discover the worker's strengths as well as areas needing change or further development.

Consultants may review case records before conferring about unique or troublesome cases. Internal committees of direct-service workers and managers, engaged in quality assurance or peer review, use records as a primary resource in evaluating the kind and quality of services provided to clients in selected programs.

Monitoring the Process and Impact of Service

The record is a useful tool in the ongoing evaluation of services. First, the worker and client work out a contract as to the purpose, goals, and plan of service. Then, throughout the service process, the practitioner documents progress in implementing the plan, achieving the goals, and accomplishing the purpose of service. Workers also use the record to document the process of service, assessing its impact upon the client-situation and citing factors that may be facilitating or impeding progress. Records are used not just to document but also to review, evaluate, and modify service activities with and on behalf of the client.

The record, then, is both a descriptive and an evaluative document, for reporting as well as monitoring progress, and for describing as well as influencing practice decisions and actions. Systematic documentation through time can signal the need for changes in service goals and plans. The record can also provide evidence of the pattern of service and, ultimately, its outcome. As described above, the record is useful to the practitioner as well as to supervisors, consultants, and peers who seek to monitor and evaluate service delivery.

Educating Students and Other Professionals

Records have both an explicit and an implicit role in education. They are used to teach social work practice and agency procedure. Although the case method, which once was the principal pedagogical tool for teaching social work practice, has been supplanted by didactic and experiential methods, records are still used to introduce students and new workers to practice in the organization. Furthermore, they are an important tool in the ongoing education and development of each practitioner. Supervisors use the record to teach workers how to practice and how to record. Records also have an implicit role in educating other professionals about social work. When members of other disciplines read what social workers record, they learn about what social workers do and how they do it.

Providing Data for Administrative Tasks

Information about clients and services is used to track clients through the system and inform administrative decisions about client needs, service patterns, workload management, personnel performance, and allocation of resources. Automated recordkeeping systems, now widely used in both large and small organizations, enable administrators to select and process information to help them manage the agency and its resources. Some of the information used in managing the agency comes directly from client records. In addition, workers prepare other forms and reports for management purposes alone. For example, many workers fill out daily logs and monthly statistical reports that are used by administrators to learn about and to evaluate the pattern of practitioners' activities.

Providing Data for Research

In the early years of the profession, research was considered a principal purpose for records. Although it is not clear how often they were used in research, records were thought to be an important source of data on human behavior, social needs, and the role of the social services. Certainly, records were influential in the formulation of social work practice theory (Richmond, 1917). More recently, large-scale studies using case data have strongly influenced agency policy and social work practice. (For example, Fanshel, 1977, has influenced child welfare services.) Perhaps assuming that research must involve similarly large-scale efforts, few agencies now say that they use their records in research. Indeed, many large-scale agency-based research projects do not use data from existing records (see, for example, Toseland, 1987) but use specially designed research instruments. Further, agencies may have difficulty justifying funding for activities labeled "research." Nonetheless, many agencies and practitioners use their records in research. For example, they conduct systematic studies of their clients' needs and their agency's service delivery patterns, or they use single-subject methods for monitoring client behavior and goal achievement.

A Brief History of Social Work Recording

The history of recordkeeping in social work reflects the history of the profession and its developing theories, methods, and roles. New approaches to practice are mirrored in new recording themes and forms. As social work practice has become more complex and varied, social work records, which document practice in action, have become similarly diverse. Yet, the development of social work records also reflects changes in agency structure. As the record has become more important in the management of the organization, the focus of the record has changed. The development of recording in this century can be understood by observing that shifts in the content and focus of the record are linked to changes in its purpose and use.

The first important book entirely devoted to case records, *The Social Case History—Its Construction and Content*, was published in 1920 by Ada Eliot

Sheffield. She described the record, which had developed with the growth of social casework, as

> a body of personal information conserved with a view to the three ends of social case work; namely (1) the immediate purpose of furthering effective treatment of individual clients, (2) the ultimate purpose of general social betterment, and (3) the incidental purpose of establishing the caseworker herself in critical thinking. (pp. 5–6)

It is clear that in common practice of the day, the first of these purposes was dominant, since records were focused on demonstrating the relationship between the client's need and the treatment that was offered. Reflecting this purpose, the record was likely to contain

> a certain range of facts [which] has come to be generally accepted among case workers as uniformly having significance for their purpose. This range would include such items as usually appear on face cards: the client's name and address, the date and place of birth, the nationality, addresses of physicians, employers, and so on. (p. 20)

Recording this information called for "no act of judgment," but was the responsibility of a trained worker. The record would also include information requiring judgment, bearing upon the "client's prospects of successful citizenship: family history, health, employment, education, finances, character" (p. 21).

One senses that, like other authors who later wrote about records, Sheffield wished to move the record—and casework practice—to a new level. She suggested that the worker go beyond this "factual" information to "key conceptions which would give the facts significance." (These conceptions are precursors of today's assessments.) In further work with the client, the worker's aim was to "frame a hypothesis as to what a fact means, and then search for confirmation or disproof in recurrent instances" (p. 38). Sheffield also emphasized the role of the record in advancing knowledge and social betterment. The record was to be a social specialist's report, identifying typical instances of social maladjustment and relating them to defects in the social order.

In 1925, Mary Richmond described the reasons for keeping records. Her description of their uses is as pragmatic—"workers get sick"—as it is wide-ranging. Records could be used in supervision, training, improving treatment, helping the public to understand social work, as well as in studying practice. In response to the question of whether checkings (checklists) could be substituted for narrative records, Richmond presented what she considered irrefutable evidence for narrative records. Not only had checkings been tried with "disastrous results," but her own work could not have been drawn from checkings: "How could these marks have made the sequence of events clear to any one else? Only the fullest and most careful recording made these apparent to me for instance" (p. 216).

In 1928, Ernest Burgess, a sociologist, proposed that caseworkers make their records useful for sociological interpretation by replacing selective narratives with full verbatim reports of the client's statements during interviews. This, he argued, would make the record more valuable to the caseworker and to the researcher, by revealing the "person as he really is to himself . . . in his own language," and would make the record "really objective and open to anyone to interpret" (p. 527). Burgess suggested a very complete record, for it was to include "a verbatim account of the family history, in both husband's and wife's versions; the conception of each regarding his [or her] role in the family and community, philosophy of life, ambitions, attitudes, and plans; attitudes of individuals and the group in family interviews; and interviews with such representative local persons as neighbors, employers, and landlords" (pp. 529–530). In addition, the record was to include, in summary form, a diagnostic statement and a treatment plan, a closing case review, and any conclusions that might be applicable to similar cases.

It is not surprising that Burgess's proposal was met with a strong reaction. Several authors responded by pointing out that, contrary to his contention, verbatim records would be longer than summary narratives—and therefore more expensive to produce—and would necessarily involve selection. And this was not the only criticism of Burgess's proposal. Eliot (1928) argued that it required that "one . . . train and trust a recorder to remember passages supposedly most symptomatic of attitudes relevant to the situation or its solution, and this introduces another chance for bias: in the training of the recorder, in the recorder herself, or both" (p. 540). By asking "Can one be simultaneously scientific and sympathetic? Can one simultaneously experience and reflect? . . . Can one preserve objectivity in a subjective experience?" (p. 542), Eliot was raising a fundamental and persistent question in practice and in recording. Swift (1928) also differed with Burgess, his comments typifying the views of many of his contemporaries as well as those of many future practitioners. He stated that "as used by the caseworker, the ultimate purpose of a case record must be treatment . . . [and therefore the] emphases are not the same as they would be for research purposes" (p. 535). Nonetheless, despite these and other limitations, the verbatim or process record still is used today, but for educational rather than for research purposes. The costs of preparing, transcribing, and reading process records prohibit their constant use.

Whereas the use of records in research is a recurrent issue in the social work literature, research has never become a predominant function of such records. For the two decades following the publication of the Burgess article, the acknowledged purpose of the record was treatment. This focus is apparent in Margaret Cochran Bristol's *Handbook on Social Case Recording*, published in 1936. Here, as in Gordon Hamilton's *Social Case Recording*, first published in the same year, the process of recording, as well as the record itself, has importance in assisting treatment. Bristol stated at the outset that

> the values in case recording are not confined solely . . . to those which are derived from the record after it is prepared. During the process of preparation, critical

> thinking and careful organization of material are stimulated and the worker is compelled to think through the situation and to make an analysis (or diagnosis) of the problems as she might not otherwise be impelled to do. (pp. 5–6)

Bristol emphasized the qualities of accuracy, objectivity, brevity, ease of reference, clarity, color, uniformity, and up-to-dateness for the record. In achieving these qualities, she recognized the difficulties in making records both objective and brief: "Without doubt, one of the most effective methods of shortening the record is by the careful selection of material. Although this procedure may decrease the objectivity of the record, it may increase its value, provided the caseworker has been objective in securing and selecting the material to present" (p. 59). Bristol suggested that the records of the future would resolve this basic conflict, through the use of "more carefully defined terminology, which in turn will permit considerable abbreviation of records without a sacrifice in their objectivity" and through an "increasing emphasis . . . upon the responsibility of the worker to make and record interpretations competently and accurately without the necessity for extensive and detailed descriptions of minute objective phenomena on which her interpretations were based" (pp. 77–78). Bristol envisioned a selective, diagnostic record, not one that was descriptive.

Unlike Sheffield, who suggested that the record focus on common characteristics among clients, Bristol and Hamilton believed that the focus of the record should be individualization. What was unique about the client and the situation formed the core of casework and of the casework record. Both authors also recognized the close relationship between good practice and good recording.

Through Hamilton's work, these concepts became accepted principles of professional practice. For Hamilton, there could be no prototype for the record that could be used as a guide by the practitioner. The content and the structure of the record were inherent in the case itself: "There is no such thing as a model record, no routines which will make the case inevitably clear, accessible, and understandable. Records should be written to suit the case, not the case geared to a theoretical pattern" (p. 2). Furthermore, recording skills would be developed in concert with other practice competencies and would simply reflect the practitioner's diagnostic judgment. According to Hamilton,

> A good record would be that in which, issues having been apprehended early, there is a minimum of fact or thinking irrelevant to the problems under consideration. In the hands of the skilled practitioner, only such material, after the initial study, would be recorded as has bearing on shifts in the hypothesis, with more accurate interpretation and with corresponding developments or changes in treatment. In an ultimate sense only the trained diagnostician can write a good record, for only he can pluck from the unending web of social experience the thread of probable significance. (p. 209)

The record was to be "the writer's attempt to express, as practitioner, the meaning of the case" (p. 44).

Hamilton's themes, with variations, were further developed during the 1940s and 1950s. In both casework and group work, students and novice practitioners would begin with the process record. They would try to reproduce, with as much accuracy as possible, their interaction with clients during interviews and group meetings. Worker and supervisor would then carefully study these records to find the essence of the client's communication and of the treatment process. In this way, knowledge of the case and practice skills were both being developed. Ideally, experienced workers would then move on to diagnostic summary recording, returning to process recording only as an aid to treatment in difficult cases. In reality, this transition from process to summary records was sometimes difficult, and the resulting records were of poor quality.

Three articles published in 1949 revealed the difficulties in moving individual workers and the profession as a whole from process to diagnostic summary recording. Little wrote that agency records were needlessly detailed and attributed this to the failure of schools of social work to prepare students for their responsibilities as practitioners. She said that "the caseworker has not been expected to formulate his tentative diagnosis and the direction of his activities" (p. 15). Sytz proposed methods of teaching diagnostic recording skills in the classroom, and of conceptually linking the process of recording with casework and group work practice. Sackheim described criteria developed in her mental health clinic for selecting information for a condensed, diagnostic record:

1. Meaningful data about the patient
2. Movement in therapy
3. Activity of the worker and client
4. Emotional interaction between worker and client

"What further," she asked, "should be included in a record that would not be excessive detail?" (p. 20). Despite Hamilton's assurance that practice and recording skills would develop simultaneously, then, it was apparent that social workers needed education in diagnostic recording as well as guidelines for selecting information for the diagnostic record.

The attention directed to the record in teaching and learning practice and in assessing and refining diagnostic skills was gradually transforming the purpose of recording. In the minds of many practitioners, the primary purpose was supervision—an assumption supported by some research findings. In their study of recording in two Chicago family service agencies, Frings, Kratovil, and Polemis found that records were being used most frequently in supervision. In 1960, Aptekar wrote that "in most agencies, records are meant to be read by the supervisor" (p. 16).

By the middle 1950s, the diagnostic record was firmly in place. It was selective and analytic. The worker prepared the record for its primary audience, the worker's supervisor. The record was intended to show the supervisor the worker's diagnostic thinking and approach to the case. But, although in theory recording was to be a thinking-planning process, in practice records were often prepared after the work had been completed. As a result, analyses were often retrospective reconstructions of, rather than prospective aids to, the worker's thinking processes.

The 1960s and 1970s brought major changes to social work and to its environment. These changes had a significant impact upon the form and function of the social work record. The community demanded broader accountability from all service professions. Not only were agencies to provide quality services; they were to demonstrate that their services "worked." In response to funding requirements, many organizations moved to supplement or replace diagnostic, process-oriented recording with more systematic documentation of service activities and their effects. During the 1970s, many large and some smaller agencies and hospitals began using automated management information systems and other computer technology in their recordkeeping. New practice models that incorporated innovative recording procedures were introduced into the field. For example, behavioral intervention incorporated ongoing measurement and charting of target behaviors; family therapy introduced routine audiotaping and videotaping of sessions with clients.

Concern for the confidentiality of personal information contained in health, social service, and educational records led to legislation to protect personal privacy. The Freedom of Information Act (1966) and the Family Educational Rights and Privacy Act (1974), for example, established procedures for protecting client privacy in federally financed programs and public education. By the late 1970s, most states had enacted privacy legislation that extended those rights to many clients in health, mental health, and social service organizations. In general, these policies placed limits on information collection and dissemination and provided clients with access to their own records. During this same period, the National Association of Social Workers acted to revise and update its code of ethics (1979) and policy guidelines (1975) regarding the handling of confidential information. The social work literature in the late 1970s reflected professional concerns about changes in privacy policy (McCormick, 1978; Reynolds, 1976, 1977) and described the effects of new policies on recordkeeping procedures in social agencies (Schrier, 1980; Wilson, 1978). Although the literature as a whole showed that professionals were apprehensive about client access (for example, see Prochaska, 1977), some authors described innovative, practical, and positive responses to client access in their own practice (Freed, 1978; Houghkirk, 1977).

New recording models that emerged during this period were dominated by concern for accountability and the documentation of client change. Goal Attainment Scaling (Kiresuk & Sherman, 1968) was developed for use in community mental health centers. This approach, which organizes accountability around program goals, offers a method of describing the intended outcomes of service concretely, linking goals to measures of client behavior, and evaluating client change and goal attainment through time. The Problem-

Oriented Medical Record (Weed, 1968), which organizes accountability around a list of the patient's problems, was developed originally as an aid to medical education. Ideally, the health team generates a list of the patient's problems; then each member of the team organizes his or her activities and chart notes around these problems. However, the team component is absent in many of the health and mental health settings that have adopted the problem-oriented approach; each health professional may generate a problem list independently. Moreover, another method of organizing progress notes is used more often than the problem list. This method, the "SOAP" format, organizes progress notes into four categories (S = subjective information, O = objective information, A = assessment, and P = plan). Several articles in the social work literature introduced the Problem-Oriented Record and suggested adaptations of the model for social work records (Hartman & Wickey, 1978; Johnson, 1978; Kane, 1974). Finally, time-series measures, an integral part of the behavioral model of practice, were introduced to a wider social work audience as a component of a new practitioner-researcher approach to practice (Bloom & Fischer, 1982; Jayaratne & Levy, 1979; Nelsen, 1981). Time-series or single-subject designs, which organize accountability around repeated measurement of target behaviors, thoughts, or feelings, received strong curriculum support from social work education. However, these designs and measurement procedures have not yet been widely adopted as a component of agency-based recording practice.

The social work record has always been an accountability document. Prior to the 1960s, the practitioner was accountable through the record to the supervisor, to other professionals working with the client, and to the organization. During the 1960s and 1970s, the record became a vehicle for accountability to a much wider audience, including accreditation, oversight, and funding organizations, and clients and their families. Furthermore, the focus of accountability changed. Prior to the 1960s, accountability focused on the process of service and the quality of diagnostic thinking; during the 1960s and 1970s, accountability focused on service activities and their impact on the client.

The ability of social workers to respond to accountability requirements has been facilitated by the widespread introduction of computers into social agencies and social work departments. Beginning in the 1970s (Fein, 1975; Young, 1974a, 1974b) and accelerating in the 1980s with the development of personal computers, computers have facilitated recordkeeping through word processing and data processing. Word processing assists in a variety of clerical functions, including preparing narrative records and agency reports. Data processing involves the collection, storage, retrieval, and reporting of coded information that may be used in case, fiscal, personnel, and organization management. Because direct-service workers do not yet have direct access to terminals in most agencies, their task continues to involve writing, typing, or dictating information that is then entered into the computer for processing by others. Although computer-processed records of the 1980s may look quite different from records of the past, the social worker's role in producing the record has changed little.

Contemporary Recording

The history of recording in social work reveals three related themes that help to explain the complexity and diversity of contemporary recordkeeping. In the first place, form has followed function. That is, as new uses for records have emerged, new recording formats have been developed. Each model of recording is associated with and suited to particular functions. Secondly, each recording approach carries with it implicit assumptions about how and what to record, and about how practice should be conducted. For example, the assumptions underlying process recording differ markedly from those of the problem-oriented record. Thirdly, in the field as a whole, newer forms of recording coexist with rather than supplanting older methods. They coexist within the social work record, which typically incorporates both traditional narrative summaries and computer-ready forms. These methods coexist within agencies where workers trained at different times and in different practice approaches may use different styles of recording.

Contemporary social work records are quite diverse in style and format, reflecting variations in service delivery patterns, practice and recording approaches, and organizational settings. They include many different items, such as computer-ready fill-in forms, narrative reports, worker-client contracts, legal documents, videotapes, charts, copies of reports from other agencies, and more. The complexity of the record reflects the complexity of today's practice, the many uses for records, and the broadened definition of accountability. However, records are also becoming remarkably similar in purpose and content, focused on documentation of service delivery. In recordkeeping as in practice, the 1980s were a period not of innovation but of retrenchment. With fewer workers seeing more clients for briefer periods, and with greater demands for documentation, social service organizations are working to streamline their records.

These generalizations are based upon the findings of two national studies of recordkeeping, the first project conducted from 1979 to 1983 and the second during 1987 and 1988. These projects included surveys of recordkeeping policies, procedures, practices, and problems in more than 200 agencies, in 22 states and all regions of the country, as well as interviews and discussions with more than 300 direct-service workers, supervisors, and administrators from social service organizations and departments in 12 states. In all, more than 500 social workers have contributed information to these studies.

These studies indicate that the contemporary social work record usually contains the following information:

Identifying information

A social history, which may be brief or extensive

An opening summary, including a statement of the presenting problem, the reason for referral, and the purpose of service

The worker's assessment of the client-situation

Goals

Plans

Progress (interim) notes

A closing summary

Many records also contain the following information:

A psychosocial diagnosis, based upon the Diagnostic and Statistical Manual—DSM-III (American Psychiatric Association, 1980; revised 1987)

A worker-client contract

Follow-up information

Variations in the content of the record result from differences in emphasis in different fields of practice. For example, a DSM-III diagnosis is routinely documented in mental health and substance abuse agencies but is documented in child welfare, schools, or aging only if pertinent to the case. A psychosocial history is included less often, and follow-up information more often, in agencies serving elderly clients than those serving other client groups. In general, agencies establish minimum guidelines for information to be included in the record, leaving the decision about additional content to the worker. Whereas including a worker-client contract is routine in some organizations, it is left to the worker's discretion in others.

There is considerable variation among agencies and practitioners as to whether and how they document the process of service in records. Some agencies document little process information in the formal record, although workers may keep notes of what transpired in sessions with clients. Some agencies use a one-page form for summarizing the content and process of each session with a client; others suggest that workers summarize a series of sessions at regular intervals. Some agencies use process recording or audiotaping or videotaping to facilitate case review and supervision, but few agencies routinely use these time-consuming and costly methods. Regardless of whether other process information is included in the record, critical incidents such as suicide threats or violent behavior should always be documented carefully. The worker should record promptly and fully a description of what took place, an assessment of the situation, the worker's immediate response, and a plan for further action.

The primary uses of records are:

Service documentation
Case continuity
Interprofessional communication

In addition, most agencies routinely use their records in demonstrating adherence to policies and standards; in accreditation, utilization, and peer review; and in meeting reimbursement requirements. They frequently use records in supervision and education, in evaluating the impact of services, and in informing management decisions. Some agencies routinely use their records in court, but many agencies and practitioners rarely if ever have had their records subpoenaed. Only a few social work agencies use their records in research.

Problems and Solutions

The 1980s were a period of cutbacks for social work agencies and departments. Social workers have been asked to carry larger caseloads of clients with more difficult and entrenched problems and to solve these problems more quickly and with fewer social supports. At the same time, the demands for documentation have increased. It is not surprising, then, that agencies cite a litany of recordkeeping problems, many of which clearly result from the lack of resources. Survey II, conducted in the late 1980s, found the most frequently cited problems to be:

1. Insufficient time available for recordkeeping
2. Recording takes too much time
3. Workers resent or resist recording
4. Insufficient clerical help
5. Lack of storage space
6. Records not up-to-date
7. Records poorly written
8. Funding and accreditation reporting demands unrealistic

Additional problems persist. Some agencies find that records are neither useful nor used; that important information is missing, while insignificant information is included; that recording forms are redundant; that guidelines are out of date or unrealistic; and that information is difficult to retrieve.

As the demand for documentation has increased, so has the complexity of the recording process. In selecting and preparing a record, workers are faced with a number of dilemmas. They must include sufficient information in the record to support its various functions but limit the content to save time and to control costs. Workers must include significant personal details that characterize the client-situation and that explain the basis for decisions and actions in the case; at the same time, they must protect the client's privacy and avoid redundancy. Workers must make the information in the record accessible and useful to its diverse audiences. They must find time to record when there is insufficient time to respond to real and emergent client needs.

If they are to fulfill this difficult but important task, practitioners at a minimum need:

Educational Preparation Recording is especially difficult for practitioners who have not been adequately prepared for the task. Some workers find that they do not possess the writing skills they need. For some, grammar, spelling, and punctuation are a problem. Others have not been taught how to select and summarize important information succinctly. Because recordkeeping is usually taught in the field rather than in the classroom, social workers' experience with recordkeeping is idiosyncratic. That is, workers know the recording style that they learned in their field work agencies. Some receive excellent preparation, learning a recordkeeping approach that will continue to serve them well throughout their careers; others do not. Furthermore, many students spend much more time on process recording, which they seldom will use in practice, than on perfecting the summary recording style they will need. Many practitioners find that there is insufficient carry-over from the records they wrote as students to the records they are expected to prepare after they graduate.

Explicit and Reasonable Guidelines If practitioners are to prepare well-written, timely, and useful records that are also cost-effective, they need explicit and reasonable guidelines regarding the content, structure, and frequency of documentation. Minimum standards regarding what information should be included in the record, how that information should be organized, and when information needs to be entered into the record can help the worker focus the recordkeeping task. Standards should be sufficiently flexible to enable the worker to characterize fairly the special nature of the client-situation and the service process. At the same time, standards should simplify and routinize some of the worker's decisions about recording, create order within each record, and encourage consistency among records.

Adequate Resources Good social work records depend on adequate agency resources. At a minimum, the agency should provide clerical services, equipment, and adequate time for preparing records. Faced with budget cuts, many agencies have reduced the number of clerical workers, deferred purchasing such time-saving equipment as dictaphones, increased caseloads, and decreased time for recording. As a result, workers have had to perform clerical functions, recordkeeping has become more cumbersome, and records have fallen behind. If their records are to improve, agencies need to address these resource problems.

Recording is more than a practice skill; it involves complex professional judgments. In making decisions about what to include in their records, social workers need to consider the following questions:

1. What are the functions of the record? How will information in the record be used? What content and what structure will fulfill these functions best?
2. How can the record best meet accountability requirements? What information should be included in the record to achieve accountability to the client, to the organization, to the profession, to the community, and to funding and accrediting agencies?
3. How can the record best represent the essential elements of service, such as its purpose, plan, process, and progress? How can it best represent the practice modality or service approach?
4. Who will have access to the record or to information in the record? What do privacy laws, regulations, and policies require of records in our agency? How can the content, access, and use of the record be limited to protect client privacy? How will the record affect the client if the client gains access to it?
5. Is there a customary form or structure for the record? Are there established standards or formats for recording in the field? Will use of the record be facilitated by adhering to the common format—for example, the problem-oriented record in health organizations?
6. How can the costs of recording be minimized? Can the costs in time, personnel, and commodities for preparing, transcribing, storing, retrieving, and using the information in the record be limited while the record still fulfills its purposes?

The purpose of the following chapters is to guide social workers in making these important choices. The choices are not and can never be easy ones, because recording in social work today involves mediating between conflicting goals. On the one hand, records should be concise to save resources and to protect the client's privacy. On the other hand, they must be inclusive enough to facilitate service delivery, meet accountability standards, and afford legal protection to the practitioner and to the agency. Even with a clear sense of purpose and explicit guidelines for selecting information and organizing their records, social workers will continue to experience some tension in recording. This tension is inherent in the task itself, because it involves the responsibility for making records that are both efficient and sufficient.

2 Content of Social Work Records

This chapter opens with a brief overview of the diversity of recording in social work today. It then proposes a rationale for selecting pertinent information for each record from the array of available material about the client, the situation, the environment, and the service provided. This rationale is service centered rather than client centered or worker centered. The approach attempts to reconcile the three conflicting goals of contemporary recording—accountability, efficiency, and privacy—while at the same time retaining the essential relationship between the record and the practice it documents. An outline of the primary elements of the record's contents, from identifying information through follow-up, is next, followed by a detailed consideration of each of these elements.

Overview

Social work records are as varied as the practice they document. Each record depicts the unique characteristics of the client-situation and the service transaction. It also reflects the worker's approach to practice in general, to the case in particular, and to the recording process. A record is shaped by the characteristics of the service organization, especially its auspices, its accountability structure, its mode of service delivery, its clientele, and its personnel. Finally, the record is shaped by how it will be used and by who will have access to its contents.

Because social work records are so diverse, making generalizations about their content is fraught with difficulty. Such generalizations may be too superficial to be useful or too specific to be accurate. Nevertheless, although there are differences among records, there are also common characteristics. Furthermore, generalizations about the nature of the record and about its relationship to practice are greatly needed. Therefore, this chapter offers generalizations not only about what is but also about what should be included in social work records.

The Service-Centered Record

A contemporary social work record should be, above all, a record of service. The essential function of the record is to document the bases, substance, and consequences of professional decisions and actions taken in the course of providing services to the client. The record today can no longer be considered a "client record" that serves as a repository for all available information about the client and the situation. Furthermore, the official record cannot incorporate or be limited to the worker's notes—jottings of names, events, working hypotheses, and "hunches." If records are to be efficient, they must be focused and succinct. If they are to protect client privacy, they must be circumscribed. If they are to be accountable, they should be service centered (that is, focused upon information that shows what service decisions and actions were taken, why, and with what impact). They should focus on the information that demonstrates that services were intended to meet the special needs of the client, were delivered in accordance with professional standards and agency policies, and were evaluated for their impact.

Information is relevant for the social work record if and only if it shows how:

the client-situation and the available resources
form the basis for
service decisions and actions, including
the purpose, goals, plan, and process of service,
and how these, in turn,
have an impact upon
the client-situation and the available resources.

Social work decisions and actions are based upon observation and inference. Professional judgment is formed, in part, through observation of the client-situation, the environment, and the transactions between persons and environments. Professional judgment is also formed through the application of knowledge and values to such observations. If documentation is to be meaningful, then, it must contain three components: observations, assessments, and the criteria used in formulating assessments. Records that contain observations but not assessments, or assessments without the observations or criteria upon which the assessments are based (which occurs more often), do not fulfill the goal of accountability.

The following are examples of assessments insufficient to fulfill the goal of accountability:

The patient receives secondary gain from illness.

Jamie has school adjustment problems.

According to Mr. Leonard, Jack has limited vocational skills.

The J family's interaction is characterized by enmeshment.

Martha is clearly inadequate in her role performance.

Mrs. N shows insight.

Mr. T has strong coping capacities.

Unlike Martin, Claire is developing normally.

Rather, assessments should be clearly linked to the observations upon which they are based. The record should contain specific and relevant descriptions from such sources as:

The worker's observations of actions or situations
Observations of other professionals
Information provided by the client or others in the client's social network
Information found in records, reports, or other documents

Moreover, records should include not just the assessments themselves but also some reference to the criteria used in formulating them. Among the criteria that social workers use in making assessments are:

Knowledge of social policy, agency procedures, and the availability of social resources

Knowledge of human development, health and illness, and mental health classification systems (such as DSM-IIIR)

Knowledge of practice concepts, principles, and interventions

Professional values and ethics

Stated client preferences

In general, although the examples of assessments listed above are typical of those found in social work records, they are far too global to be meaningful and too abstract to form the basis for service decisions and actions. Assessments not only should be linked to observations and the criteria used in formulating judgments, but also should be specific and linked to plans for action to be taken. For example:

Reason for Social Work Referral: Teacher asked for evaluation of home situation. Student is having school adjustment problems.

Background: James transferred to Metropolitan High School in October. He and his mother left St. Louis in May to look for work in the Chicago area. When she could not find work, she moved on to Detroit and then to Cleveland. James and his mother moved in temporarily with her sister and her five children. James says that there is little food and too much noise. Mrs. K and her sister argue frequently. James, born 3/11/75, is placed in a class two years below age level. His teacher indicates that he comes to school poorly dressed, is not clean, and has not eaten.

Assessment: It appears that James and his mother are homeless or nearly homeless. Because they are new to the city, Mrs. K may be unaware of the services available in this community. Among the emergency services for which they may be eligible are: family shelter, school breakfast program, food bank, food stamps, and job service.

Plan: Appointment scheduled with Mrs. K on February 2. Once immediate needs are addressed, I will discuss James's educational history and performance with her. I will observe him in the classroom this week.

Information about the bases, substance, and consequences of service decisions and actions should be fully documented. However, information about the client-situation itself should be recorded only if it is clearly relevant to the delivery of services. Information about the client-situation that demonstrates why services were offered, how services were delivered, and what impact services had is pertinent for the record. Other information about the client-situation, however interesting, is not. Recording information unrelated to service delivery invades the client's privacy and is time-consuming; meanwhile, such documentation does nothing to further the goal of accountability. The primary criterion for including information about the client-situation in a service-centered record is its relevancy to service delivery.

To fulfill its essential function, a record must document and substantiate the bases, substance, and consequences of professional decisions and actions through time. A service-centered record develops as the service transaction develops; its focus shifts as service moves from phase to phase. When, during the initial phase of service, the worker and the client are concerned with exploring the problem, the need, or the eligibility for service and with developing a service contract, the record focuses upon:

The reason for the service request, referral, or offer
Descriptions and assessments of the client-situation
Available resources, services, and barriers

Once the service contract has been formulated, the record focuses upon implementation, and it documents:

Worker and client decisions regarding service
The purpose and goals of service
Plans
Service activities
Progress
Assessments of movement and impact

Finally, the decision to terminate or otherwise end service to the client changes the focus of the record to:

The reason for termination or transfer
A review of the client-situation throughout service
A review of service provision
An evaluation of service and of its impact on the client-situation
Plans for future service
Follow-up

The content of the record is temporally linked to the practice it documents, and, as in practice, the record does not focus entirely upon exploration, then upon formulation, then upon implementation, and finally upon termination. Rather, entries in the record emphasize different processes during different phases of the service encounter but include information relevant to other phases as well. For example, exploration does not end with the initiation of a plan of service but continues throughout the service transaction. Similarly, new information about the client-situation is added to the record as it becomes known, and the purpose and plan of service are reformulated as necessary.

This need to update client information and to alter the direction of service makes timely records appear unsystematic. Why not write records retrospectively, at long intervals or after service is terminated, when the direction of service is clear and the record can be more systematic? Retrospective recordkeeping may be feasible in some cases, especially those in which service takes place over a short period and is relatively routine. However, records can only be accurate and useful in service delivery if they are up-to-date and, as a result, reflect not only the purposiveness but also the responsiveness of service. Records of long-term or complex cases that are written retrospectively may appear to be more systematic than records kept at more frequent intervals.

However, the appearance of purposiveness may actually have resulted from the loss of information; the record may not fully or accurately report the client-situation or the service transaction.

The essential function of the social work record, then, is to describe, explain, and evaluate the service transaction it documents. The service-centered record is also intended to facilitate ongoing service delivery. Therefore, it must be a "living and working" document rather than a retrospective review of activities long past. In summary, if a record is to fulfill its primary goals in today's practice environment, it should include content that is:

Selected to reflect the bases, substance, and consequences of professional decisions and actions

Composed of observation and inference in the form of descriptions and assessments of the client-situation and the service transaction

Grounded in the knowledge, values, and ethics of the profession

Linked through time to the practice it documents

Elements of Content

A social work record is composed of some or all of the elements of content shown in Figure 2.1. Ideally, these elements are linked together, as information for one phase of service forms the basis for decisions and actions both in that phase and in subsequent phases. Although in practice information may not be gathered or documented in this temporal order, and phases of service may not be linear but cyclical, elements of the record will be described in this sequence for the purpose of clarity.

Client Characteristics Demographic information is usually entered into the record early in the service transaction. Some of this information, requiring no act of judgment, may be gathered and recorded by clerical workers or by clients themselves and entered into the record prior to the first encounter between the worker and the client. Based upon information reported by the client and the client's family, and supplemented by information in public documents and other service records, client characteristics are used:

To determine eligibility for services
In service delivery
In accountability
In administrative planning
In research

FIGURE 2.1 Elements of Content

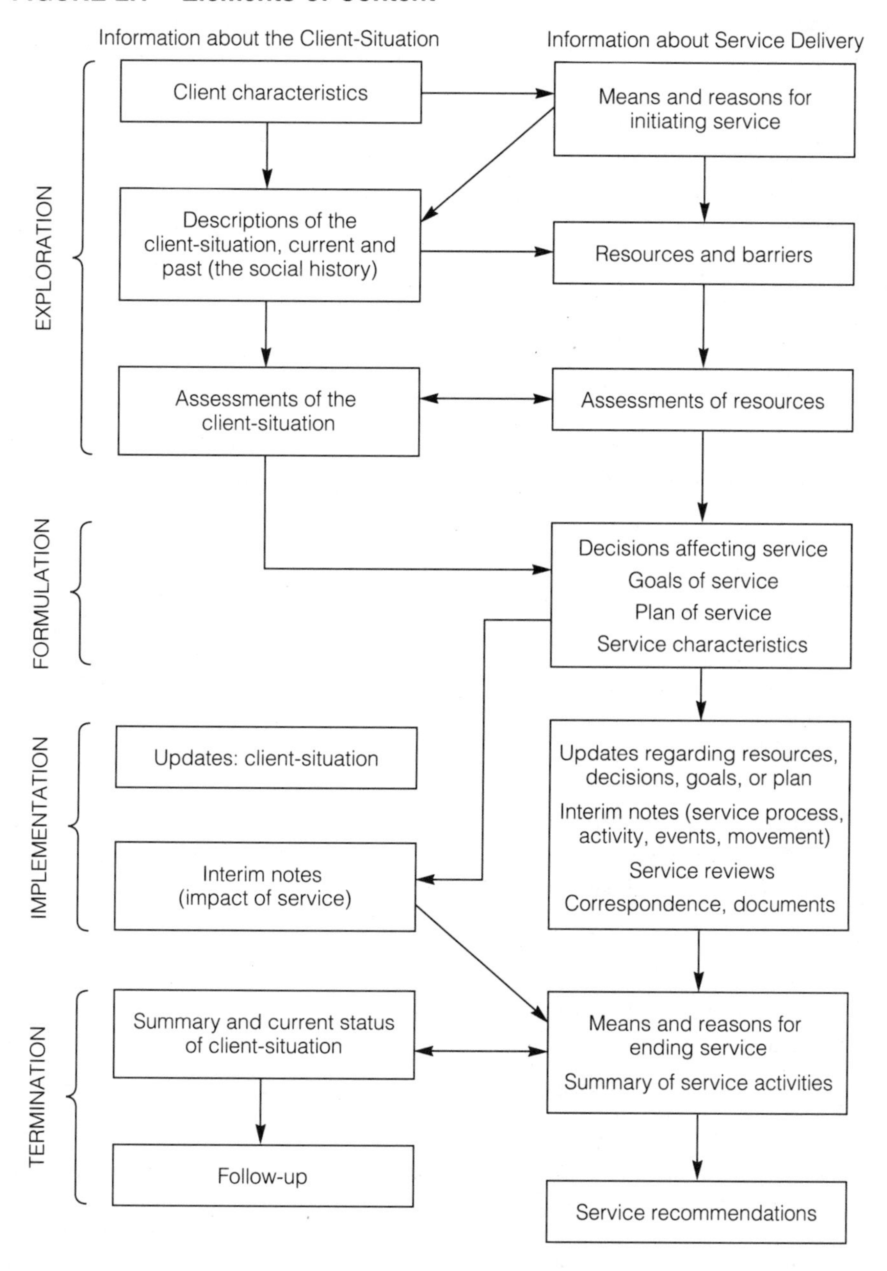

Clients (individuals or families) are identified by such public information as:

Name
Address
Birthdate
Sex

and such private, verifiable information as:

Level of education achieved	Family composition
Current employment	Race
Income	Religion
Marital status	Ethnic group
Citizenship	Languages spoken

In addition, the following information is retained by some agencies, depending on the field of practice, service program, and funding source:

Insurance coverage
Medical diagnosis
Tested IQ
Military status
Type of commitment
Guardianship
Census tract
Social security number[1]

Means and Reasons for Initiating Service Clients seek, are referred for, or are offered service for a wide variety of reasons. This information is recorded because it forms the basis for:

Understanding and responding to the initiating party's view of the problem or service need

Understanding the client's perception of the agency and service

Engaging the client and others in the service process

Evaluating how the agency's services are perceived in the community and how clients come to the agency

Entered into the record at intake, the means and reasons for initiating service represent the referring party's view of the need for or potential benefit of service. If the client did not initiate contact with the agency but was referred or offered service, it is also important to document the client's perception of the problem or the need for service.

---

1. See Chapter 7 regarding the potential for invasion of privacy when social security numbers are used in social service records.

The reasons for initiating service must be clearly differentiated from the purpose of service as an element of the record. Although in some cases the "presenting problem" is the "problem to be worked," in many cases the purpose of service emerges from the process of exploration. The definition of the problem or service need at entry is transformed into the purpose of service just as the applicant for service is transformed into a client.

Usually both the means and the reasons for initiating services can be stated succinctly. For example:

> Mr. D became a member of our cardiac patient group upon his admission for bypass surgery, 1/26/88.
>
> Agency initiated services after Mrs. B called our office. She said that she had been concerned for the past year that her daughter, Linda, was slow. Linda is three years, five months old; she does not speak or respond well to verbal cues.
>
> The S family was referred for service by the juvenile court. Regina has been repeatedly truant from school in the past three months. On 8/2/87, she was arrested for shoplifting at R department store.
>
> Ms. P called our Crisis Line on 2/15/86. She said that she had just broken up with her boyfriend and was thinking of suicide. Susan R spent over an hour with her; after assessing the risk of an imminent suicide attempt, Susan R determined that an emergency admission would not be needed. Ms. P agreed to her appointment today, 2/16/86.

Sometimes, the means for initiating services are immediately apparent, although the reasons are not. For example, a client may be selected for outreach or preventive services on the basis of personal or social characteristics rather than on the basis of a perceived need. In such cases, the means for initiating services should be documented with a statement that the client-situation is to be assessed to determine whether the need, interest, or eligibility for services actually exists.

Descriptions of the Client-Situation, Current and Past The social work record contains information about the client-situation, current and past, so as to place the client's problem or need in its historical and ecological context. This information is documented for a number of important reasons, among them:

To afford the client, family, and significant others the opportunity to "tell their story" and thus review and share their experiences

To individualize the client, the situation, and the relevant environment

To locate sources of problems and locate resources for resolving them

To discover strengths and coping abilities as well as needs and deficiencies

To focus attention and services on relevant issues and points of intervention

To convey pertinent information to other service providers

To document the bases of social work decisions and actions, including those related to service delivery within the organization and those involving referral for services elsewhere

Even when this component of the record focuses on the present and the recent past, it is usually called the "social history." A social history may be brief or extensive. A brief social history concentrates on personal, interpersonal, social, and environmental information pertinent to understanding the current client-situation and places the central problem in its relevant ecological context. An extensive social history moves beyond these issues to seek historical antecedents, recurrent themes, and long-term patterns.

The worker may gather the social history from a number of sources. The principal sources are the client and members of the client's family. In addition, information may come from:

Other service providers, such as physician, educator, psychologist, attorney, nurse, nutritionist, or other social worker

Other significant individuals in the client's social environment

Agency records

Tests and examinations

Direct observation

These sources vary in their knowledge and their objectivity. Furthermore, information may be freely offered or compelled, and the nature of the information and the context of service may encourage candor or concealment. As a result, it is often important to identify clearly the sources of information, its verification by other sources, and the context in which information was revealed. This practice helps to establish the reliability, timeliness, and accuracy of the information. For example:

Mrs. S reluctantly told me of previous calls to the police. She said that she would tell because I would find out anyway, but if her husband found out, he would probably hit her again.

Dr. R told me of a brief encounter with the F family shortly after the accident occurred.

The interview took place in a crowded and noisy office; Mrs. W repeatedly referred to the fact that she did not want others to hear what she was saying.

Agency began investigation because of a report by the school. At first, Mrs. B would not let me into the house; after about 15 minutes she said that, since the neighbors might see us, I might as well come in. She said again and again that she would only tell me what she had to in order to get the school off her back.

The following information was collected from the record of an earlier admission to this program, 5/16/84–10/18/84.

Mr. K described Mrs. K's reaction to the fire in detail. Later, Susan K gave a similar account.

Thomas's school behavior was described by his teachers and his mother. I observed similar behavior during an hour in his classroom on 9/15/88.

The social history is both a process and a product. As a process, it involves exploration of factual and affective content, allowing the worker and the client (or significant other) to review, sort through, and share significant events and circumstances. Although social-history-taking is an essential part of the information-gathering phase of service, it is clearly intended and perceived as part of the helping process. Moreover, the social history process is ongoing; as service progresses, new information is revealed, becomes part of the service transaction, and is documented in the record.

The social-history-taking process involves exploration of the client's experiential landscape. The client (or significant other) reviews familiar territory in a new way with a worker who is both guide and follower. The worker guides the client through areas of interest and concern, and responds to information as it is revealed. The worker and client scan the entire client-situation for salient issues, needs, and resources. As they surface, these areas are explored in depth. Exhibit 2.1 presents a social history outline that can be used in scanning the client-situation.

At the same time, the worker draws attention to specific factors that knowledge and experience indicate may be of critical importance in this client-situation. Some organizations provide the worker with a social history form that outlines specific areas for focused exploration. Workers would focus their exploration on these areas as well as others suggested by:

Client characteristics
The presenting problem or the reason for initiating services
The field of practice or service program
Agency policies and practices

Focused exploration should, above all, be informed by:

Theory and research regarding factors that cause, maintain, remediate or are in other ways linked to the problem or need

EXHIBIT 2.1 Social History Outline

PERSONAL INFORMATION

Cognitive and Physical Development: Specific milestones, e.g., rolling over, sitting, other motor activities; first word, language development; toilet training, other self-care, habits; critical experiences, for example, mother's pregnancy, child's birth, illnesses; unusual family events, for example, death, separations, divorce; development of siblings, other family members; important events and experiences in psychosocial maturation; client and family attitudes, expectations; tested IQ.

Health: Current and past illnesses, accidents, disabilities, signs, symptoms, complaints, diagnoses; previous hospitalizations, treatments, procedures, medications, prostheses; health behavior, including diet, exercise, substance use, sexual practices; attitudes, expectations, adaptation to past, current, anticipated future health status.

Mental Health: Current and past cognitive, affective, social and behavioral functioning; onset and duration of any current difficulties; critical events related to current status; current or past mental health diagnosis; previous hospitalizations, treatments, procedures, medication; attitudes, expectations of client, family, others in social environment.

Critical Behaviors and Patterns of Response: Critical behaviors, patterns linked to current situation or of concern to client, family, or others in social environment; antecedents and consequences of those behaviors; controlling conditions, such as cues, reinforcers; distressing or stressful behaviors and habits such as smoking, bingeing and purging; antisocial behavior at home, work, school, or in community.

Knowledge, Information, Cognitive Patterns: Client's and others' interpretation of current situation and of related events; knowledge, information, and beliefs regarding human behavior, social services, and so forth; current and recent efforts at problem solving; self-concept; insight; values, preferences regarding means and ends of service.

Feelings, Emotional Responses: Client's and others' emotional responses to current situation, critical events related to situation; current level of anxiety, discomfort; motivation for change, action; commitment to service; attitudes toward future, potential for improvement in current situation; self-esteem.

Education: Schools or other educational programs attended; level of performance, achievement; experiences, attitudes, expectations regarding ability, achievements, value of education and credentials; desire for further education; behavior in classroom; study habits, level of basic skills.

Employment: Paid, volunteer, and in-home work experiences; current employment, employer, position; critical incidents in work history; knowledge, skills, interests, aptitudes, attitudes, expectations; job-seeking skills, work habits.

Finances: Current and recent sources and amount of income; savings, investments, holdings, assets; monthly outlay; financial responsibilities, debts; means of defraying costs of current situation, such as insurance coverage of hospitalization; attitudes, expectations, priorities regarding income, use of resources.

Legal Issues: Current and past incidents involving police, civil court action, or criminal court action; past incarcerations; parole, probation status; involvement as perpetrator, victim, or witness to acts of violence or other antisocial acts; immigration status; custody, guardianship.

INTERPERSONAL RELATIONSHIPS

Marital and Family: Current and past marital or family situation, including descriptions of members of household, roles, responsibilities; relationship to absent parents, siblings, children, members of extended family; milestones and critical events in marital or family development; attitudes, beliefs, values regarding marriage, family; relationship of family to neighborhood community, culture; issues in family structure and function, for example, sexuality, care of children, intergenerational alliances.

Peer Groups and Informal Social Network: Description of informal peer relationships, including social, recreational, sexual relationships; membership and participation in formal organizations, groups; interpersonal behaviors, skills, concerns.

Work Relationships: Description of relationships within the work environment, including relationships with supervisors and others in authority, peers, subordinates; critical incidents in work relationships.

SOCIAL INFORMATION

Culture: Values, preferences, and expectations of behavior; issues of prejudice, discrimination; opportunity, access, availability of resources; attitudes toward services, service providers; language and custom differences from community; resources.

EXHIBIT 2.1 Social History Outline (continued)

Community: Formal or informal resources; demography, economy, ecology, physical characteristics; critical incidents involving client and the community.

Institutional Relationships: Relationships with schools and other educational organizations, employment and volunteer associations, religious groups, legal system, health and mental health organizations, social welfare agencies and programs.

PHYSICAL ENVIRONMENT

This includes a description of the physical environment, with special attention to the safety, adequacy, upkeep, and accessibility of:

Housing
Neighborhood
Work environment
Transportation

Knowledge of service processes, available resources and the potential effect of different approaches to service

Informed especially by current knowledge in the field, the social worker uses focused exploration to develop, and then substantiate or refute, hypotheses regarding critical factors that may influence the client-situation. Once the worker identifies these critical factors, he or she can use them to formulate a plan of service.

Three examples of the use of current knowledge in focused exploration follow. The first is a situation in which parental child abuse and neglect are the presenting problem. The purpose of the social history is not to investigate whether abuse or neglect occurred, but to explore in depth the relevance in a particular case of factors known to be associated with child abuse and neglect in other cases. Given this client-situation, the worker explores intensively factors in the parents' family of origin and the current family situation that have been linked in the literature to child abuse and neglect. These include:

Socialization to violence

Substance abuse

Parent-child attachment problems

Scapegoating of one or more child

Situational stress, such as job loss or economic hardship

Structural inadequacies, such as the lack of affordable child care

Skill deficiencies, such as inadequate parenting skills

Knowledge deficiencies, such as lack of information about child development and children's developmental needs

Social isolation

Knowing that one or more of these factors, if unchanged, can lead to continuing abuse and neglect gives direction to the process of exploration and, subsequently, to a plan of service. Social work intervention can be directed to factors specifically linked to the problem in a particular case.

Family Dynamics: Mr. M has been staying at home most days since he was laid off. He watches TV and drinks beer. By evening, he is often drunk and "ready for a fight," according to Mrs. M. She feels that he is a good man down on his luck—and if the court takes their children, Terry and Jerry, he'll "take it real bad." Although she did not volunteer the information, Mrs. M has also been the target of abuse.

Impression: The immediate causes of abuse appear to be linked to Mr. M's job loss seven months ago. Mrs. M is working while he is home all day drinking. No one member is the target of abuse; rather, all have been targeted.

Plan: Mr. M is now involved in a job search program. He has been referred to AA but has not yet attended. Both Mr. and Mrs. M were referred to a parenting skills group, which she is attending. Terry and Jerry have been enrolled in a socialization group at school.

The second example involves the use of knowledge to inform focused exploration in a situation in which an elderly client is experiencing dementia. In this situation, the purpose of the social history is to investigate personal, social, and environmental factors that may indeed be the cause of cognitive deterioration. Familiarity with current literature is essential in establishing hypotheses and guiding social-history-taking. Dementia may be irreversible if caused by Alzheimer's disease or multiple infarcts, but it may be reversible if linked to other factors such as:

Rapid onset of symptoms
Changes in the client's physical environment
Misuse of medication
Malnutrition
Infection
Physical trauma

Emotional trauma, such as the loss of a loved one
Depression

Familiarity with current knowledge about the client-situation is essential to competent social-history-taking and social work assessment. Focused exploration leads to appropriate health and social service planning. Physicians, for example, can use this information in making their own judgments about diagnosis and treatment. Social workers can use this information to plan with some clients and their families for increasing supervision and care over time, and with others to seek active medical evaluation and treatment of the patient's condition.

Mrs. H (daughter) reports that Mrs. O has had poor memory for two years, since Mr. O died. Mrs. H described her mother as changing from a cheerful, active person to an old woman "overnight." Although they do not live in the same part of town, Mrs. H visited her mother several times a week during the first year after Mr. O's death. She found her mother absentminded, complaining, and uncaring about her home or appearance. Finally, after being "yelled at once too often," Mrs. H stopped visiting regularly. She would occasionally take her mother shopping, but she hired a housekeeper to do most of the work around the house, the marketing, and so forth. Although she visits infrequently, Mrs. H reports that she and her brother have, in the past year, taken over all finances and watched their mother lose interest in herself and others.

Specific causes: Mrs. H is aware of no illness or physical trauma, although she admits that her mother may have fallen without anyone knowing about it. In addition, medication and nutrition have not been supervised or supported by others. Loss of husband, role, and relationship with daughter is evident.

Impressions: At this time it appears that dementia may be caused by some specific agent, such as over- or undermedication or malnutrition. Also, Mrs. O may be suffering from depression, which may have caused, but certainly is contributing to, her current mental status.

Plan: Interview scheduled with Miss T (Mrs. O's housekeeper) on June 14. Following that interview, I will meet with Dr. F about these findings and impressions.

The third example involves focused exploration in cases of serious mental illness, such as schizophrenia or major depression. In such cases, the worker should be guided not just by such classification approaches as the DSM-IIIR or the P-I-E (Person-in-Environment) coding system (Karls & Wandrei, in press), but by knowledge about the factors that exacerbate or ameliorate episodes of severe mental dysfunction. The social history process should seek information that goes beyond differential diagnosis to discovering the client's strengths, capacities, and resources as well as needs and limitations. It is therefore important to explore such factors as:

Early social development and adaptation
Age and stage of first symptoms or episodes of severe dysfunction
Educational history and experience
Social and vocational skills
Work history and experience
Family history
Quality of current and past family relationships
Sources of stress, satisfaction, and social support
History of hospitalization, treatment, and medication

This information is useful in understanding the client's background and the course of the problem, as well as in planning services that build upon the client's strengths and meet the client's current and potential needs.

Exhibit 2.2 presents a focused social history of a client experiencing a long-term mental disorder.

In some agencies, the social history is a separate document or section of the record; in other agencies, such information is included in the opening summary and assessment. A social history may be organized topically or chronologically. Social history information is usually entered into the record early in the process of service and updated as new information becomes available. Some organizations have a standard outline or social history form that workers use in selecting and documenting social history information. Other organizations leave the selection of information and the organization of the social history to the discretion of each worker. Over time, most workers develop an approach to social-history-taking and documentation that they can use again and again.

Exhibits 2.1 and 2.2 are both examples of the use of an open-ended narrative style in documenting social history. In contrast, Exhibit 2.3 presents an example of a brief social history in which a standard agency form is used. Note that Exhibits 2.2 and 2.3 present essentially the same information but use different formats.

Resources and Barriers In response to the problems and needs identified during the exploration process, the worker considers the resources and services both needed and available to the client. The client may already have an established relationship with formal or informal resources, such as church groups, self-help groups, or social service agencies. The worker may need to inform the client or refer him or her to other resources. In addition, the worker may need to develop new resources or advocate for the client in new or established service relationships. This information is useful:

EXHIBIT 2.2 Social History in the Case of a Client with a Long-Term Mental Disorder

Background Information: Mr. C, who is now 29 years old, was first known to this community mental health center when he was 22 years old (August, 1983). He had been discharged to the community from Lorall State Hospital following a four-month stay. He was hospitalized after locking his parents into a bedroom and setting the house on fire. At the time of discharge, his diagnosis was "paranoid schizophrenia," and he was treated with thorazine. Upon his return here, he moved into a basement room of his older sister's farmhouse. After a few weeks with the sister (Mrs. W) and her family, he moved out.

For the next three years, he lived alternately with his sister, two aunts, in supervised housing, and on the streets. He received SSI benefits, which were delivered to his sister's house. He attended the clinic irregularly for medication checks and to talk with his case manager. He also was rehospitalized on four occasions. Case notes indicate that, upon discharge from inpatient treatment, he would attend the medication clinic and meetings with his case manager. However, within two or three months, his attendance would become irregular, his behavior would become increasingly disturbed and troublesome, and, eventually, he would stop coming to the clinic. This would be followed by readmission to Lorall (for one to three months), usually through the emergency room at Ranger Hospital.

His last contact with this clinic was in June 1986. Following readmission to Lorall (8/86–10/86), Mr. C returned to his sister's house for a week; following a fight, he left town. What happened subsequently is unclear. He reports that he traveled "out west," was hospitalized briefly on two occasions, and "lived on the street." He returned to this community in March.

Current Situation: Mr. C was treated at Ranger Hospital from 4/28/89 to 5/9/89, when he was discharged to supervised housing and the outpatient treatment program. He has had no contact with his sister or his mother since his return to town, although he believes his sister "spotted" him in town. (His father is now deceased.)

Family and Developmental History: According to the extensive materials collected in 1983, Mr. C is the fourth of five children and the only son. He was born when his father, a disabled farm laborer, was

57 and his mother 38 years old. His next older sister (Mrs. W) is 14 years his senior. According to Mr. C's father, his wife's parents, sister, and nephew all were "feebleminded" and "had nervous breakdowns." Mr. C was described by everyone in the family as shy and fearful. He was physically abused by his father throughout his childhood. At age nine, he was given a BB gun for Christmas. After that, he spent many hours in the woods shooting at birds and small animals. He never brought friends home or visited other homes. His only significant peer relationships during his childhood appear to have been with his cousins, many of whom live in this county.

Mr. C attended school until age 16, when he dropped out in the ninth grade. His grades in school were poor, and he was held back twice, in grades four and six. His school records indicate that he was a "loner," but he was not troublesome in the classroom or in conflict with his peers or the community. He indicates that he does not read or write well.

There is little information available as to whether Mr. C has ever had a job. This is a very sensitive topic that Mr. C avoids discussing. Mr. C was visibly upset when Mr. V (the vocational counselor) described his role in the home program during Mr. C's first group home meeting. Mr. C attempted to leave but was told that he must remain until the end of the meeting.

Areas for Further Exploration:

1. What are Mr. C's feelings toward and experiences with work?
2. Is it appropriate to reconnect Mr. C with Mrs. W and Mrs. C? How could they be a resource for Mr. C?
3. What serves as a trigger for medication noncompliance and withdrawal from services?
4. What is Mr. C's reading level? What is his vocational potential?

Initial Impressions: Mr. C has a cyclical history of good adjustment and medication compliance, followed by noncompliance and deterioration. Clearly, his sister has been an important resource in the past, although there has been no contact in three years. Vocational development may be a problem, since his social skills and language skills appear to be very limited. Perhaps more important, he experiences even the discussion of work as stressful.

M. Grover, B.S.W.
5/20/89

EXHIBIT 2.3 Social History in the Case of a Client with a Long-Term Mental Disorder

Wesson County Mental Health Center (WCMHC)
Brief History Form

Client Name: Darryl C #83-4291 DOB: 3/12/61
Date: 5/20/89 By: M. Grover, B.S.W.
Information from: Darryl C, WCMHC records
Initial Diagnosis: Paranoid schizophrenia, 8/83 ______
Lorall State Hospital, B. Benton, M.D.
Hospital Admissions: Lorall State, 4/83–8/83; 4/85; 8/86–10/86
Ranger Hospital, 1983, 1985, 1986, 1989

WCMHC:
Current: Supervised housing
Medication clinic (thorazine)
Case management

Past: Nine reopenings, 1983–1986
Services: Medication clinic; thorazine maintenance; case management
Status at termination: No show, medication noncompliance

Benefits: SSI reapply DPA ______ DVR ______

Brief History:

Father:	Wolfgang C, deceased. Farm laborer, was disabled. Much older than his wife. History of abusing Mr. C throughout childhood.
Mother:	Myra C, 67 years old. History of "feeblemindedness" and "nervous breakdowns" in her family. No contact since 1986.
Siblings:	Four sisters, three older and one younger. Greta W, next older sister (14 years older), has allowed Mr. C to live with her family in the past. No contact since 1986.
School:	Dropped out at age 16, in ninth grade. School grades poor; failed fourth and sixth grades. Described as a "loner," a "poor student" but not a discipline problem.
Work:	No work history available.
Marital:	Not married
Children:	None
Housing:	Lived briefly with Mrs. W and family; otherwise, has lived on the street, in shelters, or in hospitals. Currently living at The Haven (supervised housing).

In planning and implementing services
In demonstrating accountability to the client and the organization

Such a review should indicate not only the formal and informal resources available; it should also note any obstacles to available resources as well as any inadequacies in the community's resource base. Workers should document, for example, when needed services are unavailable in the community or when the client cannot be served because of understaffing or restrictive eligibility for existing programs. Such information will demonstrate unmet client needs to decision makers at all levels of the organization and community. It also will justify the service plan and help service professionals to evaluate its impact. The following example describes barriers to needed resources:

In the past week, Mr. and Mrs. L's attempts to find suitable services for Mickey have been met with a series of disappointments. Marymont, the local outpatient treatment program, has lost funding and has closed intake indefinitely. (There are indications that half of their clients will be terminated or transferred to Cold River, 80 miles away.) They also found that respite care has a four-month waiting list.

Assessments Throughout the record, descriptions of the client-situation and of the service process and progress are usually accompanied by assessments of the information presented. In assessments, the worker analyzes the critical factors in either the client-situation or the service transaction according to a specific frame of reference or set of criteria. Assessments show the worker's thinking process and the bases of the worker's decisions and actions. They are used:

In planning, implementing, and evaluating service

In supervision, peer review, and quality assurance

In demonstrating accountability to the client, the organization, accrediting bodies, and funding sources

In communicating with others in the organization who are also offering services to the client

In the best records, assessments are separated from descriptions and are clearly labeled as "worker's assessment," "impressions," or "working hypotheses." Assessments of the client-situation acknowledge strengths and resources as well as needs and limitations. Assessments of the service transaction recognize limitations in the provision of service and its impact as well as acknowledging progress and improvement. Furthermore, the criteria used as the basis for professional judgments are stated explicitly. These criteria, which reflect agency policies, procedures, and practices as well as the worker's own knowledge and skill, are drawn from:

Theories of human behavior in the social environment—for example, the behavior of social systems, or the ego's mechanisms of defense

Assumptions underlying a particular approach to practice—for example, stages of group development, or the ABC of rational emotive therapy

Classifications of behavior developed for use with specific client groups—for example, diagnostic classes in the DSM-IIIR, or levels of social functioning according to the adaptive behavior scale developed by the American Association of Mental Deficiency

Social policy and agency procedure—for example, guidelines for Medicare reimbursement for skilled nursing facilities; application procedures, eligibility standards, and availability of county aid

Previous experience with this and other clients

In poor records, descriptions and assessments are admixed, so it is not clear what the worker has observed and what he or she has inferred. The criteria against which the observations have been judged are not made explicit, although judgments may be couched in professional-sounding jargon. Finally, analyses tend to be of the "Aunt Fanny" variety; that is, they are generally applicable rather than specifically relevant to this client-situation or service transaction (Kadushin, 1963). For example:

Poor: Mr. F described the first time that Randy was picked up for shoplifting. Mr. F received a call at work and immediately went to the police station. Randy and Mr. F decided not to tell Mrs. F about the incident, so that she would not be upset. This is one of many instances in which Mr. F colludes with Randy, implicitly suggesting to Randy that what mother does not find out about is okay. Mr. F felt that he had done all he could in handling the situation. He "read Randy the riot act" and told him that if this got out it might be trouble for him in his job. [Mixes description with analysis; criteria are implicit.]

Better: Mr. F described the first time Randy was picked up for shoplifting. Mr. F received a call at work and immediately went to the police station. Randy and Mr. F decided not to tell Mrs. F about the incident, so that she would not be upset. Mr. F felt that he had done all he could in handling the situation. He "read Randy the riot act" and told him that if this got out it might be trouble for him in his job.

Impressions: This is one of many instances in which Mr. F colludes with Randy, implicitly suggesting to Randy that what mother does not find out about is okay. [Separates description from assessment.] It appears the intergenerational ties between Mr. F and Randy are undermining the structure of the family. [Makes criteria explicit.]

Poor: **Impressions:** The client appeared to be anxious during the first interview, although no more anxious than most clients who are coming in to see a social worker for the first time. After about 15 minutes, she seemed to relax. [Overgeneralizes.]

Better: [Omit; avoid extraneous observations.]

Decisions Affecting Service It is important to document the substance and rationale for major decisions that affect the kind, quantity, and quality of services delivered to the client. This information is used:

In implementing service and evaluating its impact
In documenting adherence to accepted standards and procedures
In promoting continuity of service
In accountability, supervision, and peer review

Some decisions affecting service involve professional judgments made by the worker or by others in the service environment. Particularly when service involves policy implementation, as when the client's eligibility or need for a service program or a social provision is being determined, decisions are made largely by service providers. Other decisions affecting service are made primarily by the client or by others acting on the client's behalf. For example, the client may choose whether to seek, accept, or use available services; the client may select one of several recommended agencies or decide to follow through on a referral.

Social work is increasingly adopting models of practice that involve mutual worker/client decisions. Mutual decisions regarding the purpose and process of service are called the contract. This signifies a move away from the medical model, in which professional decisions were dominant, to a legal model, in which the roles of worker and client are more coequal and differences in opinion are negotiated. Mutual decisions affecting service include general agreements as to the goals and methods of service and specific agreements regarding, for example, the scheduling of meetings, fees, tasks, and actions.

When a written contract is used, a copy of it should be filed in the record. When a verbal or implicit contract is used, a brief statement of its major components should be documented, including, where applicable:

Who participated in the decision making
What decisions were made
What alternatives were considered and why they were rejected

When decisions are made by the worker or by others in the service environment, the participants, the substance, and also the rationale for such decisions should be carefully delineated. Social service decisions are frequently based upon such criteria as the worker's observations of the client-situation, the client's preferences, the availability of resources, previous client history, social or agency policy, or the actions of the client or of others in the client's personal environment. Complete documentation of decisions would explain which decisions were reached and their bases in observation and assessment. The following example presents such an explanation:

Because the S family situation is not classified as emergency status, they were offered two options: wait listing (six to eight weeks) or referral to the NCH outpatient program. They chose wait listing but will call if an emergency arises or if they decide on an alternative service.

Purpose of Service Clarity of purpose gives structure both to the service transaction and to the record. The purpose of service is a statement of the goals of service; it specifies what action the worker, the client, and others will take to achieve the goals. Arriving at the purpose of service may involve mediating among the views of the client, persons in the client's natural environment, the worker, other professionals, and the community. It may involve reconciling various views with what resources are available to the client. The purpose of service, then, describes what is to be achieved, whereas the plan of service describes how the goal will be accomplished.

A statement of purpose unifies the record and forms the basis for:

Locating appropriate points of and approaches to intervention

Establishing a plan of service

Communicating with other professionals who are also involved in service delivery

Evaluating the impact of service

Yet, this element of the record is often absent from social work records; even when it is included, it may be stated in vague terms or in process language.

Poor: Improve social functioning. [Vague]

Act as advocate in the client's attempt to get the landlord to comply with city ordinances. [Process]

Improve communication among family members [Vague] through the use of family therapy. [Process]

Better: Improve client's social functioning in employment and relationships with extended family.

Improve client's housing conditions, especially heating.

Change family's pattern of communication from blaming-withdrawal to explicit requests-responsive listening.

Plan of Service The plan sets forth the actions to be taken to fulfill the purpose of service. A detailed statement of the plan is particularly useful in maintaining continuity of service when the worker is absent and another service provider takes over the case. The plan is used also:

In demonstrating adherences to agency policy and procedures
In facilitating supervision, consultation, and peer review

In communicating with others who are providing service to the client
In evaluating service implementation

Although in practice the planning process varies widely, the role of the record in documenting the plan remains constant. No matter whether the worker develops the plan independently or in concert with others, or whether planning is part of the service process or preparatory to it, the plan gives form to the future. Some client-situations and service approaches appear to lend themselves to detailed planning, though others do not. When service calls for action in the environment, for activities in the group, or for behavioral intervention, the record can clearly show when, how, and who will undertake each step. Yet, even insight-oriented therapies can benefit from prospective documentation of a plan of service. Such a plan might describe the critical issues the worker and client will explore next or how the worker will employ interpretation. A plan may, for example:

Describe agency or program referrals:

Refer Mrs. T to Family Service for homemaker service.

Describe epilepsy self-help group and ask to make a referral.

Suggest issues for exploration and intervention:

Discuss John's current development and changing needs for parental guidance with Mrs. K.

At next meeting, encourage Carl to ask the group for suggestions on how to deal with conflict with his roommate.

Discuss school situation in depth with Rachel; avoid direct confrontation, but explore what others want her to do and compare with what she wants.

Following its success in the classroom, teach Mr. and Mrs. M how to use time-out whenever Tom has a tantrum.

Outline a sequence of steps to be taken by worker, client, and others:

---

a. Meet with Mr. and Mrs. T to assess their awareness of Mr. T's long-term care needs; meet with Dr. Q if needed.

b. Explore financial and employment situation, home environment, available individuals, and resources if Mr. T returns home.
c. Discuss alternative discharge arrangements and preferences with Mr. and Mrs. T.
d. Suggest interviews with nursing homes, home health agencies, and meetings with physical therapy and nurses.

By next interview, Mr. N will have polled residents of house to see if they are having problems with the landlord and if they are willing to attend a meeting. Worker will locate a meeting place and will find out about building code and procedure for reporting complaints.

Suggest contingencies:

Mr. P and I have agreed to meet again on 8/28. If he has not by then been recalled for his job, he will enroll in the training program.

If place in group home is available, begin preparation for move. If not available, place name on list, seek temporary support from:

a. Respite care
b. Family members
c. Church

The record of the plan of service is most useful if it is:

Up-to-date and covers the ongoing and subsequent phase of service
Specific enough to be implemented by another service provider, if needed
Amenable to review and evaluation

Service Characteristics Like client characteristics, service characteristics may be documented in a separate section of the record to be easily accessible for use:

In service delivery
In accountability
In administrative planning
In research

In some agencies, a checklist identifies the program or service modality. For example:

Services

( ) Individual counseling	Resource provision:
( ) Marital counseling	( ) Transportation
( ) Family counseling	( ) Call-in
Time-limited groups:	( ) Meal center
( ) Financial management	( ) Information and referral
( ) Widow's outreach	( ) Advocacy

In other agencies, a form is used not just to identify the services provided but also to document the client's movement through various services within and outside the agency. Some agencies use a single form, such as the flowchart or the service log presented in Chapter 5, for the purpose of tracking services.

Still other organizations use a battery of standardized forms to document each aspect of the agency's involvement with the client. This method of service recording is typical of large public organizations that deliver nondiscretionary services based upon entitlement or legal mandate—for example, public assistance or child welfare services. In many of these organizations, this information is computerized, allowing the service provider, managers, and oversight authorities to follow individual cases and groups of clients.

Interim Notes Once the plan of service has been initiated, interim notes describe and assess the client-situation and the service transaction at regular intervals. These notes may be brief or extensive, depending upon what information is to be included and upon the frequency of notations. In many agencies, interim notes are called progress notes, implicitly indicating that an important criterion used in selecting information for this element of the record is that it should demonstrate movement and improvement. Until recently, with the introduction of some new recording structures such as Goal Attainment Scaling and the Problem-Oriented Record, few guidelines for the content of interim notes existed. Despite the availability of these new structures, however, interim notes are still often unfocused and unstructured.

Depending upon their content, interim notes may be used:

To document new or additional information about the client-situation or about the provision of service

In altering the purpose or plan of service

In determining when to terminate service

In evaluating service

In accountability

In demonstrating adherence to accepted practices

In supervision, consultation, and peer review

In administrative decision making

Interim notes may include any or all of the following information:

1. Descriptions of the status and any changes in the client-situation since the previous entry
2. Assessments of the status and any changes in the client-situation since the previous entry
3. Descriptions of service activities and the service process since the last entry
4. Critical incidents reports
5. Assessments of the purpose, plan, process, and progress of service
6. Changes in the purpose or plan of service

Interim notes document new information about the client-situation that is relevant to the provision of service. Sometimes this information is not available during earlier recordings; sometimes it reflects changes in the client-situation since service was initiated. Such information is relevant for the record if it corrects or amends previous descriptions, if it substantiates or refutes assumptions, or if it reflects progress or lack of progress in achieving the purpose of service or in implementing the plan. In describing the current status and significant changes in the client and in the relevant environment, social workers should be particularly careful to document changes that represent a new cause for service, a new resource or barrier to service, or unanticipated consequences of service. This information serves as a basis for assessments and as an impetus to alter the purpose or change the plan of service. The following example describes changes in the client's environment in the context of reassessing the feasibility of a preferred service plan:

In the interview 3/30, which included Mrs. Q, her daughter Ms. Q, and her son-in-law Mr. N, it became apparent that Mrs. Q's preference of moving to her daughter's home would not be feasible at this time. Mr. N's layoff has been changed from temporary to indefinite. Ms. Q has taken a job and has placed her son Darren in day care. Mr. N will seek employment in another state.

Interim notes also document service activity. In the past, social workers were advised against recording specific service activities in their records. These "behold-me-busy" details were considered extraneous to the purpose for keeping records, which was to aid the worker in diagnostic thinking. Today, however, documentation of each activity with or on behalf of the client may be decisive in obtaining reimbursement from funding sources or in corroborating testimony in court. Furthermore, such documentation is useful in demonstrating the level of effort and the quality of service rendered to the client; it is certainly used in substantiating decisions and judgments. Although it is inefficient and seldom appropriate to include a full report of all activities with and on behalf of the client, social workers should routinely note the date, setting, and participants involved, as well as the subjects discussed and decisions made. This information should be recorded for each interview, session, phone call, or other encounter with the client, with members of the client's family or social network, and with other service providers.

9/23/88: Office interview with Mr. and Mrs. K. Final interview for marital counseling, initiated 4/17/88. Reviewed changes that have taken place in their relationship with each other and with Mr. K's father. Planned for usual follow-up phone interview on 10/20/88 to assess situation and possible need for reopening.

3/18/86: Met with Raven's teacher, Mrs. G. She indicates that Raven's classroom participation and overall performance have improved somewhat during the past two weeks. She has noticed that other students, especially Garnet and Ethel, are trying to distract Raven. On my suggestion, Ms. G will (1) separate Garnet and Ethel, (2) positively reinforce them for school-directed activities, and (3) have Raven lead reading group this week.

Critical incidents should always be fully and immediately documented in the record and at the same time should be reported to the supervisor or other designated manager. The following situations are examples of critical incidents:

A client threatens or attacks another person.

A client is threatened, attacked, or mistreated.

A client threatens suicidal behavior or exhibits antisocial behavior.

A client reports that he or she was the victim, perpetrator, or observer of child abuse or neglect.

A critical incident report should include the following information:

The date, time, setting, and participants involved

What was revealed, in detail

The behavior observed, in detail

What was said by each party involved, in detail

Any action taken by the social worker and others during and subsequent to the critical incident

Any further action planned

For example:

12/22/87, 8:00 A.M.: Mrs. R phoned. She said that Mr. R had been drinking all night, was "on a rampage," and was threatening her and their daughter Mary (age seven) with his shotgun. I told her that I would call Officer James, who had responded to her call on 12/16/87, and would come with her or another officer to her home. We arrived at about 8:40 A.M. She and Mary were waiting in the garage. I drove Mrs. R and Mary to the Women's Shelter, as I had done on 12/16/87. Officer James entered the house and, I later learned, arrested Mr. R again. Rhonda F. (a worker at the shelter) and I will talk with Mrs. R today (for the third time) about getting an order of protection.

Typically, interim notes summarize briefly the service activities that have taken place and document more fully critical incidents. However, some records include detailed descriptions of the service process itself or even verbatim excerpts from sessions with clients. The purpose of including information about the service process is to demonstrate something important about the client or about the service transaction. A worker is often guided by a particular theory of human behavior or a model of intervention in selecting process information for the record. A family therapist, for example, may wish to record a component of the process to show a particular pattern of family interaction that has changed as the result of social work intervention. In the example that follows, the worker uses process information to demonstrate an important feature of group development. This process information also indicates Sarah's and Leslie's commitment to the group.

During meeting number three last week, Leslie called the group "our group." Later Sarah said that when one of the kids asked her where she had gone during math class, she said "my group," which in her opinion was better than saying "my shrink." Everyone laughed and looked at each other and at the worker.

Impression: The group is beginning to develop an identity and some cohesion.

Interim notes include the worker's assessment of the progress of service. This assessment may be based upon any of a number of criteria, such as:

Progress in implementing the service plan
Movement through successive stages of a treatment process
Efficiency, pace
Impact on the client-situation

Perhaps the issue in the provision of social work services of most concern and controversy during the 1970s was practice effectiveness. Social workers were asking themselves and each other such questions as: Are social work services effective? How can services become more effective? What criteria should be used to monitor and assess the impact of service? As a result of these questions, social workers began to experiment with new approaches to practice and with new ways of documenting and evaluating service effects. These efforts have had a direct impact upon social work recording.

In fact, social workers have always described the effects of their services on the client-situation. For example, they have described client statements that reveal insight:

After I interpreted her behavior as yet another example of her ambivalence about achievement and success, Ms. G said that she had been giving this idea a great deal of thought recently. She could think of several situations at work that also showed that she was avoiding being "too successful." She had worked hard but had not sought "showy assignments" that would have brought her work attention at the highest levels. Yet, she resented doing all the work and being treated as an assistant rather than an associate attorney.

Social workers have always recorded information that revealed the development of the worker-client relationship, movement through successive stages in the process of treatment, or steps in implementing a service plan. But effects were often described in terms of the process of service. What the effectiveness issue has done is to focus attention not just on process goals but also on outcome goals, on specific rather than global outcomes, on observable rather than implicit change, and on systematic rather than random observations of the client-situation.

Social work records can benefit from these innovations. The purpose of service, once defined, leads the worker and the client to select some specific indicators of movement toward achieving their goals or accomplishing their tasks. For example, the client and the worker may choose to monitor the client's thoughts, behaviors, or feelings; or the client's attitudes toward, or skills in, interpersonal relationships; or the development and utilization of a community resource. These records become part of the interim notes and are used to evaluate the progress of service and its impact in achieving intended outcomes.

Martha's diary from 11/15–11/29 showed four incidents of moderate anxiety and one incident of panic.

She used relaxation techniques on all five occasions. Anxiety dissipated in 30 minutes.

Change: Number of incidents decreased 10 percent; no change in time elapsed after initiating relaxation.

Plan: Reinforce relaxation training.

Mr. and Mrs. L each completed the Index of Marital Satisfaction (Hudson, 1982) before service was initiated (9/19) and again after six interviews (10/30). Scores were:

	9/19	*10/30*
Mrs. L	88	65
Mr. L	70	66

Assessment of progress based upon such "outcome" measures alone can be misleading. Are social work services actually responsible for the change (or no change) in the client-situation? Are services producing unintended or unfavorable consequences? To what extent are the real effects of service being measured? Social work is not practiced in a vacuum; personal factors, factors in the client's natural environment, and the activities of other service providers influence the client-situation and have impact on whether the purpose of service is actually accomplished (Kagle, 1982). If such factors are operating in the case, it is important that the worker report them in the interim notes so that measures of effect are properly interpreted. In the following example, Susan's attendance was being used as a measure of service effects. If the record had not documented the actual cause of poor attendance, the attendance data would have been misinterpreted.

4/4: Susan's poor attendance in school in March (six absences) had been attributed to her continuing relationship with Chad. However, she revealed today that her mother returned to State Hospital early in March. Susan had stayed home for a week last month when her brother Larry (age nine) had the flu.

No matter what indicators of movement are used, the progress and impact of service cannot be assessed properly unless the purpose, plan, and process of service have been clearly defined. When the worker's thinking is diffuse and service unfocused, interim notes become similarly confused. Left without guidelines for selecting what is relevant, the worker may produce long and rambling notes or may fail to include key information. In either case, the core issues of service and of the client-situation are obscured and the record as a whole is weakened.

Service Reviews Although interim notes document the worker's ongoing observations and assessments of the case, service reviews document periodic, formal reexaminations of service decisions and actions. Such reviews often include the opinions of colleagues and other service providers, supervisors and consultants, and clients and others acting on the client's behalf. The process of review may be a regular case management activity, as, for example, in a child welfare agency where all cases of children in foster care are reviewed at regular intervals or in a school where all individual educational plans (IEPs) for special education students are reviewed annually. The process of review may be initiated as part of a research or quality assurance project, such as in a hospital social service department, where a client group may be selected as the subject of peer review. A case may be chosen for review at a case conference or for consultation because of special problems encountered in service delivery.

Service reviews are documented for the purpose of accountability. In general, their content should include the date, names of participants, recommendations, and decisions. Following the review, the worker may also need to update the purpose and the plan of service to reflect these recommendations and decisions.

Foster Care Six-Month Review

Name: Tanya N, eight years, four months old

Date: 5/12/87

Present: Mrs. R, foster mother
Mr. T, central office
Mrs. A, foster care supervisor
Ms. M, caseworker

Absent: Miss N, Tanya's mother. Miss N was notified by mail and phone of the scheduled meeting. At the time of the meeting, Ms. M called her by phone. Miss N said that she could not attend the meeting because she was sick.

Worker's review of the case was presented. Tanya's mother has visited Tanya only once; Miss N says that she has been sick most of the time.

Tanya is doing well in school. Mrs. R says that she is doing well at home and has stopped wetting the bed.

Plan: Encourage visiting; plan return home by end of year. Look into mother's health and job status. She may be eligible for JPTA program.

Means and Reasons for Ending Service Service may be terminated by plan or may end prematurely as the result of independent client action, decisions made by others in the service environment, or unforeseen circumstances that affect the client, the worker, or the service transaction. The circumstances surrounding service termination are documented because they are used:

In accountability
In evaluating service
In planning future services to the client

Generally, the means and reasons for ending service are briefly documented, in the manner described in the section pertaining to the means and reasons for initiating service. Often this element of content is incorporated into a closing summary along with a summary of service, a description of the client-situation throughout service and at the time of termination, and any recommendations for further service or follow-up.

Summary of Service Activities and Outcome Social service records usually include a closing summary, a recapitulation of the process of service, and a description of its outcome at the time of termination. Unfortunately, this review often is completed long after service is terminated; as a result, the closing summary can be too sketchy, general, or unfocused. Workers often delay completing the closing summary, which they perceive to be time-consuming and useless, written only to be placed in storage. However, the closing summary, if properly made, can be efficient, if brief, and useful, if it serves one of two purposes. A closing summary is useful when service has been limited or conducted over a short period of time; this summary then replaces the interim note, describing and evaluating the service process and its impact. Secondly, a closing summary is useful when service has been long-term and the record lengthy; this summary can be used then to abstract salient information from the body of the record, making information about the service transaction easily accessible if the client returns for additional services. The summary should include a brief review of:

The reasons for initiating service
The client-situation throughout service
The purpose, plan, and process of service
Significant events in service and in the client-situation

In addition, it should include new information regarding:

The status of the client-situation at termination

An evaluation of service and its impact on the client-situation and the available resources

---

Ms. T called the crisis line on 1/12, saying that she was depressed, drinking a lot, and "at the end of her rope." She came for an interview on 1/13 and was immediately accepted for individual, group, and drug therapy.

She has attended one individual and one group session per week through 6/18, when individual sessions were terminated.

Individual therapy focused on making decisions about what she would do upon graduation. Her initial depression followed a breakup with her boyfriend, Nathaniel, but appears to be more pervasive, linked to uncertainty about the future and failed relationships in the past. She was able to understand the relationship between her depression, her parents' divorce, and her ambivalence about Nathaniel. She took active steps to develop additional job and educational options, and to select among her options; she developed new friendships and learned to anticipate and manage events that might make her anxious or depressed. It became clear that her bingeing and purging and alcohol dependency were related to anxiety and depression. These problems showed no increase during therapy, but they were not the focus of the intervention, by client decision.

Ms. T has experienced a gradual lifting of depression, aided by drug and group therapy. This is reflected in her own statements, in her appearance, and on psychological tests. She feels much stronger now, but will continue with group and drug therapy follow-ups. She will call me in two weeks to check on progress.

Follow-Up Many agencies routinely follow up on closed cases with one or more phone calls. This procedure is useful in evaluating the impact of services, since changes may occur after service has been completed or has ended. Follow-up is also used for assessing the client-situation to identify whether further services are appropriate. Documentation of formal or informal follow-up contacts between the client and the agency are used:

In demonstrating adherence to agency policies

In documenting service activity

In evaluating the impact of service

In maintaining continuity of service, if the case is reopened or if the client is referred for services elsewhere

Follow-up reports should contain information on the current status of the client-situation, any recommendations for further service, and any action taken with or on behalf of the client.

Three-month follow-up: Mrs. R was unable to manage her mother at home, even with home health care. She reported that Mrs. P moved to Apple Valley Convalescent Home last month.

Mr. S said that he and Mrs. S feel as if they are on a honeymoon. He worries that it might wear off, but he said they would call if they needed a "refresher." He asked if I would call his sister, who has just separated from her husband. I suggested that he tell her to call me between 1:00 and 3:00 today.

Impression: Mr. S's attitude at follow-up stands in contrast to his initial reluctance to commit himself to the casework process. He has gone from skeptic to convert! His ambivalence still shows in his fear that the honeymoon will wear off. Nevertheless, Mr. and Mrs. S have made significant strides toward acceptance of each other and have learned to resolve conflict rather than withhold themselves and their feelings.

Conclusion

This chapter has suggested guidelines for selecting information for the record. Because records today must fulfill the competing goals of accountability, efficiency, and privacy, they should be service centered and should focus on documenting the bases, substance, and impact of services. This chapter also has provided detailed descriptions of each element of content that may appear in a social work record, along with examples of recording in narrative form.

However, in practice a record may not include all of these elements of content. In many cases, service is limited, and the record may briefly document who the client is and what services were provided. Furthermore, most records use forms or checklists in addition to or instead of narrative reports. Forms and outlines standardize recordkeeping, assure that specified information is documented, and simplify information storage and retrieval.

Chapters 3, 4, and 5 describe various recordkeeping structures used by social workers in agency practice, private practice, and education for practice. These chapters concentrate on how the structure of the record influences how the record is made and used. However, it is important to remember that a record's structure also influences its content. The adoption of a particular form or format can determine not just how information is presented but also whether and which information is selected for the record.

3 Records Used in Social Work Education

This chapter describes, evaluates, and presents examples of three recording structures used in educating students. The first of these is the **process record,** an approach to recordkeeping that has a long history in social work, dating back to the beginning of the twentieth century. Social workers originally produced process records to document the social conditions under which their clients lived (Burgess, 1928). However, ever since Mary Richmond (1917) used process records in her study of social casework, these records have been written and used principally to facilitate students' learning of practice skills and development of diagnostic thinking.

The second recordkeeping structure presented here is the **teaching/learning (T/L) record,** developed by this author in 1982. Using narrative summary rather than process form, the T/L record incorporates far more description of the service transaction and of the process of decision making than does a typical agency record. The T/L record is intended to facilitate the development of interpersonal and cognitive practice skills along with summary recording skills.

The third recordkeeping structure presented in this chapter is actually a combination of three or four recording structures used in sequence. This approach is called **essential recording** because it teaches the student to distill the essence of the client-situation and the service transaction for the record. Essential recording not only can aid the student in developing summary recording skills, but it also helps the student produce records that are useful in supervision. In essential recording, students audiotape or videotape all or most of their sessions with clients, providing student and supervisor with direct access to what happened in the service transaction. Using the tapes themselves or transcripts made from the tapes, students then prepare summaries of each session. Finally, students use their session summaries as a resource when they prepare narrative reports for the official agency record. Tapes, transcripts, session summaries, and narrative reports are all available for review and use in supervision. Thus, essential recording aids the student in developing cognitive and interpersonal practice skills as well as summary recording skills.

As a general rule, records prepared primarily for educational purposes should not become part of the client's official record. Process records and early drafts of reports that students revise under supervision, for example, should either be destroyed or become part of the student's record with the client's name obscured. Records produced by students in their early stages of professional development may include distortions of fact and biased judgments that are potentially harmful to the client. If such material were to become part of the client's record, it might be damaging to the client, to the student, to their relationship, and to the organization. Such information may be disseminated within or outside the organization, to the client's detriment. Other professionals may use such information to make poor or uninformed decisions. Clients who read the record or who are informed of its contents may take action against the worker or the organization. Furthermore, such information can undermine others' view of the student's competency and of the social work program's level of professionalism. Even when records prepared primarily for educational purposes are accurate and fair, they are generally focused more on the student's behavior and thinking than on the client-situation. Moreover, such records may not be written in a form that is useful to other service providers. Thus, students should not place process records or other educational records in their clients' files; instead, they should prepare standard agency reports that are first reviewed and approved by the supervisor and then become part of the client's record.

Process Recording

The process record has had an important place in the history of social work. First used in studying the client and the situation when an important purpose for practice was social investigation, the process record has changed with the altered orientation of the profession. In earlier times, social workers documented everything they could remember about what their clients said and did, about what they themselves said and did, and about what they observed, believed, and surmised. By the time Hamilton wrote *Social Case Recording*, process recording was used not just for the purpose of social study but, more importantly, for "indicating the manner in which one person appears to relate himself to another person during the therapeutic experience" (p. 92). The focus of interest had broadened from the client-situation to the service transaction as well. However, although the record that Hamilton described contained a great deal of information about the process of service, not all information about service process was recorded in process form. Workers no longer reproduced everything in the transaction but selected particular information to process-record because of its importance in characterizing and individualizing the client; they summarized the rest. Over time, the amount of information workers "processed" decreased and the amount they summarized increased. Today, process recording is seldom used in day-to-day practice. Records still contain information about the process of service, but it is likely to appear in narrative summary rather than in process form.

The process record is still widely used in social work education. Students may process-record all or portions of their interviews or meetings with clients. Preparation, documentation, and review all contribute to the learning experience. Preparation for process recording requires that students concentrate on what clients say and how they behave throughout the encounter. Students must also remember their own statements, feelings, and behaviors. Documentation itself causes the student to review the sequence of events and to reexperience the service transaction. Finally, reviewing the written record allows students to assess the meaning of the client-situation, the service encounter, and their own performance. Exhibits 3.1 and 3.2 present excerpts from student process records.

The process record may be used in field instruction and in the classroom to develop students' assessment skills, self-awareness, and use of self in the service encounter. Students and their instructors find it particularly useful to have process records transcribed, leaving a wide margin where students can note their reactions and analytic responses as they review their records. Later, instructors can add their own comments. In addition, process records, like any other form of recording, can serve as a basis for discussion in supervision and in the classroom.

Although process recording is too time-consuming to be cost-effective in agency practice, time is not as significant a limitation for social work education. However, there are two other limitations of process recording that suggest that it should not be the only recording method used in social work education. Rather, process recording should be used in combination with other learning approaches. First, as Timms (1972, appendix) demonstrated, a process record is not a verbatim report but a selective reconstruction of the service encounter. Thus, if a student and an instructor wished to study the actual service process, they would gain a more accurate picture of what took place if they used audiotapes or videotapes. Taping reproduces the interview and allows the student to observe himself or herself. Although taping may seem invasive and may have some reactive effects, it can be introduced naturally into most service encounters as a means of improving the quality of service. Second, because process recording is not used regularly in practice, its use does not allow students to develop the recording skills they will need

EXHIBIT 3.1 Excerpt from a Student Process Record: Mental Health Crisis Line

		Worker Comments
Worker:	Crisis Line; Mary speaking.	
Client:	Hello. [*pauses*] Is this the place . . . you call for help if you are in trouble?	
Worker:	Yes it is. Can I help you?	
Client:	Well, I don't know. [*pauses*]	*I was really nervous.*
Worker:	We try to help everyone who calls. Nothing that's bothering you is too big or too small.	*I sound like I'm in sales, not social work.*
Client:	You sound kind of young. Are you?	*This upset me—did I handle it right?*
Worker:	Yes, I am. Does that matter?	
Client:	I guess not. [*pauses*] I do have a problem . . . and I really don't know where else to turn. [*pauses*]	*Jumped in too fast.*
Worker:	That is what we are here for.	
Client:	Yeah.	
Worker:	Sometimes it's hard to start. Just tell me what you are feeling right now.	*This is about the best thing I did.*
Client:	Well . . . I am feeling lost . . . tired . . . alone.	
Worker:	Yes?	
Client:	You see, I really have no one any more.	*I could have asked her about herself.*
Worker:	You seem to feel very lonely right now.	
Client:	Yeah. [*pauses*] I have been crying a lot tonight. Just watching TV and crying. I was watching this really sad show, and I started feeling like there is nothing to live for.	
Worker:	You started to cry when you were watching a sad show.	

EXHIBIT 3.1 Excerpt from a Student Process Record: Mental Health Crisis Line (continued)

		Worker Comments
Client:	Yeah. It was about a family that had all kinds of trouble but stuck together. The father lost his job. Then the mother got cancer. The father took care of the kids while the mother was in the hospital. She was real bitter but then she realized how lucky she was . . . and they all lived happily ever after.	
Worker:	Has anything like that happened to you?	*Pretty good.*
Client:	No. That's why I was crying. Because they all loved each other . . . and I'm alone.	
Worker:	You're alone and lonely. Are there any other problems you're having right now?	*I really don't seem to want to hear how lonely she is!*
Client:	A lot of other problems. Like my job. And like my health. I feel sick all the time.	
Worker:	Could you tell me some of your symptoms?	*Am I trying to be a doctor?*
Client:	I feel tired all the time. Can't get out of bed. I've been late to work, missing work.	
Worker:	So feeling sick and staying home is affecting your job. But you called because you thought we could help you with something. Can you tell me a little bit more about what made you decide to call?	*I am willing to talk about her job, her sickness, but not her loneliness.*
Client:	It's how lonely I feel. I thought that if I just had someone to talk to I wouldn't feel so lonely right now.	*She brings up her loneliness again, but I change the subject again.*

Worker:	And we've talked a little, but I really don't know very much about you.	
Client:	There's not very much to tell. I'm divorced, 45 years old. I work at N——[*department store*]. My kids are grown; my folks are dead. And I come home at night to an empty house.	
Worker:	Sometimes talking to someone else helps.	
Client:	Yes, it does. Talking to you has made me feel less lonely.	*She is indicating some interest.*
Worker:	And we can talk a little more. But I wonder if you have ever thought about talking about your problems with a counselor?	
Client:	Well, when I was getting a divorce, I saw a counselor. But the marriage was already a lost cause.	
Worker:	Uh-huh.	
Client:	Yeah. I have thought about going to a counselor, and I thought about it before I called tonight.	
Worker:	Have you thought about getting in touch with that counselor again?	
Client:	It was in another city.	
Worker:	I could refer you to a counseling agency here.	
Client:	You could?	
Worker:	Yes. In fact, if you give me your name and phone number, I could have an intake worker from the agency call you and make an appointment.	*But I am trying too hard.*
Client:	I don't know.	
Worker:	No obligation, of course. You could talk about anything: your job, your health, your loneliness.	*Selling again!*
Client:	Uh-huh. Well, I'm not sure.	

EXHIBIT 3.1 Excerpt from a Student Process Record: Mental Health Crisis Line (continued)

		Worker Comments
Worker:	Or I could give you the name of the agency, and you could call them.	*I was scared that I'd lose her—and felt anxious through the rest of the interview.*
Client:	I suppose I could give you my name and you could have them call. I wouldn't want them to call me at work, though.	
Worker:	No. You could tell me when they should contact you at home.	
Client:	Well, I guess that that would be okay. So long as no one at work knew. Is this going to cost a lot of money?	
Worker:	Well, I can't tell you exactly how much, but the agency has different programs, and different fees for different clients. And they have a sliding scale.	*Unclear.*
Client:	What does that mean?	
Worker:	The fee is set by how much you can afford to pay.	
Client:	That sounds okay.	
Worker:	Then I'll take your name and number. And when you want to have the agency call. [*takes information*] I'm glad you are willing to consider counseling.	*Is she committed or am I?*
Client:	Just thinking about it.	
Worker:	I know.	
Client:	Well, thanks. It helped. Goodbye.	
Worker:	Goodbye, Mrs. T.	

EXHIBIT 3.2 Excerpt from a Student Process Record: Developmental Disabilities, Parents' Group

Meeting Number 11

Date: 11/11
Members present: Mrs. B, Mr. and Mrs. W, Mr. and Mrs. Z, Mrs. F, Miss C
Goals for the meeting: Discuss use of community resources and the need for additional resources to meet the needs of families caring for children with developmental disabilities.

I opened the meeting by describing our planned agenda. We would discuss what kinds of community services each family uses in caring for their developmentally disabled children and also what kinds of needs they had that could be met by additional services. What did they use and what did they need? Mrs. W said that she was sorry more of the parents were not at the meeting, since this was a very important subject. Mr. W nodded; he said that whenever the meeting was planned around a "serious matter" rather than a party or a sports activity, most of the parents did not show up. (The agenda for the meeting had been proposed by the Ws.) Mrs. Z and Mrs. C nodded in agreement, and Mrs. C said that the regular members (those attending tonight) are the only ones who seem to see the group as more than a place to go in the evening. The discussion of the "others" (that is, those parents who are not part of this core group) continued for several minutes.

I said that I had sent a letter to each parent, to inform them of the meeting and the planned agenda. I wondered if anyone had any suggestions about how to encourage other parents to attend meetings. Mrs. W said that all she could suggest was to have meetings where there was a party or a baseball game rather than meetings about important things. Mrs. B said that she could understand why some of the "others" came if it was a social event . . . the meeting was "fun" and gave them something to do in the evening. Not everyone enjoys sitting around and talking about their kids. (They come to the meeting to get away from them.) Mr. W said that he thought the other parents should take some responsibility and should see this group as a way of making life better for the kids, rather than just as a social club. The group then discussed the purpose of the group—social club or helping the kids. Mrs. B said that different people had different reasons for coming to the meetings; she asked if that was all right. The Ws continued the theme of "responsibility, not fun."

EXHIBIT 3.2 Excerpt from a Student Process Record: Developmental Disabilities, Parents' Group (continued)

Mr. W said, as he had said many times before, that he thought the group should be like the Jaycees, with formal meetings, elected officers, and so forth. Mrs. B, looking very disgusted, said that his attitude might be a reason why parents didn't come to the discussion meetings. Mr. W responded by citing their lack of responsibility for the kids.

I said that what we had been discussing was very important, but that it was also important to get to the agenda for the meeting. Could we discuss participation and the purpose of the group again at the next meeting and move on to community resources? There was general agreement that we should move on to the agenda, but disagreement on how to handle the issues of attendance and purpose.

I said that the meeting next month was a holiday party, but that the January meeting had not yet been planned. Since the January meeting would mark the beginning of the second year of the group, could we use that meeting to talk about the past year and about plans for the future? This would give everyone an opportunity to discuss the purpose of the group as well as the agendas for future meetings. There was some discussion of this suggestion. The Ws thought the suggestion was good, but that the other parents either would not show up or would suggest parties and games. Mrs. B thought we should take a vote on the January agenda, which passed unanimously.

The meeting was more than half over by the time we got to the issue of resources. Mrs. F, who had been restive through the earlier discussion, asked if we could just move on to the resources that were needed rather than beginning with what resources were being used. Without waiting for approval from the group (meaning approval from Mr. and Mrs. W), she went on to say that what she really needed was a bodyguard for her son, a housekeeper for herself, a taxi service to and from the doctor, and a gun to rob a bank so she could pay for all of the things she needed. Everyone laughed, but she said this wasn't a joke. Her son, Manuel, now 12 and quite large for his age, was getting into fights in the neighborhood, walking home from the bus. She used to meet him at the bus, but this year she had let him walk home alone. He is old enough, and the teacher thought it would be good for him. But he is getting into fights because the kids call him names, and he "goes crazy." He needs to learn how to take care of himself, but the neighborhood kids won't leave him alone. She went on to describe many problems that she was facing at this time.

Mrs. F said that she also had many problems, not big ones that required a new program, but many small ones that added up.

I suggested that we make a list of all the small and large problems each family was facing, and that maybe we could come up with some common themes. This might help us in trying to find some solutions. Over Mrs. W's opposition, the group spent the rest of the meeting listing problems. These will be discussed at a future meeting. I also made an appointment to meet with Mrs. F about her problems with Manuel.

as practitioners. Therefore, a student's experience should not be limited to the use of process recording but should include other forms of recording as well.

Summary

Primary Function: Social work education.

Current Usage: Field instruction.

Organizing Rationale: The worker records as completely as possible all or selected portions of the service encounter. The record includes client statements and actions as well as worker statements, actions, and feelings. The record may resemble the script of a play or it may be organized into paragraphs, using "I said" and "(client's name) said." It is useful to have the record transcribed, leaving a wide margin for comments by the worker and the supervisor.

Strengths: The practitioner learns to remember the service transaction in detail. The record is a useful learning tool.

Limitations: It is time consuming and costly.

It does not teach recording skills needed for agency practice; it should be supplemented by other forms of recording.

It is selective rather than duplicative; it should be supplemented by approaches which more accurately portray the encounter.

The Teaching/Learning (T/L) Record

The teaching/learning record was developed by the author to meet the special learning needs of social work students in field agencies. It is intended to assist in the teaching and learning of cognitive and interpersonal practice skills and of narrative recording skills. The student prepares an extensive record of the service transaction, one that incorporates far more information about the process of service than is included in most agency records; the record then serves as the basis for the development of practice skills. In preparing and reviewing the record, the student has the opportunity to describe and assess the client-situation, the service transaction, and his or her own practice skills. At the same time, the record provides the field instructor with a "window" into the service process and into the student's professional development. This information allows the field instructor to collaborate with the student in making decisions about service and to assess and facilitate the student's progress in knowledge and skill development.

Although the T/L record, shown in Table 3.1, is more extensive than the records kept in most social service agencies, it is prepared in the same narrative style most agencies use in records and reports. As a result, students have the opportunity to practice the recording skills they will use as practitioners. The acquisition of these writing skills is critical to professional development; yet, although social workers are expected to possess these skills, their development is often neglected. Today, many practitioners find that writing is their most difficult task. Therefore, developing narrative recording skills with the intensive supervision offered in the field can help to prepare students with the recording and writing skills they will need in a variety of practice roles. Exhibit 3.3 presents excerpts from a T/L record.

TABLE 3.1 The Teaching/Learning Record

Content of the Record	Teaching/Learning Issues
Initiating Service	
A. Reason for service request, referral, or offer. Describe the circumstances as well as the persons and organizations that brought the client and worker together.	How do the methods of case-finding influence the client and the worker?
B. Description of relevant client-situation factors. Describe the client. Be sure to include important: Behaviors Feelings Values, preferences Strengths Unmet needs	Who is the client? What is a social history? What should it include?

The family and natural social network: Identify and describe those in the client's interpersonal environment who are interested parties. What are their expectations of the client, of service? Identify persons or groups who are potential resources or barriers (for example, work, neighbors).

How do we identify how others feel? Is culture or ethnicity a factor in this case?

The physical environment: Identify and describe any aspect of the environment that acts as a resource or barrier (for example, distance from public transportation).

Does the physical environment have a bearing on this case?

Formal social organizations: Identify and describe current and past relationships with social organizations (for example, school, public aid) that bear upon the current situation. Identify agency or public policies that may influence the client-situation.

Can organizations be a barrier and a resource?

C. Describe the process of data collection, including where and from whom the information was obtained. Characterize each interview by answering the following questions in summary form:

How did the interview begin? Was the purpose of the interview made explicit?
Who did most of the talking?
What techniques were used to encourage the source to talk?
What techniques were used to show interest, acceptance, and so forth?
What emotions did the source show?
What information did the worker share?
What decisions or plans for the future were made? How did the interview end?
What were the strengths and weaknesses of the interview?

How did the student feel before, during, and after the interview? What were your assumptions about the client? How did you test them out? How did you show warmth? empathy? genuineness? What did the client get from the interview? What information is lacking, and how can you find it out?

D. Assess the current client-situation by answering the following questions in summary form:

What are the client's most salient needs? problems? strengths? preferences?
What are the relevant existing resources in the natural social and physical environment?
What are the relevant existing barriers?
What are the relevant current relationships with social organizations?

How do we know what is important? How do we know what is not important? How does the setting influence the focus? How do you organize a summary?

TABLE 3.1 The Teaching/Learning Record (continued)

Content of the Record	Teaching/Learning Issues
E. Explore the range of interventions, services, and resources. List: Problems and needs: / Relevant interventions, services, and resources: 1. / 1. 2. / 2. 3. / 3.	How do you find needed resources? What do you need to know about them (for example, eligibility)?
Establishing Goals (and Contract)	
A. Describe the process of formulating and planning goals by answering the following questions in summary form: How did the interview begin? Was the purpose of the interview made explicit? How was the range of possible goals and services presented? What were the client's views and preferences? How were the worker's and the agency's views presented? What goals were selected? To what extent is the client committed to the goals? (Give examples of statements, behaviors.) What plans were made? What interventions, services, and resources are involved?	How does this phase of the process differ from data collection? How do worker and client values influence goals, and plans? How does agency policy influence goals and plans? How important is client motivation? Will referrals be followed up? What are the benefits?
What are the client's responsibilities? How were these responsibilities explained? What are the worker's responsibilities? How did the interview end? What were the strengths and weaknesses of the interview?	Action? Were responsibilities appropriately distributed?
B. Briefly describe the contract. Describe and give a rationale for any decisions made with or on behalf of the client.	What is a contract?
C. Describe any barriers to implementing plans or reaching goals. How can barriers be minimized?	

Interim Notes

A. Interviews with clients:
   1. Describe the interview by answering the questions under Initiating Service, C, above in summary form.
   2. Describe worker and client activities since the last report.
   3. Describe any changes in the client-situation or other persons or environments that demonstrate:

      Movement toward goals
      Barriers
      New problems, needs
   4. Describe and give a rationale for any decisions made with or on behalf of the client.
   5. Briefly describe any changes in goals or plans.

How has the relationship changed through time?

Compare this phase with earlier phases of the process. What factors in the client-situation or the service environment are influencing goals and plans?

B. Interviews with other resource persons:
   1. Identify the resource person and the setting of the interview.
   2. Describe the purpose of the interview.
   3. Describe the content of the interview by answering the following questions in summary form:

      What information was learned?
      What information was shared? (Include the signed release of information in file.)
   4. What was accomplished regarding goals and plans?

What is privacy? Confidentiality? How do these values influence our contacts with clients, others? Are other professionals or organizations influencing service?

Terminating or Transferring Service

A. Briefly review the process of service by answering the following questions in summary form:

   What was the client-situation at the time service was initiated?
   What were the service goals and plans?
   What interventions, services, and resources were involved?
   What did service accomplish?
   What is the current client-situation?

Why review the service process? What were the intended or unintended benefits of service? Compare this phase with other phases in the process.

B. Describe the reasons for termination or transfer.

How did you feel during the last interview?

TABLE 3.1 The Teaching/Learning Record (continued)

Content of the Record	Teaching/Learning Issues
C. Describe the termination or transfer process by answering the following questions in summary form: How and by whom was termination or transfer introduced? Why was it suggested? What feelings were expressed? Were the process and progress of service reviewed? What plans were made? How did the interview end? What were the strengths and weaknesses of the interview?	How did the client feel? From the social work perspective, was termination planned? If you could start over, what would you do differently?
Follow-Up	
A. Briefly describe the persons and settings. B. Describe the current client-situation. C. Describe any plans for referral, service, or contact with the client or others.	Why do follow-up? What does this information tell us about services to the client?

EXHIBIT 3.3 Excerpts from a Teaching/Learning Record: Shelter for Runaway Youth, Casework Services

Reason for Service Request: Nancy was picked up by the police in D——, 40 miles from here. She had hitchhiked there and was walking along the highway, trying to get another ride at about 12:30 A.M. Saturday, when the state highway patrol spotted her. She said that she did not want to go home, so she was brought back to A—— to the shelter. Her mother was notified at about 7:30 A.M. that she was in residence here. Mrs. R did not know that Nancy was gone.

Description of the Client-Situation: Nancy R is a physically mature 14-year-old ninth-grade student. Nancy lives with her mother, two younger brothers, and her mother's boyfriend in a small house near the highway. Nancy was truant from school three days last week. Her grades were average (Cs) until this year, when she has been absent from classes frequently. She now is failing most of her classes.

Nancy is very attractive and pays a great deal of attention to her appearance (wears lots of makeup, fusses with her hair). She seems very bored and uninterested when she talks with me about school or her family situation. When she is with the other kids in the shelter, she is talkative and involved. When I ask her about her feelings, plans, and so forth, she says she doesn't know. Asked to describe school, she says it is boring and like a prison. Asked to describe her family, she says that everything was fine until Bill (her mother's boyfriend) moved in. He orders her around, orders everyone around. She says that she will not go back to her mother's house unless Bill goes; when asked where she would like to go, she says that she wants to stay at the shelter.

Mrs. R appears to be a very tired woman. She said that Nancy has been fighting with her "stepfather." Bill says that Nancy needs discipline, so he has been disciplining her. Nancy never used to help around the house or keep regular hours. Bill makes her help out and be in by a certain hour. Nancy does not like this; last week Nancy and Bill had a screaming fight that turned into a hitting fight. After the fight, Nancy left the house. Mrs. R thought that she had gone to stay with Lana, where she had stayed other times. That was why Mrs. R did not know that Nancy was missing when she was picked up in D——; she thought that Nancy was at Lana's. Mrs. R works the evening shift as a nurse's aid at S—— Hospital. Nancy used to babysit the younger children while Mrs. R was at work. Now Bill, who works days, is home while Mrs. R works, and most of the fights between Bill and Nancy seem to happen then. Mrs. R says that Bill is sorry he hit Nancy, but he says that she tore his shirt and that made him real mad. Mrs. R wants Nancy to come home but says that she will have to get along with Bill better.

Nancy's school counselor said that Nancy's school behavior was not really a problem until this year. Many students seem to have a "bad year" during junior high or high school, a year when their grades go down. The counselor did not notice anything unusual until a few weeks ago, when Nancy began to skip classes. She was called in to the counselor's office and told that a special report on her attendance would be sent to the counselor each day. Since that time, Nancy has been attending classes, although she has been absent from school six days in the past month.

No other agencies are active with the family. The police filed a report, which means that if Nancy runs away again the case will have to go before the juvenile court. She can stay in the shelter for one week only; at the end of the week, other plans must be made. . . .

Interview with Nancy (Day 4): I had left a note on her door asking Nancy to come to my office after she returned from school. (This was

EXHIBIT 3.3 Excerpts from a Teaching/Learning Record: Shelter for Runaway Youth, Casework Services (continued)

her first day back at school.) My purpose for the interview was to discuss with Nancy the family interview that was planned for that evening.

We began by talking about what had happened when she went back to school. She said that all the kids seemed to know that she had run away and was staying at the shelter. She described at length many encounters she had had with kids at school that day. In general, it appears that she is getting a great deal of attention from other students about her "adventure." She said that she told Lana (her best friend) that she had a "shrink" (me!) and that she might not have to go home.

This is when I introduced the subject of the family interview. She seemed surprised about it, although I had spoken to her about it several times before. I explained again about the time limits, and that some arrangements would have to be made by the weekend (three more days). I explained that her mother would take the evening off to be home for the interview. She asked if Bill would be there. (I did not handle this part well.) I told her that I thought that it would be important to have him there, since he was living with her family. Nancy said that she would not go if he were there, that he was not her father. I then went into a long explanation about how he was willing to work on the problem and about how her mother felt it was important that she and Bill work things out.

Weaknesses: I realize now that I did most of the talking in this interview. Nancy really had no chance to tell her side of the story. Nancy went to the family interview without realizing that I would be there to support her in expressing her feelings. It would not surprise me if she views me as just another person who is trying to get her to do things that she does not want to do, when my real purpose is to support her and to be her advocate. In looking back over what occurred in the interview, it seems that what was important to her about school (her friends' reactions) was not what was important to me (the family interview, her schoolwork). Also, her attitude gets to me.

Strengths: Not many. I am in touch with how exasperating Nancy can be. I know that she gets prestige from being a runaway. The time factor that I find so important does not seem to be important at all to her. . . .

Client needs and problems:	**Services, resources, and interventions:**
1. Living arrangement	Return to mother's home Extended family (?) Foster home Group home
2. Relationship with family	Counseling agency
3. School problems	School social worker Counseling agency After-school program
4. Running away	Counseling agency Police Juvenile court

Family Interview (Day 4): Purpose of the interview: to establish a contract. Nancy and I arrived at Mrs. R's house about 15 minutes early. After saying hello to her mother (who was in a bathrobe) and her brothers, Nancy went off to her room and her mother went to get dressed. I sat in the living room with Bill, who was watching TV. He did not talk to me for the half hour I sat there.

The house is clean but small and threadbare. The boys share a room, and Mrs. R and Bill share a room on the main floor. Nancy has a room in the basement. The house is in a neat working-class neighborhood.

Finally, the interview began. Mrs. R and Nancy sat on the couch. I sat opposite on a chair. Bill sat in front of the TV, which remained on. I began by explaining the need to make some plans by the end of the week. I described the possibilities: coming home (with counseling), foster care, group home. Surprisingly, Mrs. R did most of the talking. She said that she had been thinking a lot. She wanted Nancy to come home. Nancy would have to follow some rules but nothing too hard. Nancy, who was very subdued, asked what rules. Mrs. R talked about curfew, cleaning up around the house, and babysitting. Nancy said that that would be okay. She expected to do some work. But what about Bill?

Bill had been watching TV up to this point. He said that he did not want any more trouble with Nancy. He had talked it over with Mrs. R. To him, Nancy had it easy. But this was Mrs. R's house, and she wanted to pamper Nancy. That was her business. He said several times that he did not want any trouble.

We all agreed that Nancy would return to the shelter for the night; I would bring her home after school the next day. Before we left, I restated the contract, that Nancy would agree to perform some chores and follow the rules we would agree upon; that Bill would allow Mrs. R to be the disciplinarian; and that each would call me if

EXHIBIT 3.3 Excerpts from a Teaching/Learning Record: Shelter for Runaway Youth, Casework Services (continued)

there were any difficulties. In addition, all three would be involved in counseling at the family agency, beginning next month.

Strengths: Nancy and Mrs. R seemed to be able to talk together. Nancy was reassured that her mother really cared for her. Mrs. R is a much stronger person than I first thought. She is able to solve problems and make decisions. We did not go too far into the relationship between Nancy and Bill; this was part of the plan, since they agreed to go for counseling, where this relationship would be handled in depth.

Weaknesses: Should have been more specific about what would happen when Nancy returned home. Depended too much on Mrs. R's ability to keep things going. What will happen when she is at work and Bill and Nancy are at home together?

Assessment: At this point, Nancy needs to know that she still has a place in the family. Mrs. R showed a great deal of strength in her role as mother. But will she be able to discipline Nancy? It seems that this crisis, which began with the fight between Nancy and Bill and included Nancy's running away, had some positive effects. Mrs. R has taken some action. Bill seems to be taken aback by the anger he showed toward Nancy. It is hard to know whether any real change will take place; Bill and Nancy each want the other to change.

As far as Nancy's school is concerned, the school counselor is aware of the family situation and is keeping up with Nancy's school attendance. I will consult with her regularly. Nancy is not engaged in her education; a plan should be developed to involve her in classroom work and other activities in the school.

Summary

Primary Function: Social work education.

Current Usage: Field instruction; field seminar.

Organizing Rationale: The student records in narrative summary style following the outline provided (left column). Some teaching/learning issues, relevant for discussion in field supervision or in the field seminar, are also included (right column).

Strengths: The student records sufficient information about the process to facilitate the teaching and learning of interpersonal and cognitive practice skills. The student uses the narrative style used in many agency records and reports.

Limitations: Time-consuming and costly.

Selective; does not actually reproduce the service transaction. To study process, and the student and instructor should use videotapes or audiotapes.

Essential Recording

Social work students have taped their sessions with clients for at least thirty years (Itzin, 1960). Audiotapes and videotapes of classroom exercises help students model and monitor elementary interviewing skills (Ivey, 1987); they are also used in teaching, learning, and supervising advanced clinical practice, notably family therapy. Audiotapes and videotapes offer practitioners, supervisors, and educators an opportunity to observe practice "in action." Reviewing tapes helps the student practitioner develop a deeper understanding of self and of clients, and gives supervisors direct access to what has transpired in the worker-client transaction. Tapes are a powerful and dynamic tool for use in the development of cognitive and interpersonal practice skills and practitioner self-awareness.

Tapes can also be used to facilitate the development of recordkeeping skills. Good records are not just clear, concise, and well-written; they also focus on the most salient information about the client-situation and the service transaction. The purpose of essential recording is to teach students how to distill the essence of the case from what takes place in sessions with clients, and how to prepare well-written and meaningful narrative reports. Students tape sessions with clients, review the tapes, and prepare narrative summaries of each session for use in supervision. Taping has many advantages over process recording, affording students the opportunity to observe themselves and their clients more objectively. Tapes also may be used in the service process, allowing clients to become more aware of their own behavior. Of course, some clients decline to be taped, and others are uncomfortable at first. Some practitioners are concerned that the tape recorder may affect the service process, because both the worker and the client respond to its presence. However, routine taping is usually accepted by the client if it is accepted by the worker. Moreover, over time both the worker and the client come to forget or ignore the machine.

Through the essential recording process, students learn to observe their clients carefully, to reflect on their own and their clients' communication, and to write narrative summaries based on careful and thorough analysis of the content and process of service. After listening to the tape of a session (and in some cases preparing a verbatim transcript for use in supervision), the student prepares a session summary in narrative style. These summaries are presented to the supervisor for review and are used by the student when it is time to prepare narrative reports for the client's record. The social history, the opening summary, interim notes, the closing summary, and other narrative reports prepared in conformity with agency guidelines become a part of the client's record, but session summaries, tapes, and verbatim transcripts do not. These educational records, like process recordings, are part of the student's rather than the client's record; the client's name and other identifying information should be obscured.

Essential recording offers supervisors the opportunity to listen to the tapes directly and to review tapes, transcripts of sessions, and session summaries with their students. Supervisory meetings are enriched by this wealth of materials. Moreover, after students have completed each step of this process, they are well prepared to write in the official client record. By that time, they have reviewed tapes, written session summaries, and discussed these materials in supervision. They should be quite knowledgeable about the case and skillful in its documentation.

Essential recording includes five or six steps.

1. The student seeks and is granted permission from the client to tape sessions.
2. The student tapes sessions with the client.
3. Each tape is transcribed into a verbatim record. (This step may be omitted.)
4. The student prepares a session summary for each session, using either an unstructured or a semistructured format. (See Exhibits 3.5 and 3.6.)
5. The student and the supervisor review and discuss each tape or verbatim record and each session summary from the perspectives of practice and recording.
6. The student prepares narrative reports for the official client record, using the customary agency format.

Educational programs that wish to use essential recording will find that this approach may not be feasible for use in every case. However, students can learn a great deal about practice and recording by using essential recording in just one or two cases. Moreover, field agencies may need to be persuaded that essential recording will not interfere with their services to clients. They may be concerned about client resistance, confidentiality, and cost. First, agencies need to know how clients will be asked to participate in the taping process. The student should present taping as a means of offering quality services but not as a requirement for receiving services. Agencies should tell clients who will review the tapes and how they will be used. If appropriate, the student should ask the client to sign a release form agreeing to be taped and indicating that he or she understands how the tapes will be used. Secondly, agencies need guidelines for the confidential handling of tapes. In general, tapes should be used only in supervision and should be erased once services are completed. Unless specifically approved by the client, other uses of the tapes may invade the client's privacy (see Chapter 7). To protect against unwarranted use, tapes should be stored securely. Finally, the student may need to share the cost of equipment, tapes, and transcription.

Exhibit 3.4 is the transcript of a tape that recorded the first session between a student practitioner and a family referred for counseling by a school social worker. Exhibits 3.5 and 3.6 are session summaries of this interview. Exhibit 3.5 is an unstructured, open-ended narrative; Exhibit 3.6 presents similar information using a semistructured form.

Summary

Primary Function: Social work education.

Current Usage: Field instruction.

Organizing Rationale: This approach combines existing recordkeeping structures in a process in which students produce and review a series of products with the goal of distilling the essence of the case and then presenting this information in well-written narrative reports. Students produce tapes and session summaries prior to preparing the customary agency record.

Strengths: Essential recording teaches students to describe and analyze the case, using the narrative style they will be expected to use as practitioners. The process focuses the student's and supervisor's attention on what actually happens in the service transaction, facilitating the development of cognitive and interpersonal practice as well as recordkeeping skills.

Limitations: The process is time-consuming and may not be suitable in some agencies or with some clients. This limitation may be overcome by using essential recording with only one or two of the student's cases. Videotape equipment may be prohibitively expensive, but audiotaping equipment is inexpensive. Tapes may be vulnerable to breaches in confidentiality.

EXHIBIT 3.4 Example of Essential Recording: Family Service Agency, In-Home Counseling Program

Transcript of Audiotape: Session Number One, 3/30/88

Worker: Okay. I am a student at the School of Social Work at the University and you are all a family that has been assigned to me. You were referred by . . .

Mrs. G: Angela Martin.

Worker: Exactly. Exactly. She said that you might be able to use services and the reason that I have a tape recorder is because since I am a student, I am supervised and that's for everybody's best interest. Okay? I want to make sure that I can provide the best services for you and my supervisor listens to these tapes before I come to see you again next week and offers suggestions.

Mrs. G: Oh, okay.

Worker: I guess it would be helpful if you gave us an idea of what's going on with you and your family now.

Mrs. G: Okay, well, the reason why I was talking to Angela and I was telling her that me and May, we lost count of, you know, we got kind of a generation gap. And I remember when she was little we could talk, and now that she's older and goin' different places and things, we can't. I don't seem to be able to talk to her like I used to. And I feel I'm losin' control of somethin', you know. And so I just wanted to know, maybe there's someone that could be neutral and could listen to us talk or something and maybe they could find out what the problem is. That you know, it's not that I'm pickin' at her or anything. I want her to understand that I love her, that's why I'm doin' this, you know—to try to keep the relationship between me and her to where when we get older she can always come back to her mother.

Worker: How do you see it, May?

Mrs. G: Well, go ahead. That's what it's about. Tell how you feel.

May: They're always pickin' at people.

Worker: Picking at people?

May: (*Crying*) Like if I go somewhere and she tells me a certain time to get back and I forget that certain time she's always hollerin' at me. She says, "Your brother don't act like that."

Mrs. G: Mm hmm. Anything else, May? Okay, so she's right about that. Only one thing is her brother is older than her, and he don't go as much as she does. You know, May is 12 years old, and he is 14 and will be 15 in July.

Worker: Donald is 14?

Mrs. G: Yes.

Worker: And, May, you're 12?

Mrs. G: Uh huh. Okay, I don't mind her goin' but, you know, I would like it if she come back, or if she's goin' somewhere else, to let me know if she wants to go somewhere else. Several times I had let her go somewhere, and I sent over to where she's gonna be, and she's not there. Then I want to know why, you know, why she didn't come back and let me know anything about where she's gonna be at. So, yes, I do yell at her, and maybe that's where she thinks I'm wrong, but then I don't feel that I'm too far wrong because I don't spank them, you know, cause I could get a little out of control by that, so maybe I do yell a little too much at her.

Worker: Donald, what do you see going on in your family?

Donald: Not much.

Worker: Not much? May, you said that there's a lot of picking on you. Is that what you said?

May: See, if I have my feet on the wall, my mother yells at me to get my feet off the wall.

Mrs. G: Because you wipe your feet on the wall.

May: If I mess with the TV, they yell at me. I get in trouble, like nobody else. I'm gettin' tired of it. I just don't like nobody pickin' at me too much. (*Begins to cry*)

Mrs. G: Okay, well, she do have a stepfather which is Clarence's father—we aren't married—so maybe that's why she feel that he's pickin'. You know, 'cause he's her stepfather. But as far as her feet bein' on the wall and everything, she's the only one that does it. She's the only one that does it.

Worker: So, you feel as if all of this attention, that the picking, is on you. Is that what you're saying? And that's what makes you feel bad, is that right? So if there weren't all that picking you wouldn't feel bad. Is that it? I'm trying to understand what you're saying.

May: Yes, if they wouldn't pick on me I'd be okay, but they pick on me too much.

Worker: Tara, you're 10? How is it when your Mom gets mad at May? How do you see it?

EXHIBIT 3.4 Example of Essential Recording: Family Service Agency, In-Home Counseling Program (continued)

Tara: As I see it, it's not really hollerin'. She's just trying to tell her right from wrong.

Worker: May, how long do you think people have been picking on you? Is it a long time or is it recent?

May: Sorta long. It started when I was 10.

Mrs. G: Yes. When she started in the double digits, 10, 11, 12 years old. Because, at first I thought it was the girls that she would be around, but then she stopped hanging around them, okay. The problem at that times changed. It didn't stop, it just changed from one thing to another. And then, after that, like right now I can talk to her a little bit more than I could a couple of months ago. So I think it was the crowd she was hanging around.

Worker: Oh, so things have gotten better.

Mrs. G: A little better, yes. I tell you, her only problem is she is under her stepfather.

Worker: You say it's gotten better because May stopped being with some of her friends?

Mrs. G: Yeah.

Worker: But what have you tried? Have you tried anything specific in your dealings with May, or has May tried?

Mrs. G: No, I mostly tried to talk to her. Because Tara is my daughter and I'm quite sure she is watching some of the things May is doing and seein' if I'm letting her get by with this and get by with that, so I'm trying to get them separate and talk to them. Like, I done told May. Okay, she wanted a boyfriend. I said fine, you know, he come by and talk to me and I get to meet him or something. Don't sneak around. You know, and so she says she'd try to do that, but I haven't met anybody but I've heard her say that she like this boy, you know, but I still haven't met him. But, I trust her because when she was younger, from birth up until 10 years old, I raised her. I'm hopin' that my values that I gave her at that younger age she can kind of look back on those, although she might think that I'm being mean to her. When she leaves I don't keep track of her like I used to. I'm just hopin' that when she comes back she comes back like she leaves. Safe and without being harmed.

Worker: So, your concern is really out of love. May, do you know what time you're supposed to be home, is that clear to you? Or is it not clear.

May: Yeah, but sometimes I'll be at my friend's house and she'll want to go by the park. So I'll be at the park. Say we leave about 5:00 or 5:30, and I'm supposed to be home at 5:00 and I'm still at the park at night and when she goes home I go over to her house, right? And say she goes home at 6:00 and say I gotta go. And I come home and I get yelled at.

Worker: Because—

May: 'Cause I didn't go into the house to see what time it is, my friend's house to see what time it is.

Mrs. G: There's nothing wrong with the girls. The one she's hanging around right now. I like the girl. She's a very nice girl. You know, I don't know too much about her family background, but as for her, she seems like a really nice child.

Worker: I wonder if the rest of you feel like your mother and May are doing most of the talking. Since it's our first meeting as an introduction of the family, could each of you kind of sketch out, draw, what you all think the family is? Stick people is fine. It doesn't just have to be family members. It can also be things that are real important to you, like, May, it sounds like you have a real close friend that is real important to you. Or maybe, Donald, you have a friend who's real important. And I'd like you to draw it. Maybe you can draw the people inside or outside your house. This is going to tell us something. Okay. And I want you to be as creative as possible.

May: I don't draw too good.

Worker: Oh, I don't really care about that. Just draw something that shows who is in this family, who are the important people, and what this family is like.

Mrs. G: Now just draw a picture like the lady says.

Worker: While everyone is drawing, maybe you could tell me something about the children and about you and about Walter. Does Walter live here?

Mrs. G: Yes, he lives here. Another thing about this is, I'm getting a divorce, going through a divorce. And that's probably why May feels, you know, a little hard tension problems. Like I have an order of protection against him, but he's still here. It's because — I don't know. I want out of the situation, but just the same I feel, you

EXHIBIT 3.4 Example of Essential Recording: Family Service Agency, In-Home Counseling Program (continued)

	know, he has an aunty here, and some cousins here, but he really don't have nowhere to go. So —
Worker:	You have an order of protection against him? But he's still . . .
Mrs. G:	He's still here.
Worker:	That's hard.
Mrs. G:	Mm hmm. So that's probably some of the reason why May feels the way she feels, you know, because when she says someone pickin' on her, she's not just talkin' about me, she's mostly talkin' about him.
Worker:	Is Walter the father of Byron and Clarence?
Mrs. G:	Yes, Byron and Clarence.
Worker:	And the rest of the kids?
Mrs. G:	Well, Walter be their stepfather.
Worker:	And their father?
Mrs. G:	They don't have no real father. Walter is their stepfather and he's the only one they know. And May don't get along with him.
Worker:	What about the rest of the kids?
Mrs. G:	Well, Byron and Clarence are still small. They don't give Walter no trouble. Donald is away a lot. And Tara's easy. It's mostly him and May that get into it. So we're supposed to be drawing houses? A family unit?
Worker:	Yeah. The house and all the people you think are part of your family and your important friends.
Mrs. G:	I have a lot of people I can really turn to, but you know people don't listen like they used to. Like I've got a sister—I'm from a family of 10. I've got five brothers and four girls, 10 of us all together. Okay, so out of the 10 it's just me and her, we're real close, you know, so I can turn to her and talk to her and she'll listen, you know. There's nothing she can say or do, cause I'm going to do what I want to do anyway. And then there's my girlfriend, you know, she has a lot of problems and stuff, too, maybe that's why I kind of feel I can talk to her. And my mom is here.
Worker:	Your mom is here and your sister's here.
Mrs. G:	Uh huh. I have two sisters and two brothers here. But, like I said, my sister don't mind—she's the only sister

that I can really talk to and she's younger than I am and she's the only one that I can really talk to and know that she'll listen. And then my mother, she's very outgoing herself. I don't feel a close relationship between me and her.

Worker: Was that always the case?

Mrs. G: Always. I felt it from a child.

Worker: It sounds like you're concerned about having a close relationship with May. That's something we can talk more about next time. I want to set up a time for our next appointment. But first I want to look at each of your drawings . . .

(The interview continued for another 10 minutes. The worker discussed each picture with the artist. She asked that Walter be present at the next family session and set a time when he could attend.)

EXHIBIT 3.5 Unstructured Session Summary

Interview Date: 3/30/88
Worker: Linda T, M.S.W. student
Session Number One

Mrs. Queenie G and all of her five children attended the session. Mr. Walter G, who Mrs. G says she is divorcing but who still lives in the house, was not present. I have asked that he attend the next session, scheduled for 4/5/88.

The family structure is unclear. The genogram of the family, based on information collected so far, is on page 82.

Mrs. G, who sought help from the school social worker about her relationship with May, a special education student, did most of the talking in the interview. May also talked. According to Mrs. G, May does not follow rules. She does not come home when she is supposed to, and she does not call when she is going to be late. According to May, who cried during the early part of the interview, everyone in the family picks on her. She does not feel that she should be blamed when she forgets to come home on time. It does seem that she is singled out as the one who causes trouble. Mrs. G says that things have gotten better during the past two months, since May no longer is hanging around with the friends who Mrs. G considered a bad influence. Mrs. G seems to worry that May will get in trouble

EXHIBIT 3.5 Unstructured Session Summary (continued)

?
?
?
Queenie
Walter
14
Donald
12
May
10
Tara
6
Byron
5
Clarence

when she is out with her friends. But Mrs. G also says that a lot of May's problem is with Mr. G, May's stepfather.

Unfortunately, I did not learn much about this, or about him or the other children's father. Mrs. G did say that she has an order of protection against Mr. G but that he still lives in the house, because, according to Mrs. G, he has no other place to go. At one point, Mrs. G said she was not married to Mr. G; at another point she said she was getting a divorce from him. Mrs. G indicated that there is tension in the house, but I did not learn what actually happens. There is a lot that still needs to be explored, including: current and past family violence; the relationship between May and the other children, Mr. G, and Mrs. G; and any other problems that members of the family have at work or in school, at home, and so on.

The interview could have been improved if all members of the family had been encouraged to talk. Also, the picture drawing was a good idea, but I did not know what to do with it. Finally, I asked a lot of stacked questions (two or three in a row) and seemed to get off the track several times.

EXHIBIT 3.6 Semistructured Session Summary

Date: 3/30/88 — Worker: Linda T, M.S.W. student
Session: One — Case: G family, #88-028

1. Briefly describe what happened during the session.

Mrs. G and her five children attended. Mrs. G and May, a special education student, described conflicts regarding May's behavior. For example, May does not always come home when she is supposed to. Mrs. G wants her to call; she worries about May when May is late, out with friends. May feels that she is being unfairly blamed, "picked on."

Mr. G was not at the session. Mr. and Mrs. G are "divorcing," although their relationship is unclear. Mr. G is the father of Byron (six) and Clarence (five) but not of Donald (fourteen), May (twelve), and Tara (ten). Mrs. G has an order of protection against Mr. G, but he is living in the home.

2. List the problems, needs, and issues that surfaced.

Conflict exists between Mr. G and May, between Mrs. G and May, between Mr. and Mrs. G.

Mrs. G thinks things have improved since May has acquired new friends; she sees the problem now as May being "under" her stepfather.

May feels picked on. She is the Identified Patient (IP) in this family. Mrs. G is very worried about May's behavior, her friends, and so on. Her special place in the family (as the oldest girl and as a special ed student) makes her vulnerable.

Mr. G may be abusive.

3. What techniques or interventions were used?

We explored Mrs. G's and May's view of the problem, but other family members were not drawn in enough.

Each member drew a picture of the family. I discussed each picture but did not know where to go with it.

I explored Mrs. G's family network as a possible support.

I tried to find out about the family history but was not successful.

4. Suggest areas for future exploration or intervention.

Relationship between Mr. G and other members of family
Question of abuse, violence
Involve all family members
Problems at school, in the neighborhood

Teaching and Learning about Recordkeeping

Records of the transactions between social work students and their clients are an important vehicle for teaching and learning about practice. When students prepare and review their records, they recall what occurred in their sessions with clients and they reflect upon what it meant. The recording process, then, helps students to develop their perceptual and conceptual skills. Records aid in supervision, focusing discussion on critical aspects of the client-situation and the service relationship, and facilitating the development of students' understanding of their clients and themselves.

Students' records can also be used in teaching and learning recordkeeping concepts and skills. Ideally, education for recording should be founded upon three precepts. First, it should take place in the classroom, in the field, and in entry-level practice. Secondly, students should move from the generic to the specific, from generic concepts learned in the classroom to their specific application in fieldwork and in entry-level practice. Skill development would proceed along a continuum; those skills acquired at an early stage would not be supplanted by others but would become the foundation for skills developed later. Thirdly, education for practice and for recording should be linked and continuous; recording would not be introduced as a necessary evil of agency practice but would be integrated as a natural adjunct to practice from the beginning to the end of the student's learning experience. To this end, students would be exposed to records and recordkeeping concepts and practice in a variety of courses throughout their academic careers.

Reality stands in sharp contrast to this ideal. What has been notably absent from the experience of most current and recent students has been:

The classroom (or generic) component of the classroom-field-practice sequence

A rational continuum of skill acquisition and development

Early and continuous integration of recording with practice

The most significant of these deficiencies is that many students are not learning about records and recordkeeping in the classroom. In recent years, the primary responsibility for teaching social workers about records and recordkeeping has fallen to the field agencies. Agencies have assumed full responsibility not by choice but by default when their students have not been taught about recording in the classroom. Although teaching specific policies, practices, and procedures is the necessary province of the field instructor, teaching generic concepts is not. The field experience is already too crowded to give sufficient attention to content better taught in advance of, or concurrent with, the field experience and in the broader context of the classroom.

However, deferring to the field not only has overcrowded that component of social work education, it also has made education for recording inconsistent. Because the field experience is necessarily dependent upon the field supervisor and the field agency, a student's experience with recordkeeping reflects that supervisor's and that agency's approach to documentation. Some supervisors give careful attention to records and to recording; others do not. And different agencies record differently. Thus, an individual student's experience with recording is both unique and specialized, and the cumulative experiences of all social work students is heterogeneous and uneven.

Inadequate classroom preparation also sets the stage for a breakdown in the continuum of skill acquisition and development. Students who have not learned generic recording concepts in the classroom have no framework for understanding and placing in context the specific practices and procedures they learn in the field. Without a structure for accommodating this information, students must learn each successive agency practice or procedure anew, since no knowledge base exists. In addition to the discontinuities that arise as a result of lack of preparation in the classroom, other discontinuities arise when the skills the students develop during their student years are not the recording skills they need as practitioners. There may be differences in purpose, content, and style between student records and practice records. For example, a student who has used process recording in fieldwork and who has had no experience with other models of recording will not be prepared for the summary recording he or she is likely to use in practice. Finally, without the classroom element, the student is unlikely to perceive a connection between practice and its documentation. Students who learn about recording for the first time in the field will always identify the task with its roots in the organization rather than with its roots in practice. For their part, students and entry-level practitioners are often surprised and dismayed by the attention directed toward their records; they frequently feel they have not been adequately equipped in knowledge, skill, or expectation for the central role that recordkeeping plays in their day-to-day practice.

Any agenda to improve education for recording, then, must begin with the return of the social work record and recording concepts to a prominent place in social work education. The curriculum plan in Table 3.2 is intended to pave the way for that return. Students are introduced to generic concepts in the classroom and to specific concepts in the field. Moreover, the plan includes not just core content, relevant both to undergraduate and graduate students, but also specialized content appropriate for graduate-level students in clinical and managerial programs.

The second item on the agenda for improving education for recording is to select an approach that integrates practice with recording skills and proceeds along a continuum. Skills students learn in the classroom and the field should prepare them for entry-level practice. This means that students should be taught practice using their records, and taught to record based upon their practice experiences. The records they prepare while they are students should help them develop their interpersonal practice skills and their ability to prepare the narrative summary reports they will write as practitioners.

Unfortunately, the approaches adopted by many programs today, using process recording, agency records, or a combination of the two, do not usually fulfill these goals. On the one hand, students may spend an inordinate amount of time developing process recording skills that are useless or even a hindrance later. Moreover, because process records do not reflect what actually occurs in an interview or session (Timms, 1972), they have only limited value in teaching practice skills. On the other hand, agency records usually do not

TABLE 3.2 Curriculum Plan for Teaching and Learning about Recording

Generic Content (Classroom)	Specific Content (Field)
Core Content	
Purpose of Recording	
Service documentation	Agency's uses of records
Case continuity	
Interprofessional communication	
Evaluation	
Supervision	
Agency management or funding	
Types of Records	
Educational records	Records kept by agency
Clinical records	Recording for teaching and learning social work practice
Management records	
Reports, letters	
Privacy principles	Agency's procedures for protecting client privacy
Recording Approaches	
Elements of content	Agency guidelines on content and style
Structures	Agency forms and outlines
Recording process and procedure	Agency procedures, aids for writing records (dictaphone, computer)
Specialized Content	
Recording by modality (for example, family therapy records)	Practice in making such records
Recording by field of practice (for example, records used in mental health)	Analysis of records used in agency
Accountability systems	Analysis of agency's accountability system

include sufficient information about the process of service to facilitate teaching practice skills, and may not give students sufficient experience preparing narrative summary reports.

If process recording is used, it should be used sparingly; in addition, more time should be spent on developing narrative summary skills. Given the limitations of the traditional approaches, educators may wish to experiment with other approaches that fulfill the goals outlined here. Earlier in this chapter, two such approaches were presented. The teaching/learning record is a narrative record that combines elements of content included in a typical agency record with additional information about student-client interaction and the student's thinking process. Essential recording uses audiotapes or videotape and summary reports.

A final item on the agenda to improve education for recording is the early and continuous integration of practice and its documentation. This goal requires that records be used as a means of teaching practice and that recording be taught as a part of practice. There is a variety of techniques through which this goal may be accomplished. In courses in direct service, students might read records in preparation for discussion of practice principles; students might write records following the role plays they perform. In courses in supervision, accountability, and administration, students might compare the utility and efficiency of different recordkeeping styles and formats; they might design forms or develop procedures and guidelines to meet particular agency requirements.

All of these changes in education for recording are predicated upon the willingness of social work educators to reintroduce recording concepts and skills into the practice curriculum. Many educators are reluctant to do so because they regard recordkeeping as an agency-based function that is extraneous to practice. It may fall to the field instructors and to their students to persuade them of the importance of returning the record to the classroom.

4 Narrative and Other Clinical Records

The Structure of Records

Various recording structures may be used to guide the selection and organization of information in social work records. Recording structures vary along several dimensions. They differ in **standardization**; that is, they vary in the degree to which content and organization are left to the discretion of the practitioner or are predetermined by form or format. Highly standardized formats increase the likelihood that required information will be documented and also increase the accessibility of that information. They tend to typify clients, services, and workers and also to routinize recordkeeping. In contrast, less standardized formats individualize clients, services, and workers, allowing the record to reflect the worker's own thinking and the salient issues in the particular case. However, specific information may not be included in the record or may appear in a form that makes it less accessible to the reader.

Recording structures also differ in **scope**; that is, they may apply to the entire record or to a specific element of content, such as the interim note. They differ in **selectivity**; that is, they vary in the degree to which they encompass diverse information about client, situation, environment, worker, and service transaction, or they scrupulously restrict content to particular observations, assessments, or elements of content. They also differ in **style**; that is, they vary in the mode of expression used, from discursive narration to fill-ins and check marks.

Finally, they differ in **rationale**; that is, they vary in the underlying principles that give focus and unity to the record and that give meaning to the recordkeeping process. Some recording structures are based on functional principles: Information is recorded for a purpose and organized to serve that purpose. Other structures are based upon conceptual principles: A theory of human behavior or the assumptions of a practice approach undergird the selection and organization of information for the record. These dimensions are an aid to understanding and to evaluating the advantages and disadvantages of each recordkeeping structure.

The need to be familiar with, and to choose among, various recording structures is a relatively recent phenomenon. Until the late 1960s, social workers had few options. Process recording was used in education and, to a limited extent, in agency practice. Narrative summary recording was the prevailing model for records used in agency practice. As social work practice and its environment changed, however, this customary approach to recordkeeping was no longer generally suitable. No one form or format met the documentation needs of all practitioners in all settings, for all service modalities and all client populations. In response, new approaches to recordkeeping were developed specially for use in social service agencies or modeled upon approaches used in other fields. Today, social workers have many options. They may choose a particular recordkeeping structure for a case, a program, or an agency because it meets one or more of the following objectives:

It minimizes costs, by limiting time spent in composing or transcribing the record or by simplifying information storage, retrieval, or use.

It meets external accountability requirements of accrediting or funding organizations.

It meets internal information needs, facilitating decision making, case continuity, supervision, or interprofessional communication.

It is congruent with current agencywide or fieldwide recording standards.

It is congruent with program or practice assumptions about what information is important and about how change will occur.

It maximizes client privacy.

It is suited to client access.

This chapter and the following one review a number of recordkeeping structures that are prototypes of those used in social work agencies and departments today. In practice, most agencies use a combination of structures (for example, narrative reports and computer-ready forms) and adapt standard formats (for example, the problem-oriented record) to meet their specific documentation requirements. Here, for ease of comparison, each recording structure is presented separately, using a common framework. First, the form or format is described, analyzed, and outlined. Then each structure is evaluated on the basis of six dimensions: primary function, secondary functions, current usage, organizing rationale, strengths, and limitations. Finally, examples of the use of each form or format are presented.

Although all the formats included in this chapter follow certain conventions of organization and content, they are characteristically open and can be adapted to the requirements of diverse organizations, programs, practice approaches, and practitioners. This flexibility is both a strength and a potential problem. The formats permit workers considerable latitude in deciding what information to include in the record, and they allow workers to present that information in their own style and from their own perspective. Because these formats allow workers to document the specific characteristics of the case, they are especially useful in maintaining case continuity, communicating with other practitioners, monitoring service delivery, and facilitating consultation. However, unless agencies establish minimum standards and guidelines regarding what and how information is to be documented, records may include too much or too little information. They also may be too idiosyncratic to permit comparisons among cases or to facilitate administrative review.

Narrative Records

Narrative recording has been, and still is, the predominant style used in social work records. It is true that many agencies are automating their records and eliminating at least some of their narrative reports. It is also true that most, if not all, social work records incorporate forms, such as a face sheet for collecting demographic information. Furthermore, an increasing number of agencies are adopting structured formats, such as the problem-oriented record, for organizing their records. Nevertheless, most of the recording that social workers do continues to be in an open, narrative style that takes its content and structure not from a form or format but from:

The function of the organization
The practitioner's role
The nature of the client-situation
The purpose of service
The practice modality and related theoretical constructs
The evolving process of service

The best narrative reports are neither unstructured nor unorganized; rather, they are organized topically and chronologically. The worker selects what is significant about the client-situation and the service transaction and then organizes this information sequentially and by content area. Some organizations offer the practitioner broad guidelines for selecting information. Many organizations have customary patterns for organizing content. Yet, to a large extent the content and the structure of the record are left to the discretion of the worker.

The narrative record, then, is both the most individualizing and the most idiosyncratic style of recording. This quality is both its strength and its weakness. A narrative can reflect the special nature of the client-situation and of the service transaction; it is therefore especially appropriate in documenting clinical practice. It certainly reflects the practitioner's knowledge of human behavior, of the theory and practice of social work, of the provision of services, and of recording. However, a narrative record may also be incomplete and oversimplified or excessively long and unfocused. In addition, the quality of the record may depend more on the worker's ability to write and on the availability of time for recording than on the quality of the service provided.

There are other important problems with narrative recording. It is time-consuming and, therefore, costly. Because it takes so much time to prepare, workers often delay recording, making the record less accurate, timely, and useful. Those who need to find information in the narrative may find it difficult to retrieve because of the record's individualistic structure and cumbersome size. These problems have led some agencies to eliminate the use of narrative records entirely. Most agencies, though, cannot or do not wish to take such a step. Their goal should be to maximize the assets of narrative records while minimizing their limitations. Agencies can achieve this goal by:

- Limiting the use of narrative records to complex, individualized services, while using structured forms for short-term or routine services
- Limiting narrative recording to those elements of the record that focus upon individualization; using forms, lists, or outlines for systematic or typical information
- Establishing guidelines for what to include in the narrative; these guidelines might suggest relevant topics for records of different client groups, service programs, and practice modalities
- Establishing guidelines for what to exclude from the narrative, especially:
  - Content that is documented elsewhere
  - Content that needs to be readily accessible
  - Content that could be sufficiently documented using a more efficient style

Narrative records are the format of choice in documenting individualized services, whether they are delivered to individuals, couples, families, or groups. Narrative reports that are brief and focused are efficient. These reports can be used to document only certain elements of content, such as the social history and assessment of the client-situation, whereas other forms or formats are used to document other elements, such as the identifying information and impact of service. Because of the wide applicability and use of narrative reports, practitioners must be able to prepare well-written, meaningful, and relevant reports. Exhibits 4.1 and 4.2 are examples of narrative records.

EXHIBIT 4.1 Example of a Narrative Record: Chemical Dependency Treatment Program

Family Assessment

Outpatient Unit
Patient name: Charles M (41)
Interviews: 5/7/89, Anne M (40)
5/8 and 5/9, Charles M, Anne M, Chip M (16), Caroline M (14)
Report dictated: 5/12; transcribed 5/14

Presenting Problem: Charles M was referred for service by his employer, T Corporation, where Mr. M is employed as a regional sales manager. Mr. M has been employed by T Corporation for eight years, moving up in the ranks to his present position four years ago. His position requires that he travel extensively; he is usually out of town two weeks out of the month, meeting clients and supervising local representatives. Mr. M began drinking heavily during these trips, first with clients and subsequently by himself or with other companions. According to the company, Mr. M's job performance and his reputation with clients and within the company have deteriorated during the past year. Mr. M recognizes that his position with T depends upon his successful completion of the treatment program. He believes, however, that his drinking is not the primary problem. He feels that company politics is involved in both his referral to the program and his problems within the company.

Family Background: There is a history of heavy drinking in Charles M's family of origin. Both mother and father drank regularly; his father drank to excess. Mr. M remembers his father coming home drunk on Friday nights when he was a teenager. His father died at age 45 in a car accident. His mother is "bitter" and "bossy." Mr. M seldom sees his mother, who lives in another state. He does, however, maintain contact with his four (older) siblings, two of whom have had "drinking problems." His eldest brother has been a member of AA for 10 years; a sister, who was recently divorced, is currently attending AA meetings.

Mr. M says that there is nothing "special" in his background. He completed high school and two years of college. After four years in the service, he began his career in sales. He and Mrs. M met at college. She completed college after Mr. M dropped out. They were married, over Mrs. M's family's objections, after Mr. M was discharged from the Air Force. Mrs. M's father never accepted her marriage, considering Mr. M a "low life." There was a reconciliation between Mrs. M and her parents at the time that Chip was born, and she has grown closer to her mother since her father died five years ago. Mr. M, however, has no contact with Mrs. M's family. He does not attend family functions; rather, Mrs. M and the children attend without him.

Current Family Functioning: Although Mr. M's job is now "at risk," he draws his full salary during his treatment here. The Ms own their own home, which is in an upper-income section of the community. Both Chip and Caroline attend the local high school, have above-average grades, and participate in extracurricular activities. Mrs. M describes herself as a housewife; she has a group of friends with whom she plays bridge, tennis, and so forth.

The M family does not spend much time together. Both Chip and Caroline stay at school late and are engaged in sports and other activities on the weekend. Often, even when Mr. M is at home, each member of the family eats dinner at a different time.

Mr. and Mrs. M have been personally and sexually distant for several years. Mrs. M became aware of Mr. M's extramarital affairs shortly after Caroline was born. She threatened to leave but was convinced by Mr. M that he would give up these liaisons; he told her that he did not love these other women. She believes that this is true, that his need for other women is a "weakness," as is his alcoholism. Mrs. M says that she has thought of leaving her husband several times but never has been able to do so.

A pattern has developed over the years: Mr. M "slips up" and reveals a liaison. Mrs. M threatens to leave. Mr. M begs her to stay, promising to give up other women (which he does for a time). Eventually, the pattern repeats itself. She does not want her family or social friends to know about Mr. M's "drinking and carousing." Her mother would say that she had been warned; her friends would be sympathetic but would turn away from her. She has tried to maintain the image that hers is a "perfect family."

Assessment: This family's relationship, in the assessment interviews and in their day-to-day life together, is characterized by emotional estrangement and superficial communication. Mr. and Mrs. M's relationship, which is at the core of this family, is remarkably distant. At the same time, Mrs. M can be viewed as an enabling spouse, since her personal withdrawal from Mr. M, while maintaining a "social image," has allowed him to continue to drink and to deny the impact it has upon himself and his family.

In observing the family together, one immediately senses the need of each member of the family to maintain denial of Mr. M's drinking

EXHIBIT 4.1 Example of a Narrative Record: Chemical Dependency Treatment Program (continued)

by not really talking to each other and by involving themselves in activities and relationships outside the family. Each family member has more frequent and more significant communication with peers than with any other member of the family. At the same time, the commitment to the family secret is very strong. Both Chip and Caroline glanced repeatedly at Mr. and Mrs. M when speaking, to seek reassurance that what they had said had not revealed too much.

Recommendations:

1. Marital counseling for Mr. and Mrs. M, to begin immediately. Their relationship has been strained for many years as an outgrowth of Mr. M's drinking and extramarital liaisons. These difficulties result from, but also sustain, Mr. M's drinking behavior. They are at the core of the estrangement of the family.
2. Teen group for Chip and Caroline, next session, 5/14. Each could benefit from support and sharing of experience with peers. The group will also model the behaviors appropriate for family counseling sessions.
3. Family counseling, to be initiated two weeks after marital and group counseling have started. By that time, Mr. M's individual and group therapy, Mr. and Mrs. M's marital counseling, and the teen group will have broken through some of the denial, allowing the family to open up to family therapy.

Family Therapy Session Number Three, 6/6

Planned Interventions: The plan for this session was to discuss what changes each member saw taking place in himself or herself; what changes each saw taking place in others; what changes were taking place in the family itself; and what changes were not taking place. The worker planned to intervene by suggesting that certain changes could not take place because these changes would mean giving up things that the family could not relinquish. The worker planned to explain using this example: Dad could not give up drinking if it was important to other members of the family that he continue to drink.

Interview: Chip and Caroline were very active early in the session. Each saw change in his or her relations with parents. Chip felt that he could now bring friends home, that he could tell anyone in his family anything that was bothering him. Caroline thought her parents were changing; before, they had seemed to hate each other, and she often worried that they would divorce. Now she was not worried any more. Mrs. M said that she felt the kids were happier, relieved of a burden. Mr. M said that he never thought the kids had any troubles, and he now saw that was not true.

The example of maintaining alcoholic behavior led to an important revelation: Caroline said, "Like if Mom wanted Dad to keep drinking so that she could keep drinking too." At first, both Caroline and Mrs. M denied that this was in fact occurring. Some probing led Mrs. M to talk about her own drinking behavior. It appears that she is chemically dependent, something known to Chip and Caroline, although Mr. M appeared not to be aware of his wife's secret drinking. She drinks at home in the evenings when Mr. M is away, sometimes falling asleep in a chair. The children find her there in the morning when they get up to go to school. Mr. M's drinking was less evident to Chip and Caroline, because of his pattern of drinking away from home and away from the family. They had been quite aware of Mrs. M's drinking behavior, but they had never discussed it with each other or with Mrs. M before this meeting.

Future Plans: Mrs. M acknowledges her need for treatment as chemically dependent. She will be admitted to the program as a patient as soon as an opening occurs (one to two weeks). Until that time, she will continue to participate in family and marital counseling sessions. She will attend an AA meeting with Mr. M on Monday.

Summary

Primary Function: Individualized service documentation.

Secondary Function: Clinical supervision.

Current Usage: All fields and modalities of practice.

Organizing Rationale: Information is organized (1) temporally and (2) by subject matter.

Strengths: Because the record is not standardized, it is inclusive and can truly represent the special characteristics of the client-situation and the service transaction. Thus the record is especially responsive to individualized service approaches.

Limitations: It is time-consuming and costly.

Information is often difficult to retrieve.

The quality of the record depends upon the recorder's ability to select information appropriately, organize information clearly, find time to record regularly, and write cogently.

EXHIBIT 4.2 Example of a Brief Narrative Report: Hospital Social Work Department

Social Work Report

Referral: Joey Smith was referred to social work upon admission, 9/24/88. He was admitted through the emergency room (ER), where police had brought him. Joey had burns on his legs and buttocks, as well as bruises on his arms and legs. Mr. Smith (his father) told the ER nurse that he had bathed Joey after Joey had made a mess in his pants. After the bath, he noticed the burns and called for help. Mr. Smith said that Joey's bruises must have come from a fall off the swings at the park earlier in the day. Mr. Smith said that Joey is very clumsy and always falls and bumps into things.

Background: Joey is three years, five months old, although he appears no more than two. He is small, frail, and quite fearful of strangers. He does not smile or respond verbally, although he complies with what the ward personnel ask him to do. Joey is the youngest of Mrs. Smith's six children; the other children range in age from five to 14. All the older children attend school; three are in a special education program.

In interviews with the Smiths, Mr. Smith did most of the talking, while Mrs. Smith said little, nodding or shaking her head when asked a question. Mr. Smith is looking for work but has not been employed steadily for two years. He is sometimes able to find a day's work but usually is at home. He and Mrs. Smith have known each other all their lives—they are kin—but have been married only four years. Mr. Smith describes Joey as "slow, like his mother"; he knows that Joey is slow because he is not potty-trained, doesn't talk, and is clumsy. Joey has never been evaluated by a doctor or by a teacher.

Service Information: The physician filed an abuse report on 9/24, stating that Joey's burns were from scalding bath water and that the bruises indicate Joey's attempts to resist and pull himself from the tub. Dr. P and I immediately informed the parents of the abuse report; she explained that all suspicious injuries must be reported. The Smiths threatened to remove Joey from the hospital but were persuaded that he should stay. I asked them to bring their other five children to the hospital for checkups the following day (9/25). All were evaluated, and, although some of the children had health problems that needed treatment, none showed signs of abuse.

We have coordinated services with the Child Welfare Department, which investigated and found evidence of abuse. Although the Smiths have been encouraged to visit Joey daily, they have visited only briefly once or twice a week during Joey's two-week hospitalization. Upon discharge, Joey will return home, under department supervision. On 10/21 he is to be evaluated for the Early Childhood Education Program.

E.H., Social Worker
10/15/88

The Problem-Oriented Record

The problem-oriented record (POR) is a format that is widely used in health and mental health settings. Weed (1968) intended that this format be adopted by all disciplines in all health organizations, but he was primarily concerned with its use by physicians in training in health (as opposed to mental health) settings. The format reflects these origins and often requires adaptation for use (1) by all disciplines in mental health settings and (2) by social work practitioners in all settings. Weed divided the problem-oriented record into four major sections: data base, problem list, initial plans, and progress notes. Exhibits 4.3 and 4.4 provide excerpts from problem-oriented records.

Data Base

Collected during intake or upon admission by various members of the health team, the data base includes:

The patient's chief complaint
A patient profile (description of an average day)
Social information
Present illnesses
Past history and review of systems
Findings of a physical examination
Laboratory reports

Problem List

Working together or independently, service providers list and number all problems defined during the process of data collection. The problem list acts as an index to the record and is an accountability document. As new problems are defined, they are numbered and added to the list. As problems are resolved, redefined, or no longer the focus of service, their change in status is noted. At discharge, the problem list forms the basis for reviewing service provision.

EXHIBIT 4.3 Excerpts from a Problem-Oriented Record: Hospital Social Work Department

Data Base

Social Information: Mr. T, a 69-year-old widower who lives alone, was admitted on 4/4 with conjestive heart failure. He has been hospitalized three times in the past year in similar condition. Mr. T was referred for social service consultation on 4/7; he and his daughter, Mrs. V, were interviewed on 4/9.

Mr. T is a retired plumber who has lived alone for the past two years, following his wife's death. His home, which he owns and where he has lived for 39 years, is in a deteriorated inner-city neighborhood. He remembers walking to the local store for milk, but there are no longer any stores close by. His daily activities are limited to caring for the house, preparing meals, and watching TV. He prepares the "TV dinners" his daughter brings to him once a week. Both Mrs. V and Mr. T have noticed that Mr. T is getting to be forgetful. They think that is why he ends up in the hospital. He may overeat or forget to eat at all some days. He probably takes his medication irregularly.

Mr. T refuses to leave his house, saying that he is too sick and tired. He resists going to visit his daughter and her family and seldom leaves the house except to go to the doctor's office or to the hospital. Mrs. V says that she has tried to get him to take his medicine, to comply with his diet, and to exercise, but that she has her own job and family responsibilities. Also, her father does not cooperate with her, and it is easier not to fight with him but to bring him what he wants (fried foods and sweets).

Both Mr. T and Mrs. V said they want Mr. T to stay in his home. Mr. T seems sufficiently concerned about not being able to return home, so he is likely to comply with the medical regimen if proper supports are provided.

Unified Problem List

		Date	
Number	*Problem*	*Active*	*Inactive/Resolved*
1	Congestive heart failure	4/4	
2	Lack of compliance with diet	4/4	
3	Abuse of medications	4/7	
4	Forgetfulness	4/7	4/12
5	Depression	4/12	

Initial Plans:

T.T., Social Service:

No. 2—Lack of compliance with diet

Explore and assess current psychosocial situation to determine cause of problem.

Reinforce nutrition education.

Work with patient and daughter toward improved nutrition support.

Explore community support network. Example: Meals on Wheels.

No. 4—Forgetfulness

Participate in assessment of mental status.

Collect further information for personal and social history.

Assess effect of mental status on no. 2 and no. 3.

Progress Notes:

4/12 T.T., Social Service:

No. 5—Depression

A—Assessment: Forgetfulness appears to be related to emotional reaction to death of wife and retirement from work role.

P—Counsel Mr. T regarding grief and loss. Assess potential for increasing physical and social activities during and after hospitalization.

4/17 T.T., Social Service:

No. 2—Lack of compliance with diet

S—Mr. T is beginning to express his recognition that he needs to change his diet when he goes home. He says that he used to live for fried chicken but now he knows that he might have died from it.

O—In contrast with earlier hospitalization when he had to be cajoled into accepting diet, Mr. T is cooperating fully. He is now taking an active part rather than a passive noncompliant stance. Staff is responding positively to his decreased demands and "manipulations."

A—As depression begins to lift, Mr. T seems able to accept the need to give up old habits. With further support and education, he is more likely to maintain improvements at home.

P—Involve daughter in planning and implementing change-in-diet support upon return home.

EXHIBIT 4.4 Excerpts from a Problem-Oriented Record: Community Mental Health Center, Long-Term Care

Background (Summarized from Charts of Previous Admissions): Mr. R is a 32-year-old patient with the following history:

Ages 16–18: Three admissions to inpatient psych unit, local hospital. Psychotic episodes.

Ages 18–29: Repeated admissions to B—— State Hospital for periods of four weeks to 18 months. Diagnosis: schizophrenia, paranoid type.

Between hospitalizations, Mr. R would return to this community, where he lived with his sister and her five children. He attended group meetings and doctor appointments at the center irregularly. Psychiatrist noted that his compliance with prescribed antipsychotic medication was as irregular as his participation in the center's programs. He was aggressive or withdrawn in relationships with staff and other patients. Within a few months of his discharge to the community, he would leave his sister's home (possibly leaving town) and not return to her home or to the center for long periods of time (months). Eventually he would return to B—— State and repeat the described pattern.

Three years ago, Mr. R left again. This was the longest absence without contact either with his sister or with B—— State. Five months ago, he was picked up by police in T—— (400 miles from here); he requested that he be returned to B—— State. He came "home" to his sister's house this week.

Discharge summary from B—— State indicates that he entered the hospital in severe distress. He was agitated, combative, and actively delusionary. He demonstrated ideas of reference and persecution. After drug therapy (thorazine) was instituted, psychotic symptoms were reduced.

Case Reopened 8/18/87: Mental status examination by Dr. K on 8/22. Meeting on 8/23, attended by Mr. R and his sister (Miss R), produced the following problem list:

1. Takes antipsychotic medication irregularly
2. Paranoid ideation (suspiciousness)
3. Poor self-care
4. Combative in relationships with other patients
5. Conflict with sister
6. Prevent "running away"

K.N., Caseworker

Conflict with Sister: 9/1/87

S—Mr. R's sister, Miss R, says that she would not mind having her brother staying with her if he would do some things for her (care for the house, run errands) and give her his money (disability). She feels that he is "lazy, not crazy."

A—Mr. R and his sister have a relationship that meets each other's needs during periods when he is able to meet her demands. During previous periods when Mr. R stayed with his sister, a pattern recurred. Immediately after he was discharged, Miss R was glad to have him around to help her and to keep her company. As his willingness (or ability) to fulfill her needs decreased, she would put increased demands on him. He would then flee the situation.

P—To "short-circuit" the previous pattern of conflict followed by flight, teach Mr. R and Miss R to negotiate responsibilities in the home, and involve Miss R in a family group. This will offer her support and increase her knowledge about schizophrenia.

K.N., Caseworker

Initial Plans

Working together or independently, service providers draw up plans to respond to each of the problems listed. The plans are numbered and labeled to correspond to the relevant problem. Each plan is updated as necessary in the progress notes. Weed suggested that a plan might include further collection of information, additional treatment, and education of the patient.

Progress Notes

After plans have been drawn up and are being implemented, progress and change are noted by a problem number and label in:

1. Narrative notes: These notes (often referred to as SOAP notes) update information in the data base and revise the initial plans. They may include:

    S—Subjective information, such as the patient's and family's description of the problem

    O—Objective information, such as the practitioner's observations of the patient

    I or A—Impressions, interpretation, and assessments

Rx—Treatment or care given

P—Plans

A particular entry need not include all categories of information. If, for example, only new subjective information and changes in previous plans need to be added to the record, the interim note would include only S and P, subjective information and plans.

2. Flow charts: These notes, which collect specific information about the patient over time, are intended to act as intensive studies of the client's current and changing status. A flow chart may be used to evaluate overall health status or change in response to treatment.
3. Discharge summary: The provider of service reviews each problem and each service response.

Several changes are necessary to adapt the POR format for use by all disciplines in mental health settings. First, the data base should be expanded to include:

Relevant current personal, social, and environmental factors
A detailed personal and social history
A history of previous mental health services
A mental status examination
Findings of psychological tests

Second, the problem list should include:

Psychiatric diagnoses where relevant

Problems in daily living, especially:

Self-care and self-management

Relationships with family, peers, community, and in the work environment

The POR needs additional changes if it is to document social work services fully and fairly. Although the POR is sufficiently open-ended and flexible to accommodate social service issues and activities, its focus may oversimplify and distort:

The breadth of social work concern, by emphasizing problems rather than needs, resources, and strengths

The complexity of relevant phenomena, by emphasizing the person rather than person-in-situation transactions as the focus of attention

Integrative and systemic issues, by emphasizing partialization

The special nature of social work activities, by emphasizing case management while de-emphasizing therapeutic intervention

These limitations in focus can be ameliorated to some extent if social workers adapt the POR format to incorporate the full range of relevant psychosocial information, social service issues, and social work activities. Thus, the data base should go beyond a focus on the person and the problem to include:

Relevant interpersonal, social, institutional, and physical environmental issues

Client strengths, resources, and abilities

Available resources in the client's personal environment

If feasible, the problem list should be relabeled "Issues," "Needs," or "Goals." The list should include not just problems conceived in personal terms but also needs (for example, "maintain relationship with children despite placement in care facility") and goals (for example, "return to limited employment") stated in transactional terms. Plans, too, should be expanded to document the full range of social service activities intended to respond to the expanded list of relevant service issues. Therapeutic and organizational intervention should not be omitted but should take their place alongside case-management activities.

Finally, the progress note format might be modified. Many social work practitioners have recognized that the organization of progress notes into the SOAP format omits important social service information and also seems to discredit information provided by the patient and family by labeling it subjective. They may wish to adopt an SOAIGP format to update information in the record. Note that content has been relabeled and that new classes of information have been added:

S—Supplementary data base information provided by patient and family
O—Observations by worker and other service providers
A—Activities with and on behalf of the client
I—Impressions and assessments
G—Goals
P—Plans

Summary

Primary Function: Accountability.

Secondary Functions: Interdisciplinary communication and physician education.

Current Usage: Health and mental health organizations.

Organizing Rationale: Medical model; structured around presenting problems, which may include, but are not restricted to, disease labels.

Strengths: Facilitates accountability; the practitioner or the health team is responsible for responding to the problems listed. Facilitates peer review, medical education, and interdisciplinary collaboration.

Limitations: It is time-consuming and therefore costly.

It must be adapted to incorporate salient social work issues and interventions.

It does not address (1) whether listed problems were significant or appropriately labeled, or (2) whether significant problems were overlooked.

Time-Series (Single-Subject) Records

Time-series records document repeated measures of the behaviors, attitudes, or relationships that are the target of social work intervention. These measures are used first in the assessment of the client-situation and subsequently in the evaluation of movement toward achieving the goals or purposes of service. Although the selection and implementation of single-subject research designs, and the interpretation of findings, are complex and beyond the scope of this chapter (see, for example, Jayaratne & Levy, 1979; and Bloom & Fischer, 1982), the documentation of repeated measures is relatively straightforward.

As soon as the purpose or goal of service is established (sometimes before service is initiated), measures are selected, the measurement process is initiated, and recordkeeping begins. For example, a child's behavior in the classroom is the target of intervention. Before intervention is initiated, during the process of service, and for a period after service is terminated, a worker who is not giving service to the client in this case observes and documents what occurs in the classroom during brief periods each day. Or a group worker notes the number of times an especially shy client speaks during each group meeting. Or a worker notes the number of requests for pain medication made each day by patients participating in a pain-control program. Or an agency notes the number of new cases of child abuse reported each day in the month before and in the months after a community education program is initiated. Or a client fills out a written questionnaire before each interview. Or members of a family keep a log of each argument that occurs. Or a client keeps a diary and rates himself or herself on a scale of one to 10: "How angry was I today?" These examples show that what is measured, what kinds of measurement procedures are used, and who records the measures may vary widely.

Recording of the measures, however, always follows the same principles. What is to be recorded, when it is to be recorded, and who is to do the recording must be made explicit and kept consistent throughout the service process. To ensure that the selected measures are consistently documented, forms should be used whenever possible. The use of specially designed forms helps to organize information collection and the recordkeeping process itself. These forms should include the following information:

Instructions for use of the form (who, when, where, what)

The measure itself

When the measurement is taken

Special factors in person or situation that may influence the measurement process or the measure itself

When more than one measure is being used (and the use of multiple measures is recommended), a separate form usually should be used to record each measure. To combine on one form information from different sources using different time sequences can undermine the accuracy of the data. Suppose, for example, that an attendance record and an attitude questionnaire both are being used to document change in an individual client. It is better to use two forms, one to document attendance and the other to document the results of the attitude questionnaire. Information from each form can always be combined later on a single chart. If information from a single source using one time sequence is being used, a single form is probably more efficient. For example, to document change in all members of a group, a single attendance form for the entire group seems appropriate. Unless each group member's attendance is documented, however, the data cannot be used to assess individual patterns.

There are many factors that confound the selection, implementation, and interpretation of time-series measures (Thomas, 1978; Kagle, 1982b). For example, the measures that are selected may not truly represent the change that has occurred; the measurement process may act as an intervention as well as a means of documenting effects; and it is often difficult to link the effects measured with their causes. Nonetheless, these measures can provide important information about the progress of service.

Several examples of time-series records follow. Exhibit 4.5 presents a behavior report; Exhibit 4.6 presents a progress log. Table 4.1 presents a time chart from a supported work program. Figures 4.1, 4.2, and 4.3 present examples of time-series graphs.

Summary

Primary Function: Documentation of service effects.

Secondary Functions: Assessment of the client-situation; practice research.

Current Usage: Widespread in behavioral intervention; limited but increasing in other practice modalities.

Strengths: Focuses the worker and the client on defining and achieving goals. Specifies content and explicit procedures for recordkeeping. May be used as an interim note format and combined with goal-attainment scaling, problem-oriented recording, or narrative reports.

Limitations: The measurement process can intrude on the service process and influence its outcome.

Measured effects should be attributed to the intervention only if certain design conventions are followed. It is difficult to comply with such conventions as the ABA design in agency practice; yet, workers may make unwarranted causal assumptions otherwise.

EXHIBIT 4.5 Example of a Time-Series Record: Public School

Behavior Report

Name: Bobby L Age: Seven Grade: One Class: Self-contained
Referred by: Mr. Peterson, for "disruptive, undisciplined behavior in class"

Measurement Plan: Observe Bobby's behavior for two five-minute periods daily, selected at random. Record (1) whether Bobby is complying with expected behavior during observation period and (2) antecedents and consequences of compliance or noncompliance. Recorder: N.R.

Date	*Time Observation Started*	*Antecedents*	*Compliance* Y	N	*Consequences*
11/1	9:10 A.M.	Lots of talking in class, told to settle down, all do except three boys		X	Mr. P reprimands B only
	11:30 A.M.	N/A		X	Time-out
11/2	11:05 A.M.	Music teacher begins song	X		—
	2:20 P.M.	Playground activities		X	Removed from game
11/3	8:55 A.M.	Reading begins		X	—
	2:10 P.M.	Getting ready for play		X	Detained before going out
11/6	9:10 A.M.	Reading	X		—
11/7	11:00 A.M.	Music teacher absent, free time, sits alone	X		—

EXHIBIT 4.6 Example of a Time-Series Record: Family Services Center, Family Therapy Program

Progress Log

Family: R
Members: Mr. R (38)
Mrs. R (38)
John R (16)
Claudia R (14)
Mrs. R, senior (77)

Modality: Family therapy
Goal or Task: Redefine IP's (John's) problem in family terms
Measure: Number "John is or has problem" / "Family has problem"
By: Worker from tapes, every second session

Session	*Measure*	*Change*	*Comments*
1	8/0		Most of the statements were made by Mrs. R.
3	4/0	+	Mrs. R continues to make most of the negative statements. Claudia is both uncomfortable and pleased that John is the focus. Mr. R speaks little.
5	4/2	+	Mr. R made two statements acknowledging family issues. Mrs. R's statements are less overt but perhaps more cutting.
7	2/2	+	Mrs. R has decreased the number of negative statements made about John in the interview. However, the two negative statements voiced were made by her. She is not giving up but is less overt. Mr. R again acknowledged family difficulties.

TABLE 4.1 Example of a Time-Series Record: Time Chart from a Work Program for the Long-Term Mentally Ill

Name: Lark				Month: September	
Day	*Present*	*Pieces*	*Appearance*	*Remarks*	*By*
Mon.	yes	10	poor	fight with Lucille	M.G.
Tues.	yes	21	fair	stayed to herself	R.R.
Wed.	yes	18	poor	said she was getting sick	M.G.
Thurs.	no			called in sick	M.G.
Fri.	no				
Mon.	no				
Tues.	yes	10	poor	withdrawn, talking to self	M.G.
Wed.	yes	8	poor	have called social worker	M.G.
				will have appt. tomorrow	
Thurs.	no			social work appt.	

FIGURE 4.1 Example of a Time-Series Record Showing a Self-Anchored Scale: Mental Health Clinic

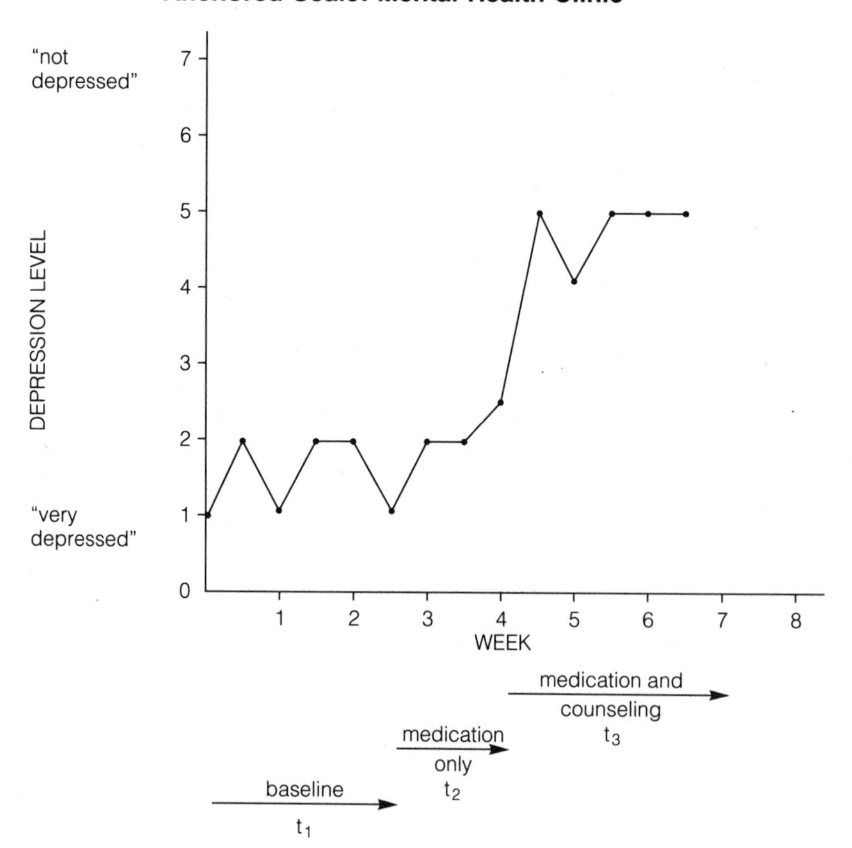

FIGURE 4.2 Example of a Time-Series Record with a Multiple Baseline: Using "Time-Out" to Decrease a Child's Tantrums

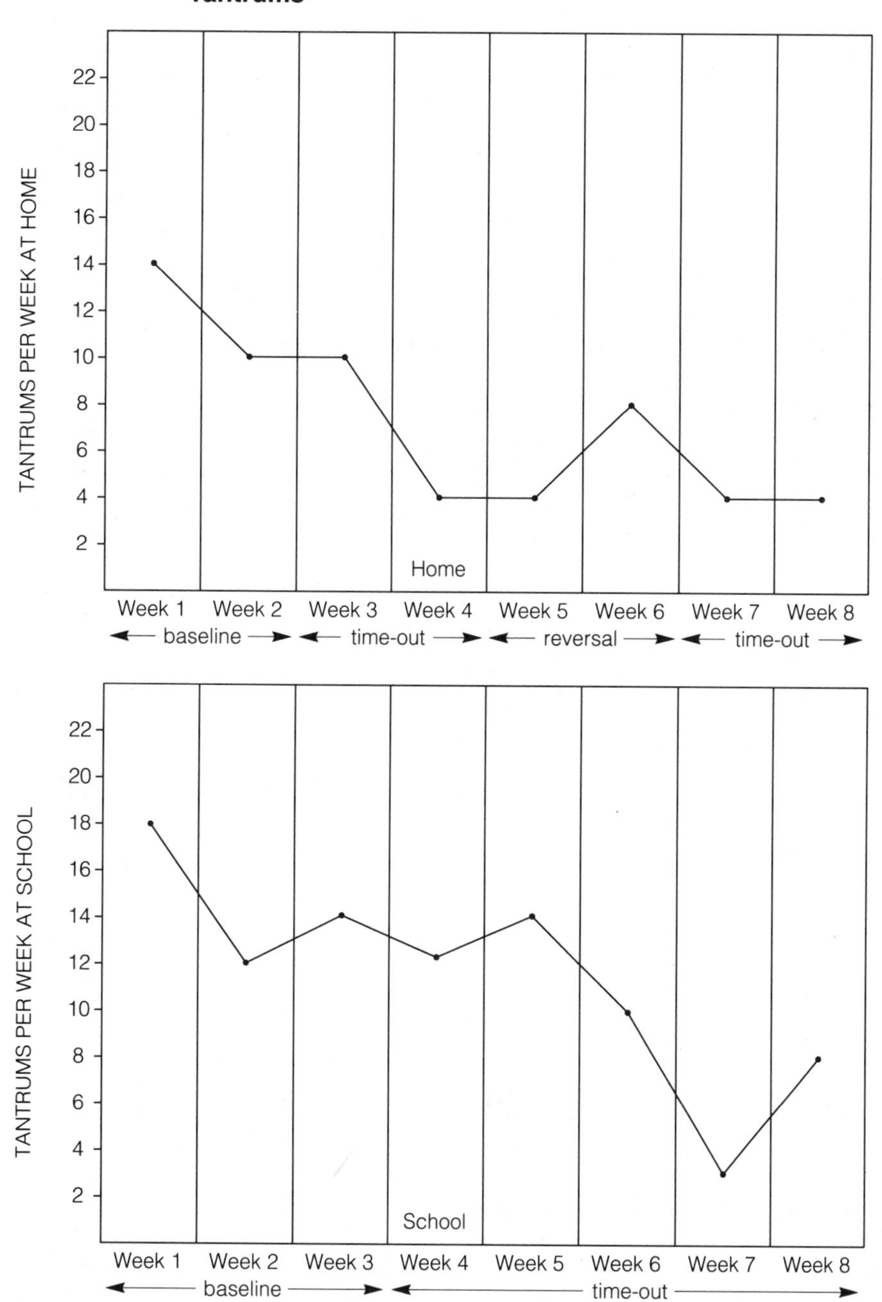

FIGURE 4.3 Example of a Time-Series Record: Measuring the Effects of a Child Welfare Community Education Plan

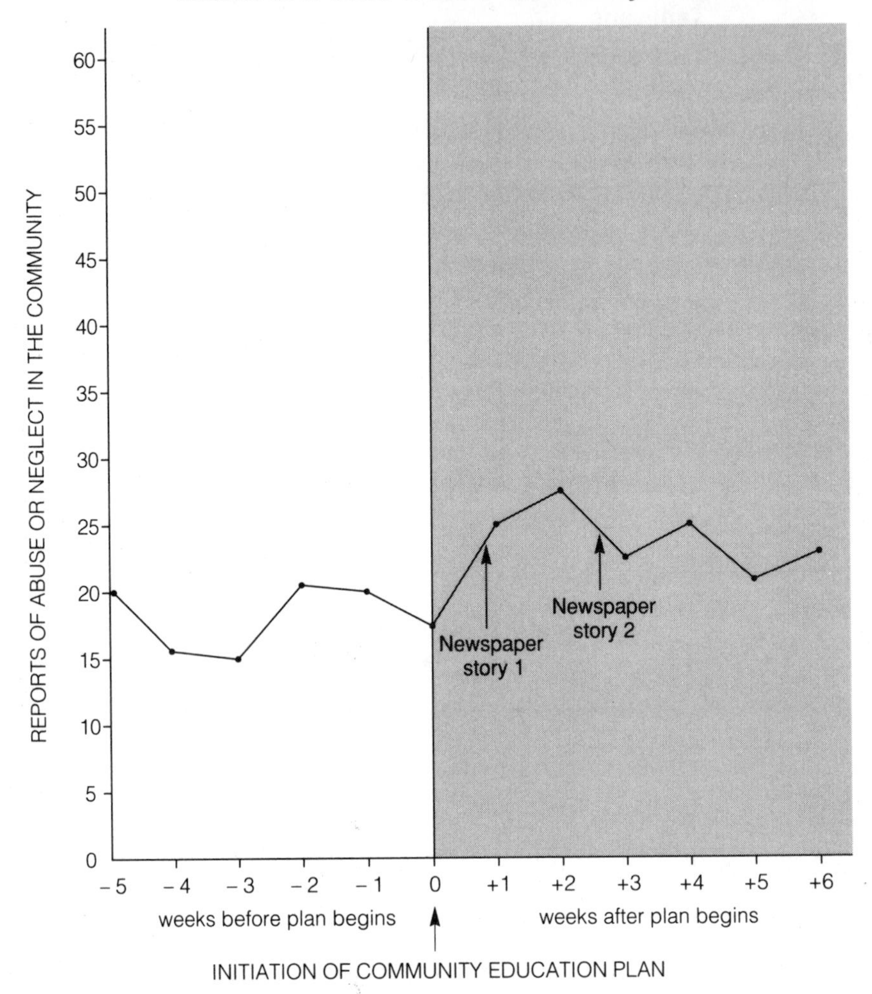

Goal Attainment Scaling

Goal attainment scaling (GAS) is a method for documenting and evaluating movement toward achieving specified goals of service. Developed by Kiresuk and his colleagues (1968, 1979) for use in mental health settings, this approach to documentation does not encompass all elements of the record. Rather, it is a format for (1) specifying goals, (2) documenting measures that represent movement toward attaining those goals, and, most important, (3) evaluating movement toward goal attainment. Above all, goal attainment scaling is a method for quantifying the progress of service.

The first step in GAS is to specify the goal or goals of service. In the example below, the worker and client decide that their goal is to improve the relationship between the client and her parents. The second step is to choose a method for documenting movement toward attaining this goal. In this example, the worker and client decide to use as their measure the number of arguments per day between the client and her parents, as recorded by the client. The third step is to develop a Goal Attainment Scale for evaluating movement toward attaining the goal.

There are five points on a Goal Attainment Scale:

−2 = The most unfavorable outcome thought likely
−1 = Less than the expected level of success
0 = The expected level of success
+1 = More than the expected level of success
+2 = The most favorable outcome thought likely

The worker (or worker and client together) prepares a verbal description of the client-situation at the outcome for each point on the scale. In our example, the worker and client prepared the following Goal Attainment Scale:

−2 = The client and her parents increase the number of arguments per day from the baseline level (three) to five or more. The parents withdraw their financial support.

−1 = The client and her parents continue the number of arguments per day recorded during baseline (three). The parents continue to threaten withdrawal of their financial support.

0 = The client and her parents decrease the number of arguments per day from the number during baseline (three) to two. The parents continue to support the client financially.

+1 = The client and her parents decrease the number of arguments per day from the number during baseline (three) to two or fewer. The parents continue to support the client financially; they no longer threaten to withdraw financial support.

+2 = The client and her parents argue infrequently (less than once per day). The parents continue to support the client financially; some long-term plans for her support are being discussed by the client and her family.

Most often, services are intended to accomplish not one but several goals. When this occurs, a separate scale is developed and used to evaluate movement toward each service goal. In addition, when goals are not equally important, each goal is individually weighted so that more important goals are given greater numerical value.

Goal Attainment Scales may be developed individually with or for each

TABLE 4.2 Example of a Goal Attainment Scale: Community Mental Health Center

Client: Leslie R
Program: Outpatient counseling

Date prepared: 2/18/8
Worker: S. K.

Measure	*Goal One (Value = 3): Improve Relationship with Parents*	*Goal Two (Value = 5): Decrease Depression*	*Goal Three (Value = 5): Decrease Substance Use*
−2	Five + fights per day Parents withdraw money	Cries several times daily; stays in bed; poor self-care; feels useless	Uses drugs or alcohol daily Stays high
−1	Three fights per day Parents threaten to withdraw money	Cries; sleeps late, but arises; self-care some days; some hope	Uses drugs or alcohol three + times per week
0	Two fights per day Parents give money, no threats	Seldom cries; usually up by 9:00; regular self-care; hopeful	Uses drugs/ alcohol < one time per week
+1	< Two fights per day No threat to withdraw money	Expresses sadness infrequently; up by 9:00; good appearance; initiates activity	Uses drugs/ alcohol < one time per two weeks
+2	< One fight per day Planning for long-term money	Expresses positive feelings, little sadness; up by 9:00; pride in appearance; making decisions	Abstains

client; they may also be developed for groups of clients—for example, for all clients who participate in a particular service program. Scores may be compared over time, across clients, or among programs. However, it is very important to recognize what the numerical value actually represents, so that the information is used appropriately. That is, the score on a Goal Attainment Scale reflects the level of goal attainment in terms of the expected level of goal attainment. These scores reflect whether expectations were appropriate, as well as whether expectations were met. Given the same outcome, low expectations will produce higher scores than high expectations. Furthermore, these scores alone cannot explain the reasons for the outcome. An unfavorable outcome may be caused by a variety of factors, among them inappropriate selection of a goal, poor measurement, uncontrollable events in the client's environment, or inadequate services. It is similarly unclear what caused favorable outcomes. If scores are to be used to assess the effectiveness of service, then, much more information about the client-situation and the service environment must be documented.

Summary

Primary Function: Accountability.

Current Usage: Mental health.

Organizing Rationale: Individualized goals and measures of their achievement form the basis for a scale that quantifies the level of goal attainment in terms of expected goal attainment.

Strengths: Focuses worker and client on outcomes that are attainable. Makes explicit the method of evaluating progress.

Limitations: The Goal Attainment Scale cannot measure whether the goal was appropriate or significant. Nor can it determine whether services were efficient, effective, or responsible for the outcomes achieved.

5 Recording Forms

Social work agencies are increasingly utilizing open-ended or fixed-choice forms as a component of their records. Some forms are actually outlines for narrative reports; most, however, are designed for short answers or check marks. Forms collect specific information used to characterize and compare clients, services, programs, processes, and outcomes. If narrative reports are intended to individualize the client-situation, the service, and the service provider, forms are intended to typify them and to ensure that certain classes of information are recorded. By standardizing recordkeeping, forms can have a similar effect upon decision making and service delivery.

Forms can also make recordkeeping more efficient by focusing the record on certain information and by decreasing the need for narrative reports. Unfortunately, in recent years the addition of forms to the social work record has had the opposite effect. In many large bureaucratic organizations today, recordkeeping consumes more of a direct practitioner's time than does service delivery (Edwards & Reid, 1989). The increasing demand for documentation, particularly for filling out forms, is due in part to the increased demand for accountability in publicly and privately funded organizations. It is also an unintended consequence of the way computers are used in social agencies: because most social workers do not have direct access to computers, their recordkeeping task has not been simplified but rather made more cumbersome (see Chapter 8).

Developing Forms

There are two major steps involved in developing a form—planning and designing. In planning for a new or updated form, the agency should consider:

The relationship of the form to the entire recordkeeping system
The purpose or function of the form
What information to include on the form to make it complete
How to limit the content of the form for efficient use

As a preparatory step, some agencies may benefit from an analysis of all their forms to assess whether there exists duplication or gaps in information collection. By preparing an index of the information currently collected on all agency forms, the agency may discover that some forms could be combined, others redesigned, and still others added. Although this step is not always necessary, it is important to begin the planning process by clarifying the relationship between the form being planned and other forms and formats in the agency's recordkeeping system. This allows for clear specification of how the information on the form is to be used and when and how information is to be entered.

Once the agency defines the purpose or function of the form, it is useful to make a list of all information that could conceivably be included on it. Expanding the range of possibilities early in the planning process increases the likelihood that the form will be complete. The next step is to limit the content to information that is necessary for decision making at some level of the organization. As in other recordkeeping decisions, the dual goals in planning forms are sufficiency and efficiency.

In developing new forms or updating old ones, agencies should recognize that good form organization and good form design encourage complete and accurate documentation. Good form organization means that information is easy to enter and can be documented in the order in which it is received. In a well-organized form:

1. There is enough space provided for writing or typing in the requested information.
2. There is a clear spatial relationship between labels or queries and the space provided for responses.
3. Checklists are exhaustive.
4. Queries are clear and can be answered briefly and specifically.
5. Information is sequenced so that it can be entered in the order in which it is received.
6. Related information is grouped together.
7. Information is listed before it is summarized or coded.

Good design form means that:

1. Instructions are placed at the top rather than at the bottom of the page.

2. Labels are small and borders are narrow to maximize the space available for responses and minimize the size and length of the form.
3. Box design is used whenever possible.

Poor: Date of Birth ___________

Better:

Date of Birth

or

(Date of Birth)

---

4. In checklists, parentheses rather than lines are used and are placed close to the appropriate caption. Of course, enough space is provided between the caption and the parenthesis so that checkmarks or blackouts are properly placed and are legible.

Poor: Sex: Male__Female__
Marital Status: Married__Never Mar__Sep__Div__Wid__

Better: Sex: ( ) Male ( ) Female Marital Status: ( ) Married
( ) Never Married
( ) Separated
( ) Divorced
( ) Widowed

or

Sex		
		(Marital Status)

---

5. On forms that will be typed:
   a. Vertical lines are placed at natural single- or double-space intervals.
   b. Vertical lines begin and end on the same horizontal space.
   c. All stops (for tabulations) are placed on the same horizontal space, whenever possible.
6. In charts, such as worker activity forms and client contact logs:
   a. The vertical axis (down the left side of the page) is used for the primary classes of information.

   b. The horizontal axis (across the top of the page) is used for subclasses of information.
   c. Single vertical lines on the horizontal axis divide related subclasses of information.
   d. Double or weighted vertical lines on the horizontal axis divide different subclasses of information.
7. When more than one form is used to collect related information:
   a. The same language is used in labels and queries.
   b. The same design elements are used.

Examples of Forms

The forms that follow in the next few pages were designed with these criteria in mind. Most of the forms presented may be used in either manual or automated recordkeeping systems. However, although these examples represent the various types of forms currently used in social service agencies and departments, they do not represent the full range of their style and content. There are simply too many different forms in use to make it possible to show them all. In fact, some organizations in which social workers are employed use more than 200 different forms in their recordkeeping systems. When differences among organizations are considered, then, the actual number of different forms being used by social workers is probably in the thousands. Nonetheless, although these forms do not represent an exhaustive survey of the field, they do offer some models for comparison and for further development.

Summary

Primary Function: Systematic information collection.

Secondary Function: Simplifying and routinizing recordkeeping.

Current Usage: Virtually universal.

Organizing Rationale: Each form is organized around a specified purpose. Except for narrative outlines, documentation requires only short answers or check marks.

Strengths: A well-organized form can simplify recording.

Information can easily be pooled, compared, and transformed into data for processing.

Specified information is likely to be documented.

Limitations: Typifies and therefore may not individualize clients, services, and providers.

May overroutinize professional documentation and service delivery.

Form 1

FACE SHEET < adult, individual >

Side 1: Personal Data

Print or type. Mark as many as apply.

(case number)

(service)

(date opened/reopened)

Client Name

(last) (first) (middle)

Address

(number) (street)

(city) (county/state) (zip) (census track)

Sex	Birth Date	Phone (day)
M ( ) F ( )	______ (month) ______ (day) ______ (year)	______ (area) ____________

Religion	Ethnicity	Language	Marital Status	Veteran Status
( )Cath. ( )Prot. ( )Jew ( )None ( )Other ________ (specify)	( )Afric. Am. ( )Asian Am. ( )Nat. Am. ( )White ( )Other ________ (specify)	( )English ( )Spanish ( )Polish ( )Yiddish ( )Other ________ (specify)	( )Never married ( )Married ( )Separated ( )Divorced ( )Widowed	( )None ( )Veteran ( )Child of ( )Parent of ( )Spouse of ( )Widow(er) of

Lives	Family Income	Source of Income
( )Alone ( )Parent(s) ( )Spouse ( )Child(ren) ( )Other relative(s) ( )Non-relative(s) ( )Nursing home ( )Foster home ( )Institution ( )Community group home	( )Less than $5,000 ( )5–10,000 ( )10–15,000 ( )15–20,000 ( )20,000 +	( )Wage/salary/investments ( )Soc. Security/pension ( )SSI ( )AFDC ( )County ( )Other ________ (specify)

Education (highest level)	Occupation	Employment Status
( )Preschool ( )Special education ( )K–8 ( )9–11 ( )High school ( )Some college ( )College degree ( )Post-graduate	( )Student ( )Homemaker ( )Professional/ managerial ( )Clerical/sales ( )Skilled/tech. ( )Unskilled **Disabled** ( )Yes ( )No	( )Unemployed ( )Retired ( )Employed—part time ( )Employed—temporary ( )Employed—full time ( )Self-employed **Seeking Change** ( )Yes ( )No

(over)

Form 1 (continued)

FACE SHEET <adult, individual>

Side 2: Service Data <mental health>

Print or type. Mark as many as apply.

1. Diagnoses—DSM-IIIR
2. ______________________
3. ______________________
4. ______________________

Source of Referral/Request

( )Self	( )Attorney	( )School
( )Personal network	( )Court	( )Employer
( )Physician	( )Police	( )Clergy
( )Psychologist	( )Social worker	( )Other
( )Outreach	______________ (specify agency)	______________ (specify)

Contact with Referral Source
( )Yes, they initiated
( )Yes, we initiated
( )No

Reason for Referral/Request

( )Depression/suicidal	( )Developmental disability
( )Anxiety/stress	( )Mental retardation
( )CMI/thought disorder	( )Education problems
( )Antisocial behavior	( )Employment problems
( )Substance use/abuse	( )Physical disease/disability
( )Psychotic episode	( )Financial difficulties
( )Situational crisis	( )Interpersonal difficulties
( )Information/referral	( )Other ______________ (specify)
( )Medication	

Services Planned

( )Information/referral	( )Individual counseling
( )Assessment	( )Family counseling
( )Medication	( )Couple counseling
( )Education	( )Group counseling
( )Inpatient/milieu	( )Crisis intervention
( )Day care—sustaining care	( )Residential placement
( )Detox/substance program	( )Early childhood stimulation
( )Sheltered workshop	( )Employment placement
( )Other ______________ (specify)	

Service Review	Plan Approval	
______________ (case opened/reopened)	______________ (signature, recipient)	________ (date)
______________ (dates of previous service)	______________ (signature, guardian)	________ (date)
______________ (previous primary provider)	______________ (signature, primary provider)	________ (date)

Form 2

FACE SHEET <family>

Side 1: Personal Data

Print or type.

(case number)

(service)

(date opened/reopened)

Name (responsible adult)

(last) (first) (middle)

Address

(number) (street)

(city) (state) (zip)

Home Phone	Business Phone (adult no. 1)	Business Phone (adult no. 2)

Family Members	Sex	Birthdate	Resides	Occupation	Education Level
Adults					
1					
2					
3					
4					
Children					
1					
2					
3					
4					
5					
6					

Family Income	Debts	Insurance/Aid

Religion	Ethnicity	Language

Family Characteristics (reconstituted, foster children, and so forth)

(*over*)

Form 2 (continued)

FACE SHEET <family>

Side 2: Service Data <Child/family>

Print or type.

(case number)

(surname)

Source of Referral/Request	If Referred, Reason for Referral
______________________	______________________
______________________	______________________

Family's Definition of Problem/Need (include differing views)

____

Worker's Initial Assessment of Family

____

Contract

Service Goals: ______________________

Service Plans: ______________________

Worker's Assessment of Client Commitment: ______________________

Service Checklist

(date) (master file)	(date) (foster file)
(date) (privacy form)	(date) (adoption file)
(date) (release-of-information form)	(date) (problem pregnancy file)

Form 3

SOCIAL HISTORY FORM

Aging

____________________ ____________________

(client name) (birth date)

Information gathered from:

Source(s) Date(s) ________

1. Description (physical appearance, behavior, affect, speech, and so forth)
2. Health History (significant illnesses, disabilities)
3. Current Health Status (mobility, self-care, medications, and so forth)
4. Family History (early life, marriage, children, and so forth)
5. Current Family Situation
6. Work History and Status
7. Community and Organization Activities (current and past)
8. Special Talents and Abilities
9. Special Needs or Problems

____________________ ____________________

(form completed by) (date completed)

Form 4

Session Summary—Individual or Couple	
Case:	
Date:	Worker:
Session Number:	Session Length (in minutes):
Who was present?	
1. Briefly describe what happened during the session.	
2. List all the new problems, needs, or issues that surfaced.	
3. What interventions were used?	
4. What new recommendations, referrals, or plans were made?	
5. What is the status of the case?	

Form 5

Session Summary—Family	
Case:	
Date:	Worker:
Session Number:	Session Length (in minutes):
Who was present?	
1. Briefly describe what happened during the session.	
2. List all the new problems, needs, or issues that surfaced.	
3. What interventions were used?	
4. What new recommendations, referrals, or plans were made?	
5. What is the status of the case?	

(*over*)

Form 5 (continued)

Session Summary—Family Side 2

6. Diagram the position of participants and the family interaction that took place during the session. (Include the worker in the diagram.)

KEY

- one-direction communication
- two-direction communication
- frequent communication
- conflictual communication
- position exchange

Form 6

Session Summary—Group	
Case:	
Date:	Worker:
Session Number:	Session Length (in minutes):
Who was present?	
1. Briefly describe what happened during the session.	
2. What interventions were used?	
3. What new individual problems, needs, or issues surfaced?	
4. What plans were made for future group activity?	

(over)

Form 6 (continued)

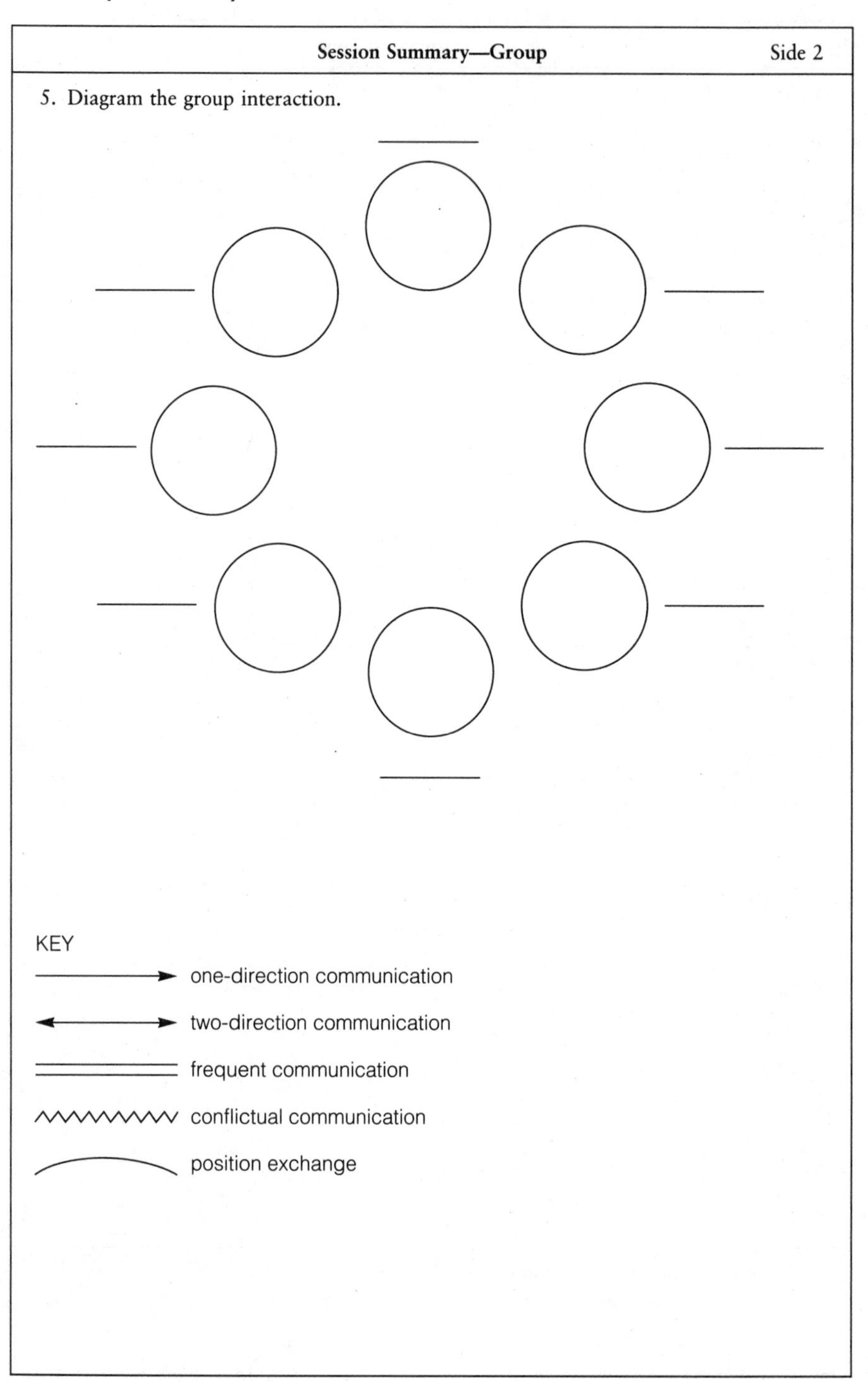

Session Summary—Group Side 2

5. Diagram the group interaction.

KEY

→ one-direction communication

↔ two-direction communication

═ frequent communication

∿∿∿ conflictual communication

⌒ position exchange

Form 7

SERVICE FLOW CHART

	Client Name
	Identification
Referral Service <if other than client> ______	Reason for Referral ______
___/___/___ (date opened) ___/___/___ (last date opened)	Client's Description of Presenting Problem ______ ______

Assessed Problems/Needs

No. 1 ______	No. 2 ______	No. 3 ______
___/___/___ (date identified)	___/___/___ (date identified)	___/___/___ (date identified)
______ (referred to)	______ (referred to)	______ (referred to)
___/___/___ (date referred)	___/___/___ (date referred)	___/___/___ (date referred)
Agency Activity ( )Client refused ( )Service denied/ unavailable ( )Service contract	Agency Activity ( )Client refused ( )Service denied/ unavailable ( )Service contract	Agency Activity ( )Client refused ( )Service denied/ unavailable ( )Service contract

(*over*)

Form 7 (continued)

Service Plan

Code
a( )Information/referral only
b( )Individual counseling
c( )Marital/family counseling

Code
d( ) Group work
e( ) ________
f( ) ________
g( ) ________

Staffings/Reviews

___/___/___ ____________
(date) (description)

___/___/___ ____________
(date) (description)

Documentation Completed

__/__ Intake summary
__/__ Social history
__/__ Goals/plans
__/__ Contract
__/__ Release of info
__/__ Interim note
__/__ Interim note
__/__ Interim note
__/__ Closing summary
__/__ Follow-up

List Each Service > 15 minutes

Month	Day	Code	Month	Day	Code

___/___/___ ____________
(date closed) (reason for closing)

	1	2	3
Resolved/improved	( )	( )	( )
No change	( )	( )	( )
Unresolved/deteriorated	( )	( )	( )
No information	( )	( )	( )

List additional information on reverse side.

Worker of Record (add name when case is assigned)

____
(worker) (date)
____
(worker) (date)
____
(worker) (date)
____
(worker) (date)
____
(worker) (date)

Form 8

CLOSING SUMMARY <health>

(chart number)

Print or type. Mark all applicable responses.

(worker)

Client Name ______

Date Admitted ____ ____ ____

Date S.S. Opening ____ ____ ____

Date S.S. Closing ____ ____ ____

Birth Date ____ (month) ____ (day) ____ (year)

Sex ( )M ( )F

Primary Diagnosis (medical) ______

Secondary Diagnoses (medical) ______

Health Status at Discharge
( )No impairment
( )Temporary impairment
( )Permanent impairment—good prognosis
( )Permanent Impairment—poor prognosis
( )Deceased

Physician ______

Service Area(s) ______

Continuing Care
( )None
( )Medication/prosthesis
( )Home health
( )Other home supports
( )ECF/nursing home
( )Hospice
( )Rehabilitation
( )Other ______ (specify)

Referred by ______

Number of interviews/consultations
( )1 ( )2–5 ( )6–9 ( )10+

Primary Problem/Need (social service)	Status at Closing			
	( )Resolved/ improved	( )No change	( )Deterio- rated	( )N/A*
Secondary Problems/Needs (social service)				
______	( )+	( )0	( )–	( )N/A
______	( )+	( )0	( )–	( )N/A
______	( )+	( )0	( )–	( )N/A

*Not addressed

Services
( )Information/referral
( )Transportation
( )Continuity of care
( )Assessment
( )Advocacy
( )Individual counseling
( )Group work
( )Couple, family counseling
( )Education
( )Other ______ (specify)

Form 9

DAILY CALENDAR <direct service>

Instructions: Using an X, enter activities for each 15-minute period. At the end of the day, tally columns.

Worker	Office	Assignment	Date ______ / ______ / ______ (month) (day) (year)

Time	*Client Services*					*Support Services*					
			Consultation				*Meetings*				
	Client Name (Status)	*Interview/ Meeting*	*Internal*	*Outside*	*Records/ Reports*	*Supervision/ Education*	*Social Work*	*Organization*	*Community*	*Research*	*Admini-stration*
___hr 00–15 15–30 30–45 45–00											
___hr 00–15 15–30 30–45 45–00											
___hr 00–15 15–30 30–45 45–00											
___hr 00–15 15–30 30–45 45–00											

___hr 00–15 15–30 30–45 45–00											
___hr 00–15 15–30 30–45 45–00											
___hr 00–15 15–30 30–45 45–00											
___hr 00–15 15–30 30–45 45–00											
Daily Tally (total Xs for each column)	______	______	______	______	______	______	______	______	______	______	______

Form 10

DAILY CALENDAR <administration>

Instructions: Using an X, enter activities for each 15-minute period. At the end of the day, tally columns.

Worker	Office	Assignment	Date ____/____/____ (month) (day) (year)

Time	*Client Services*					*Support Services*					
		Consultation				*Meetings*					*Other*
	Interview/ Meeting	*Internal*	*Outside*	*Records/ Reports*	*Supervision/ Education (Name)*	*Social Work*	*Organization*	*Community*	*Research Planning*	*Oversight/ Grants*	*Admini-stration*
___hr 00–15 15–30 30–45 45–00											
___hr 00–15 15–30 30–45 45–00											
___hr 00–15 15–30 30–45 45–00											
___hr 00–15 15–30 30–45 45–00											

___hr 00–15 15–30 30–45 45–00											
___hr 00–15 15–30 30–45 45–00											
___hr 00–15 15–30 30–45 45–00											
___hr 00–15 15–30 30–45 45–00											
Daily Tally (total Xs for each column)	___	___	___	___	___	___	___	___	___	___	___

Form 11

SERVICE LOG <case>

INSTRUCTIONS: Log each activity with or on behalf of the client.

(client name)

(worker name)

Date	*Time*		*Activity*	*With*	*Brief Description of the Purpose/Content*
	From	*To*			

Form 12

SERVICE LOG <group>

INSTRUCTIONS: Log each activity with or on behalf of the group.

(group name)

Date	*Activity*		*Participants*	*Purpose/Content*
	Group Meeting	*Other*		

Form 13

Service Agreement

INSTRUCTIONS: This form is to be completed by worker and client by the end of the third interview. One copy is to be retained by the agency and placed in the client's record. One copy is to be retained by each client.

We have agreed to the following:

1. Purpose(s) or Goal(s) of Service: ______________________________

____

____

2. Plan of Service: ______________________________

____

____

3. ______________________________ agrees to undertake the following responsibilities:
(client name)

____

____

____

4. On behalf of the agency, ______________________________ agrees to undertake the following responsibilities: (worker name)

____

____

____

This Agreement covers the period from ______________ (date) to ______________ (date)

Signed ______________________________ (client) ______________________________ (worker)

______________________________ ______________________________

Form 14

Authorization for the Release of Information

INSTRUCTIONS: This form is to be prepared in triplicate. These copies are to be distributed: 1. To the client or the client's guardian
2. To the party that releases information
3. To the party that receives information

I, ____, hereby give consent
(full name)

to ____
(name of party to release information)

of ____
(address of party to release information)

to release the following information: ______________________________

____
(description of information to be released)

to ____
(name of party to receive information)

of ____
(address of party to receive information)

for ____

____
(description of how information will be used)

My signature means that:

1. I have read this authorization or have had this authorization read to me. I understand and agree to its contents.
2. I have been informed that no other information may be released without my written consent.
3. I have been informed that I may revoke this authorization by written statement at any time and that this authorization will be automatically revoked on

____
(date)

Signed:

______________________________________ ______________
(client) (date)

______________________________________ ______________
(guardian) (date)

______________________________________ ______________
(witness) (date)

6 Practice Issues

This chapter uses a question-and-answer format to address many of the recordkeeping issues facing social workers and their agencies today. Among the issues discussed are quality, cost, retention, and special uses of records. Two issues, privacy and automation, require more extensive coverage; therefore they are not addressed here but in the following chapters.

The Quality of Records

How can the quality of records in our agency be improved? The quality of a record depends primarily upon the quality of thought and action that go into the provision of service. Ultimately, records can be no better than the practice they document. However, the quality of social work records also depends upon the way in which information is selected, retained, and presented to the reader. In many agencies, the quality of records in no way represents the quality of services.

Given that good practice is prerequisite to good recording, we must next define what we mean by quality so we can take action to achieve it. Social workers have not always agreed on what constitutes good recording. At the center of the debate is the question of focus. Should records be complete or selective, objective or subjective, descriptive or analytic? Should records concentrate on the client-situation, on the service transaction, or on the worker's diagnostic thinking? Should records be used retrospectively to document what has occurred, or prospectively to plan for the future? In large part, this debate reflects differences of opinion about the very nature of practice and about the primary function of the record. Social workers differ widely about the basic purposes of the record and about what information the record should contain. For example, those who adopt a psychosocial frame of reference might argue for a record focused on the worker's diagnostic thinking, whereas a behaviorist would argue for a record focused on changes in target behaviors over time. Those who believe that the record is primarily a tool for teaching the process of service delivery and those who view it as an accountability document also have divergent views about the appropriate content and focus of the record.

The service-centered approach to recordkeeping developed in this book attempts to resolve this debate by redefining the nature of recording, refocusing the record's content, linking structure to use, and encouraging diversity as it pertains to different fields of practice, theoretical perspectives, and service delivery arrangements. The service-centered approach is built upon the assumption that the three competing goals of recordkeeping (accountability, efficiency, and client privacy) can be reconciled if records are focused on the purpose, the process, and the impact of service. In the context of this approach, then, a good record:

Focuses on service decisions and actions

Contains information about the client-situation that forms the basis for assessment, intervention, and evaluation

Contains information about service delivery at each phase, including its purpose or goal, plan, process, and progress

Contains well-written descriptions and assessments, clearly labeled and separated so the reader knows both what the worker observed and how the worker interpreted information

Is structured so information can be documented and retrieved efficiently

Is useful in service delivery and in accountability

Furthermore, good records are concise, specific, relevant, clear, logical, timely, meaningful, useful, and grounded in fact, professional ethics, and accepted theory. Good records are well organized and well written. A good record documents the views of professionals and other experts but does not neglect the client's perspective. In contrast, poor records are unfocused, vague, biased, speculative, imprecise, and inaccessible to the potential user. Poor records often contain too much or too little information and may also be disorganized and poorly written. Poor records may even document poor practice such as inaccurate assessment, poor judgment, unethical behavior, inappropriate intervention, or disrespect for the client.

Improving records may require action at four levels:

1. Practitioner skills
2. Agency guidelines

3. Supportive resources
4. Organization atmosphere

Improving Practitioner Skills

The quality of an agency's record depends in part on the skills of its practitioners. Social work records can often be improved if practitioners prepare systematically for recording and if they develop their writing skills.

Preparation for recording should take place before, during, and after each encounter with or on behalf of the client. Before such encounters, especially early in the service relationship, the worker should prepare to seek the information necessary for the record. Reviewing agency forms, outlines, and guidelines can help the worker keep in mind what information is needed. During or shortly after each encounter the worker should make brief notes about what was learned and what transpired during the service transaction. Key words and phrases are often sufficient to help the worker remember essential information. The habit of brief note-taking is especially effective to enhance accuracy and specificity when recordkeeping takes place more than a day or two after the service encounter. Experienced workers find that note-taking helps them retain complex observations and recreate in detail the sequence of events in complicated cases. Students and new workers find that notes form the foundation for building skills in observation and assessment as well as recordkeeping. In general, note-taking improves the content of the record and aids in the recording process.

Narrative records can be improved if workers briefly outline each entry prior to dictating or writing the record. Working from their notes and from agency guidelines, the worker can organize each entry chronologically or topically. The use of headings such as "Background information," "Assessment," or "Phone interview with Dr. Slake, October 17" helps to structure the content for the reader.

Records also can be improved by eliminating some recurrent writing problems that appear in all fields of practice and at all levels of practice skill. In fact, these writing problems seem to be passed along from one generation of practitioners to the next with the old records that are handed to students and new workers when they are introduced to the profession and to an agency. These common writing problems are technical errors, poor diction, and oversimplification.

Technical errors are the easiest problems in writing to solve. In most cases, mistakes in spelling, grammar, and punctuation can be minimized if workers proofread final copies of narrative reports. In a few cases, workers have not acquired the necessary technical skills; these workers often find it useful to read texts on expository writing and attend writing classes. Technical errors are probably not as important as errors of diction and oversimplification, because such errors do not ordinarily undermine explicit communication in the individual record; the reader can usually discern the writer's meaning.

Yet, they are important enough to warrant some concern. Recurrent errors in spelling, grammar, and punctuation implicitly undermine the reader's perception of the worker's education and professional competence. To locate technical errors, look for:

Misspellings and run-on sentences
Repetitions and wordy phrases

Poor: Mrs. B's phycal needs, not to mention nutrition, are poor. It is not being attended to adequatly.

Better: **Impressions:** Mrs. B's physical needs, particularly her nutrition, have not received adequate attention.

Poor: Mr. T and Mrs. T and John and Linda and even their Grandmother have repeatedly told me again and again how much they wanna have Joseph return home in despite of the troubles that they were encountered during his last visit home which was on 4/4.

Better: Although Joseph's last visit home on 4/4 caused problems for his family, his parents, brother John, sister Linda, and grandmother have each told me that they look forward to his next visit.

Of the problems in diction frequently encountered in social work records, overuse of the passive voice and inaccurate use of language are the most significant. The passive voice not only produces awkward sentence structure; it also creates ambiguity because the writer does not identify the subject or actor. Although some use of the passive voice is appropriate and necessary, its overuse leads to an overall impression of inaction. Social workers need to be especially careful to avoid constructions in which they appear to be passive recipients rather than active participants in decisions and actions. To locate use of the passive voice, look for:

Sentences in which the actor is not identified
Use of the verb *to be* as a helping verb

Poor: Concern was raised that . . .

Better: The worker expressed concern that . . .

Poor: It was felt that . . .

Better: Mrs. T felt that . . . **Or** Worker's Assessment: . . .

Careful selection of terms used in description and assessment improves the accuracy, specificity, clarity, and meaning of the record. Workers should avoid hackneyed terms, pejorative language, and overwriting. In addition, workers should be careful to separate description from assessment. This last problem may be difficult to recognize. Sometimes workers confuse assessments with descriptions. For example, "the client appeared to be depressed" may seem to describe but actually assesses the client. In contrast, "the client wept often during the interview; she talked about losing her appetite and her interest in others since her mother's death" is a description. Sometimes workers admix descriptions with assessments. A worker often can correct this error by making sure that each entry includes observations and analysis, and by searching for diagnostic terms in descriptive passages. Jargon such as "depression" draws a conclusion. Whenever such information appears in the record, it should be clearly labeled as an assessment, diagnosis, working hypothesis, or judgment and accompanied by the observations from which it was drawn. Because social work decisions and actions are based upon both observations and conclusions, each needs to be carefully documented for the record. To locate inappropriate use of language, look for:

Meaningless, judgmental, or pretentious language
Jargon or diagnostic terms used as description

Poor: All attempts to mobilize and utilize Mr. K's environmental network were met with resistance. Mrs. K was basically hostile to all pursuance. She was not respondent to my efforts at supportiveness.

Better: Mrs. K. did not respond to several phone calls and an appointment letter. She became angry when a nurse asked her to contact me about Mr. K's discharge.

Impression: It is clear that Mrs. K is aware of, but does not wish to respond to, my efforts to offer support. It is not clear, however, whether she is resisting Mr. K's discharge or social work services.

Poor: Ms. R is very masculine in her demeanor. I often have to hold myself back from offering to buy her a dress!

Better: [Omit]

Oversimplification, the most troublesome of this group of writing problems, is symptomatic also of problems in practice. Workers who fail to document the complexity of the client-situation, the issues involved in service delivery, or the varying perspectives of interested parties may also neglect these issues in assessment, intervention, and evaluation. Workers who stereotype the client in the record may also fail to individualize the client in practice. For example, a record that includes only a teacher's assessment of a pupil as "disruptive" and that fails to include the pupil's perspective, the worker's observations of the pupil, and information about the pupil in the environment is oversimplified and biased. A worker who would base a plan of service on this oversimplified view of the client-situation is apt to make inappropriate decisions in the delivery of services. To locate oversimplification in records, look for:

Overuse of forms of the verb *to be*—for example, "The client *is* disruptive . . ."

Conclusions without supporting observations and assessments

Singular or authoritarian views of the client-situation, especially those that blame or negatively label the client

---

Poor: Mrs. S is passive-aggressive, withholding, manipulative, and narcissistic.

Better: Mrs. S sat with her arms crossed and refused to speak for more than five minutes. Other members of the family tried to draw her out. Finally, Mr. S said that this is how she gets her own way. He explained that Mrs. S often stops talking and waits for others to guess what is bothering her.

Impressions: Mrs. S is coping with the stress of her illness and hospitalization using a typical pattern. This pattern, of which Mr. S is aware, appears to be accepted by the family but has not worked here where the staff views her as manipulative and narcissistic.

Narrative reports can often be improved by including focused description and brief assessments of other viewpoints. Too often, in their efforts to be brief and specific, workers synthesize rather than analyze the complexity of the situations in which they intervene. By adding description and presenting other interpretations of Mrs. S's behavior, the above entry is immensely improved. Furthermore, intervention in the organization is initiated, since the record has reinterpreted Mrs. S's behavior to the hospital staff.

Improving practitioner skills alone, however, can seldom produce good records for an agency. Such skills can only be put to use in an agency that promotes quality recording with clear, reasonable, and adequate guidelines; with sufficient means; and with a supportive atmosphere. Toward this end, many agencies need to reevaluate and revise their recordkeeping policies, procedures, and practices.

Improving Agency Guidelines

With fewer resources for social work services and with increased demands for documentation, agencies and departments seeking to improve their records need to develop or upgrade current recording guidelines. The argument for explicit guidelines regarding the content, structure, and procedures for recording is persuasive: agencies must use their most precious resource, professional time, stintingly. It is wasteful to use such time in recording too much, too little, or too late. The opposing argument, that such guidelines undermine professional autonomy, is less persuasive. Recording guidelines do not, in themselves, diminish a practitioner's responsibility for his or her own practice; rather, guidelines that are imposed by administration without consideration of practitioner views and concerns are at fault (Edwards & Reid, 1989).

Although administrative guidelines are intended to improve recording, they often have the opposite effect. They may lead to practitioner resistance and to an increasing disparity between practice and the record as practitioners comply with requirements without changing their practice activities. In contrast, guidelines developed with the full participation, advice, and consent of those who are responsible for service and for its documentation improve recording. First, practitioners retain control over their own activities by exercising discretion at two levels—in developing guidelines and in documenting service in each case. Secondly, this approach minimizes both the disparity between practice and the record and worker resistance to the recording process. Finally, it simplifies the recording process, since many of the choices about what and how to record have been made in advance and are included in the guidelines.

An agency needs guidelines for each of its programs specifying the content, form, and procedures for recordkeeping. Rather than attempting to systematize all recordkeeping, guidelines should establish minimum standards and leave specific decisions to the worker. In general, guidelines should stipulate:

The types of records to be kept, and the purpose

The information to document in all cases, and the information to document only in special circumstances

The forms or formats to be used, and the circumstances under which to use them

When specific elements of content are to be documented, and how frequently records are to be reviewed and updated

Improving Resources

The conflicting goals of accountability and efficiency can be met only if an agency allocates sufficient resources to the tasks of preparing, transcribing, storing, and retrieving records. First, workers need enough time to prepare records. Most agencies assume that workers will find time to record during periods between interviews and meetings, or will complete the task during scheduled recordkeeping periods. However, the time available for recording has eroded. Sixty-five percent of the social work managers responding to the Records II survey indicated that there was not enough time available for recordkeeping, and 58 percent indicated that recordkeeping took too much time. Often, the time allocated for recordkeeping must be used to respond to client needs or to fulfill other duties. It is not surprising, then, that 40 percent of the managers in the Records II study indicated that their records were not up-to-date. In addition, time-saving equipment and support personnel should be available and fully utilized. During recent cutbacks in social service funding, many agencies chose to cut clerical rather than professional staff, and to forgo repairs and put off purchase of new equipment. As a result, social workers may be writing, typing, and filing their own records. Agencies with sufficient clerical staff and modern equipment can overcome this very costly use of professional resources. Clerical workers should be available for transcribing, filing, and retrieving information. Workers should be encouraged to use dictating machines and computers; their recording time should be used principally for composing and reviewing records.

Improving the Organization's Atmosphere

The culture of the organization may also need to change in order to improve the quality of records. Too often the use of the record in supervision inhibits rather than promotes accurate and timely recording. When the record is the primary source of information about the worker's performance, and when that information is regularly used as a means of finding and correcting weaknesses, recording may suffer. The worker finds himself or herself in a no-win situation: the written record is used to demonstrate the worker's weaknesses in practice, and the unwritten record is used to demonstrate his or her weaknesses in meeting administrative responsibilities. In response, the worker may avoid, delay, or stint on recordkeeping. To correct this problem, the focus and atmosphere of supervision must be altered. First, evaluative supervision should draw upon a variety of sources of information about the worker's performance, de-emphasizing the use of the record for this purpose. Secondly, the record's content should form the basis for discussion of substantive practice issues rather than for criticisms of the practitioner's work habits. Thirdly, the atmosphere surrounding any discussion of recording should be supportive rather than accusatory, to reinforce strengths and efforts at improvement rather than to discover weaknesses and to chastise lapses in performance.

Furthermore, recordkeeping must be linked clearly to practice. If recordkeeping is perceived as an administrative rather than a practice activity, it will not receive the full commitment of direct-service workers. In many social work organizations today, practitioners view recordkeeping as a meaningless and burdensome responsibility imposed by managers. They put off recordkeeping not just because other tasks demand their attention but because they do not consider recordkeeping important. If agencies are to overcome what is sometimes called worker resistance, they must reconsider the role of the record in the day-to-day life of the practitioner. Recordkeeping achieves full legitimacy among direct-service workers only if the record is useful in their practice.

Benefits of the Recording Process

I have been told that the process of recording is helpful to the practitioner. Is it helpful? If so, how? Although there is truth to this maxim, many practitioners are wary of efforts to convince them of it. They have been told that, like a bitter pill, recording is really good for them. However, when they have "taken their medicine" and completed the task, the benefits of their efforts have not always been evident. Their experience leads them to question the notion that recording is genuinely helpful.

In fact, the recording process can be very beneficial to the practitioner and, ultimately, to the client. Through documenting what has occurred, the worker recalls and reconsiders the content and context of the service transaction. This review, in turn, informs future action with and on behalf of the client. Simply put, writing aids thinking.

The act of recording clarifies thought in a number of ways. Recording involves *selection.* The worker sorts through the array of information about the client-situation and the service transaction, with the goal of documenting what is most important. Thus, recording focuses the worker's attention on the most salient features of the case. Recording also involves *organization.* Information is arranged topically and in sequence. Thus, writing aids the worker in logical thinking and in perceiving temporal, spatial, and causal relationships. Recording requires *substantiation* of fact, decision, and action. As a result, gaps in information and distortions in interpretation often become clear. Recording involves *analysis,* separating the whole into parts, as well as *synthesis,* making connections between observations and inferences. As a result, the worker may generate new options and alternative ways of conceptualizing relationships. Recording may involve *classification.* In so doing, the worker typifies the client-situation and compares it with others in the light of theory, values, empirical evidence, and accepted practices. This process can aid the worker in linking a particular case to the body of professional knowledge and ethics. Finally, recording involves *judgment* and therefore can facilitate critical thinking. As a component of the recording process, the worker develops and tests hypotheses and evaluates action and impact.

The worker may examine relationships between knowledge and supposition, between attitudes and actions, and between intention and implementation. By means of this process, the worker not only may come to understand the client-situation and the service transaction in new ways, but may also gain self-awareness and professional skill.

The record reflects practice, and, through the process of recordkeeping, the worker has cause to reflect upon practice. Writing takes place at some distance from the practice it documents, thereby allowing the worker to gain a new perspective on the case. Recording at its best can help the worker to reconsider what has taken place, to reevaluate plans for the future, and to give form and precision to inchoate ideas. Admittedly, recording is merely an aid; it is no substitute for the thinking and planning that must take place within the service transaction. Nonetheless, it can be an important means for improving service to the client, if it is not remote from practice. To be truly helpful to the practitioner and the client, the recording process must be closely connected in time and in substance to the service process it documents. Recording is most useful if it is not delayed until long after service decisions have been made and implemented, but rather temporally linked to service events. It is most helpful when the content of the record requires consideration of crucial practice issues. Given these conditions, the recording process not only evokes but also enriches practice.

Recordkeeping in Private Practice

Do I need records in my private practice? I have not been keeping records and am reluctant to do so. One of the attractions of private practice is the freedom from some of the onerous tasks of agency-based practice. Some social workers believe that private practice means no meetings and no records! However, social workers in private practice need to keep records for several reasons. First, they need records for office management. For this purpose, they need a system for tracking appointments, billing, expenditures, and income. Secondly, they need records for case documentation. Increasingly, clients who seek services from social workers in private practice are insured by third parties. To claim reimbursement, social workers must submit forms that document their assessment and treatment plan, as well as information about service delivery and outcome. In many cases, the client decides to submit bills for insurance reimbursement late in the service process or even after services have been terminated. Social workers who wish to be paid for their services, then, may need to rely on their records for the necessary information. Thirdly, social workers may need records to support their credibility in court. Sometimes social workers are sued by their clients; more often they are summoned to court to testify in cases where clients' rights, actions, or disputes are being considered. In any court action, a social worker will find his or her credibility challenged by an opposing counsel. Workers who testify that they keep no records but rather rely on memory to recall facts and events may find their testimony and professional reputations in question. For legal protection and for case documentation, social workers in private practice are well advised to keep brief case records that include an assessment of the client-situation, a treatment plan, a brief closing summary, a log of each appointment, and full documentation of any critical event, such as a threat of violence, along with the practitioner's response.

Many practitioners in private practice find that their services are enhanced by keeping clinical records as well. Some practitioners prefer to keep brief, anecdotal notes about persons and events in the client's life, about critical issues that emerge, about dynamics in relationships in families and groups, and about plans for the future. They can then review this material before sessions with clients to maintain continuity and to sustain empathy and immediacy in the relationship. They find that, over time, such notes reveal patterns of behavior, thought, or emotional response that might not otherwise have been apparent. They may also use these records in determining and evaluating progress in the client-situation and in the service transaction. Other social workers in private practice may choose to keep more systematic records to use as a tool in intervention. Depending upon the purpose of service, they document measures of status, attitude, or behavior (for example, the client's weight, level of marital satisfaction, or frequency of temper tantrums) throughout the process of service. This information, which the client or another observer may gather, is used to assess movement toward achieving specific goals.

Whether anecdotal or systematic, records kept for clinical purposes tend to be idiosyncratic, depending upon the private practitioner's own style and mode of practice. These are records that the practitioner keeps for himself or herself, not for a wider audience. Practitioners should be aware, however, that any such notes might be subpoenaed. Barker (1987), who believes that case records are "essential to competent (independent) practice," also suggests that "the prudent social worker should prepare every case record as though it was certain to be reviewed in courtrooms" (p. 5).

The practitioner who provides services outside the context of a social service organization or department faces new obligations. Private practice offers freedom from institutional constraints but leaves the practitioner without institutional legitimacy. To some extent, practitioners can establish their legitimacy through licensure and certification. However, without records, such practitioners may have difficulty in demonstrating accountability and legal credibility. Although records do not, in themselves, establish professional legitimacy, they can demonstrate the practitioner's commitment to professional standards and practices. Moreover, the keeping of records can have more than a symbolic meaning; records are evidence of the practitioner's accountability to client and community.

Records That Clients Prepare

I've seen some reports of client recordkeeping. How does this work? Client-prepared records, here called client memoranda to differentiate them from worker-prepared client records, are used as a source of information about the client-situation and as a component of the interventive process itself. Indeed, these functions are inseparable. Whenever clients keep diaries or logs, they are contributing information to the service transaction; in addition, they are using that information, adapting and accommodating to it. Often identified with behavioral interventions, client memoranda are used in a wide range of practice modalities and in service to diverse clients with a variety of needs, abilities, and concerns.

Social workers ask their clients to keep records to serve several objectives. Through such documents, the worker can discover information about the client and the situation, about behavior and its contingencies, and about the relationship between thought, feeling, and action that might not otherwise be apparent. Client memoranda supply information that may be useful in assessment, intervention, and evaluation of service to this client as well as to others. In addition to supplying information, client memoranda can provide a learning experience for the client. The client can learn awareness of self; through describing specific experiences in detail, the client learns about how he or she feels, behaves, and thinks. Clients also learn how to observe themselves and others, to express themselves verbally, and to label their perceptions and reactions. Client memoranda can also enhance the service transaction, because keeping records can encourage the client to be more active in seeking information, expressing opinions, making decisions, and reaching conclusions. The memoranda are a tangible link between the worker and client when they are not together, as well as a source of continuity and a focus of attention when worker and client meet. The process may even have a more general benefit, offering the client an opportunity to gain a sense of self-control as well as control over service and over the situation.

Client memoranda take two basic forms—diaries and logs. In both forms, the client documents relevant feelings, ideas, and experiences. The worker helps the client to focus the content by asking the client to write about particular events, reactions, or environments. The worker also suggests when and how often entries should be made. But while decisions about the actual content and organization of the diary are left to the client and made in the act of writing, decisions about the content and organization of the log are made in advance. In preparing the log, the client's task is to document a narrow range of observations, at specified times, in designated environments, using a prepared form. The content of the log is limited to those behaviors, feelings, or thoughts that are the subject of assessment, intervention, and evaluation; its structure is intended to support those limitations. The diary is an open form, broad in scope, analogous to the narrative discursive style of

EXHIBIT 6.1 Excerpts from Client Memoranda

Excerpts from the Diary of a Teen-age Girl

I really don't know what to write about. Keeping a diary of "who I am" seems like just another assignment from White [English teacher]. Sometimes it seems that no one really knows or cares who I am—especially me. . . . Today just happens to be one of those days . . . maybe because everyone tries to be so cheerful, so helpful, when I feel like—. . . . Smile, smile . . . keep up the pretense of being anything, anyone, something, someone. . . .

Excerpt from the Log of a Teen-age Girl

Fights with Mother

What Happened Before	When	Where	What	How I Felt
Sleeping	8:30	Bedroom	She wanted me to get up	Tired, angry; ruined my day
Eating, reading the paper	10:00	Kitchen	She wanted me to clean up	Tired, angry: wanted to get out
Out	7:00	Kitchen	Where had I been?	Tired, mad; why did I come home???

social work recording; the log is a more systematic form, which may either be individualized to meet the needs of a particular client or standardized for use with several clients. In selecting a diary or a log, workers should consider the results of these formal differences: A diary is likely to be highly individualistic, encompassing the client's moment-to-moment perceptions. However, because content is not prescribed in advance, particular information may not be included. A log will include designated information but not random, moment-to-moment perceptions.

Both the diary and the log shown in Exhibit 6.1 can provide a meaningful record for the client and the worker. However, practitioners should use them with discretion, carefully considering the following questions:

Should client memoranda be used? Of course, the prime factor in this decision is the client's interest and consent. However, workers should first decide whether to suggest a diary or log. On the one hand, the use of a diary or log might bring information into the service transaction, provide a learning experience for the client, and give focus to intervention. On the other hand, the memoranda may prove intrusive, especially in group or family processes. Recordkeeping may also be an unnecessarily difficult assignment for clients who are undergoing severe stress or are self-conscious about their poor education.

How should client memoranda be presented to the client? The worker's purpose and plans for the content, structure, and use of the memoranda should be presented as clearly and specifically as possible:

Poor: I want you to keep a diary. Okay?

Better: I think it might be a good idea if you would keep a diary of your experiences, your ideas, and your feelings. We've talked a lot today about your not knowing who you are and what you are "supposed to be." It seems that you keep changing, and so do your ideas and feelings. If you would write down, every night before you go to bed, just what you are thinking and feeling about who you are, we'll be able to talk about it when you come next time. Nothing fancy—just your thoughts and feelings in any form you like. What do you think?

Who should keep the diary or log? The worker should be aware that the role of recordkeeper carries power with it. Whenever the purpose of service is change, either in interpersonal relationships or in transactions between the client and others in the environment, whoever acts as observer gains power. The worker may use this factor either to alter or to maintain the existing balance. For example, the log presented in Exhibit 6.1 is only one of two used in the case; mother and daughter each kept a log of their fights. By giving both members of the transaction the role of recordkeeper, the worker tried to minimize the disruptive effect of recording upon the balance of power in the mother-daughter relationship.

How should the memoranda be used? If client memoranda are to retain their significance, they must be used regularly in interviews or sessions with the client. The content of the diary or log may form the basis for discussion of thoughts and feelings. Worker and client may develop a chart to document information over time and to compare current entries with previous entries. The log, in particular, is very useful in the assessment of the contingencies of behavior and in the evaluation of the effects of service. The diary is especially useful in gauging what issues are most salient to the client.

What are the limitations in the use of client memoranda? Although an important resource in assessment, intervention, and evaluation, client memoranda are inherently subjective in content. Therefore, to enhance the reliability and objectivity of decisions, client memoranda should be used in conjunction with other sources of information.

The Cost of Recordkeeping

How can we cut our recording costs? The cost of recordkeeping is generated by:

The amount of time (proportion of wages or salary) clerical workers, direct-service workers, supervisors, and administrators spend in producing, using, storing, and retrieving information

The amount of time spent in developing, implementing, and evaluating guidelines for content, structure, and procedure

Commodities, such as paper and storage space

Equipment, such as dictating machines and computer hardware

Studies of recordkeeping costs have appropriately focused on the time spent in producing and using records. In 1953, Hill and Ormsby reported that 32 percent (12.8 hours for a 40-hour week) of caseworkers' time in a family service agency was being spent on recording. In 1964, Goldman reported that 21 percent (8.4 hours for a 40-hour week) of caseworkers' time in a children and family service agency was being spent on recordkeeping. In 1980, the Records I survey found a wide range among agencies in the amount of time spent on record-related activities, from one hour to more than 15 hours per worker per week. On the average, direct-service workers were spending from four to seven hours per week on recording, while supervisors were spending from three to five hours reviewing records. Although these studies appear to show that the amount of time professionals spend on record-related activities is decreasing, a recent study does not support this assumption. Edwards and Reid (1989) found that child welfare workers in New York state spent an average of 23.5 hours per week on recordkeeping in 1982, an increase of 9.4 hours per week from the previous year, before a new recording system was added. During the same period, time spent delivering services to clients decreased commensurately, from 24.1 to 15.1 hours per week. Clearly, the amount of time spent on recordkeeping varies widely, with some organizations using an alarming proportion of their resources on documentation.

Regardless of the proportion of time spent on recordkeeping, agencies and clients can clearly benefit from cutting costs in this area. The Records II survey found that most agencies were not successfully managing the increase in demand for accountability and for services with limited and diminished resources. Several areas appear to be prime targets for cost-cutting.

1. *Eliminate redundancy in and among records.* In some agencies, workers keep two or more sets of records that contain the same information. They may keep a social work record and a medical record on the same client; they may write detailed personal notes as well as narrative reports for the official record. Where such practices still exist, costs can best be reduced by eliminating one set of records. If this is not feasible, one record should be established as the primary record and the other as a supplementary record. Information in the primary record should not be rewritten but should be mechanically reproduced and elaborated upon in the secondary record.

   A more prevalent problem is redundancy within a record. Often workers repeat information from entry to entry. These redundancies can be minimized if workers review and update previous entries rather than repeat information that has already been recorded. Through this practice, the record as a whole, rather than the most recent entry, becomes the working record. To make information more accessible in lengthy records, workers should prepare brief summaries of previous entries at regular intervals.
2. *Establish guidelines that discourage overdocumentation.* When no criteria are established for selecting information for the record, workers may record too much. Many practitioners find that having well-constructed outlines of the information to be included in narrative reports helps them to limit the length of the record, ensure that needed information is documented, and aid in the process of preparing and organizing each entry. Guidelines regarding information to be excluded also prove useful.
3. *Substitute brief forms, checklists, and outlines for open-ended narratives.* Many agencies use a combination of forms and narrative reports in their recordkeeping systems. But they often restrict the use of fill-in and checklist forms to client identification, worker activity reports, and management information. Costs can be reduced if narrative reporting, the dearest style, is minimized and new forms are introduced into the recordkeeping system. For example, agencies may develop a checklist for documenting referral information and a simple fill-in form for documenting the purpose of service, the service plan, and activities in service to the client. Many of the forms in Chapter 5 can be adapted to meet the needs of a particular case, program, or agency.
4. *Streamline documentation of routine cases.* Many agencies and programs use the same recording approach for all cases, regardless of type, complexity, or duration. They may realize significant savings by developing a short form for documenting routine and short-term service delivery. In general, a recording format that is sufficiently detailed and open-ended to apply to complex, long-term cases is apt to be unnecessarily complicated and costly to produce in cases where services are circumscribed. Indeed, in many social work agencies and departments,

as many as 25 percent to 75 percent of services are either routine, time-limited, or terminated before the fifth contact (Kagle, 1987).

Many agencies would benefit from devising a routine services protocol and a short recording form for use in such situations. First, the organization establishes criteria for using a short form. Cases in which the primary service is information and referral, the provision of resources, or planning a transition from one environment to another might be appropriate choices. At intake or after the planning phase of service is completed, cases are assigned to either "short" or "extensive" documentation. Secondly, those involved in service delivery and program management outline the steps that are taken ordinarily in providing the designated services. Finally, the organization develops a short recording form, combining brief narratives with a checklist format, that includes the following:

Information about the client-situation focused on:

1. Eligibility for services
2. The reason or need for services
3. The bases for service decisions and actions

A list of the steps ordinarily taken in delivering the designated services, with space for indicating when each step is completed

Space to explain added or omitted steps

Information about the status of activity and the client-situation at termination

5. *Provide cost-saving resources.* As mentioned before, some agencies have attempted to cut costs by eliminating clerical positions or by postponing the purchase or repair of equipment. Unfortunately, these are false economies. When clerical services are inadequate, records are often incomplete, out-of-date, or backlogged. Furthermore, workers may assume tasks that are more efficiently performed by clerical workers. When dictaphones, typewriters, or computers are unavailable, preparing records and retrieving information is more time-consuming and costly. By cutting cost-saving resources, agencies may inadvertently increase the demand on workers' time and diminish the quality of their records.

   The availability of clerical staff, dictaphones, and word processors can lead to more efficient use of professional resources and can improve the quality and efficiency of the recordkeeping process. Of course, these resources can only have the intended effect if they are used regularly and appropriately.

   Computerization of client records may or may not result in cost savings. As discussed in Chapter 8, in many agencies computerization has been more costly than anticipated. The start-up cost of any new system is especially high. Moreover, the Records II survey showed additional costs at the line worker level. In many organizations, computerization has added work demands without simplifying the worker's task or providing the worker with useful information.

Decreasing the cost of recording is a worthy goal. Resources that are freed up can be used in providing services to clients. However, some attempts to cut costs actually can have reverse or adverse effects. The goal of efficiency must be balanced against the need for accurate, timely, and useful records. Moreover, the objective of efficiency must be measured and evaluated. Decisions and actions taken in the name of efficiency may actually be expensive and wasteful.

Retaining Records

Records have become a storage problem in our agency. We are reluctant to destroy our records, but something needs to be done. What can we do? Many agencies and departments would prefer to keep the records of their closed cases but must eventually find a solution for the resulting storage problem. In finding a workable plan, each agency faces a number of questions:

- Does the agency need to retain all or part of the physical record or only the information the record contains?
- Does the agency need to retain all of the information in the record or only elements of the record's content?
- If the agency chooses to destroy all or part of the record, when is the appropriate time to do so?
- How can the agency improve its management of the records it does retain?

In finding answers to these questions, agencies are strongly influenced by:

- The legal requirements and professional guidelines that apply to the agency, such as:
  - Laws and regulations that require that certain documents be retained indefinitely
  - State record laws that mandate that records be retained for a specified period
  - Recommendations by such membership organizations as FSAA and CWLA that agencies make plans to destroy portions of their records
- The potential usefulness of old records in informing future service delivery, in responding to requests for records, or in administrative decision making or research

TABLE 6.1 Percent of Agencies That Never Destroy Records

Field of Practice	Percent
Child welfare	88%
Family service	22
Health	41
Mental health	27
School	38

The availability of technology for use in improving storage and in making information accessible to future users

These influences are apparent in the policies and practices of agencies and departments that participated in the Records I survey.

The survey revealed that about 35 percent of agencies never destroy their records. Child welfare agencies, which are influenced both by the legal responsibility to retain certain documents and by the widespread use of computer technology, are especially likely to retain all portions of their records. The proportion of agencies in each field of practice that retain their records indefinitely is shown in Table 6.1.

Those agencies that do destroy portions of the record do so differentially; they are likely to retain client identification and legal documents. They are likely to destroy documentation of service delivery, communication within the agency (such as interprofessional reports), communication with other agencies, and progress notes.

The length of time that agencies keep information they eventually destroy varies by field of practice. The "shelf life" of a record depends upon the customary pattern of service to clients. Agencies that offer long-term or recurrent services (schools and mental health organizations) find that their service records are useful for a significantly longer period than agencies that offer intensive, time-limited services with a briefer interim between service episodes (family service and health). Shelf life may also depend upon the relative value placed upon information from the past. Educational and mental health organizations may keep their records for a longer period, anticipating requests for information long after service has ended because of the importance given school performance and any history of emotional distress. The average length of time that agencies in each field of practice keep their records before destroying them is shown in Table 6.2.

An agency that wishes to retain its records but that must find solutions to the storage problem should first consider mechanical reproduction by computerizing or microfilming all or portions of its records. If such technological solutions are not feasible, the agency should study (1) pertinent legal

TABLE 6.2 Average Length of Retention by Agencies That Destroy Records

Field of Practice	Length of Retention
Child welfare*	—
Family service	6.0 years
Health	6.5
Mental health	11.5
School	10.0

*Few child welfare agencies in the study destroy even part of the record.

requirements and professional guidelines and (2) the current and potential uses for old records in service delivery, in responding to requests for information, in administrative decision making, and in research. Then, with the findings of this study in hand, the agency can develop a suitable policy for retention or destruction of records. The following policy is offered as a model:

Policy on Retention and Destruction of Agency Records

1. Abstract all records at closing, using a specially prepared form.
2. Retain all abstracts, storing them in an accessible place in the agency. Retain all legal documents.
3. Store all records of closed cases for a limited period of time (for example, two years following closing) in an accessible place in the agency.
4. After the limited period has elapsed, transfer records of closed cases to a warehouse to conserve space.
5. After sufficient time has elapsed following the last contact with, or on behalf of, the client (for example, six to 11 years after closing), destroy the warehoused records.

Records in Research

Our agency's records contain a wealth of information. Are they a suitable source of data for research? Agency records have been the primary data source in a number of classic research studies that have had a significant impact on the practice of social work. Richmond based *Social Diagnosis* (1917) on her investigation of narrative case records in several social service agencies; her study is an example of qualitative research using existing agency records. Fanshel based his study of parental visits to children in foster care (1977) on computerized data from child-care agencies in New York City; his study is an example of quantitative research using existing agency records. In addition to their use in these and other traditional research studies, available records are frequently used within agencies as the basis for systematic studies of client characteristics and needs, of service patterns and outcomes, and of professional activities and productivity. Intensive study of a single case using qualitative—and, more recently, quantitative—methods of inference has also been an important source of knowledge for the practitioner and for the profession as a whole.

Yet, in spite of their widespread use as a data base in both inter- and intraagency studies, records that have been kept for service purposes and under the conditions of agency practice may not provide suitable data for an agency's research purposes. As an information source, all archival records have inherent weaknesses that limit the kind and quality of conclusions they can support. Although such records are potentially useful in description, in process evaluation, and in the generation of hypotheses about relationships, they usually are not suitable for making inferences or for establishing causal connections. For example, records may be used to answer such descriptive questions as:

Who are our clients?
Where do they come from (referral in)?
Where do they go (referral out)?
What services do they receive?
How are agency resources being used?
How are clients, needs, purposes, goals, processes, and outcomes defined?

Records also may be used to evaluate adherence to established policies, procedures, and practices; thus, they may be used to answer such questions as:

Are we adhering to privacy guidelines?
Are we documenting needed information?
Are our records up-to-date?

Records also may be used to generate hypotheses about relationships (correlations). For example, they may help practitioners answer these questions:

Which client groups are selected for which programs, services, or practice modalities?

How does goal setting relate to outcomes achieved?

Unless the conditions of practice conform to the strict standards of control necessary for making causal inferences (see Campbell & Stanley, 1963; Kagle, 1982b), existing records should not be used to answer such questions as:

Are casework services effective?
Do inpatient services produce better results than outpatient services?
Did family therapy help the M family?

Furthermore, an agency's records may not offer reliable or valid data in usable form for answering appropriate questions. Before undertaking any research project involving the retrospective use of its service records, an agency should carefully assess existing records to determine whether the information they contain is sufficiently accurate, specific, complete, consistent, and accessible to make them a suitable data source for the research questions the agency wishes to answer.

A prime consideration is the accuracy, specificity, and completeness of the information in existing records. Many factors can undermine the suitability of agency records for research. The most important are the following:

1. *The effects of time.* Frequently social work practice records are written long after the events they report. Both accuracy and specificity are adversely affected by a lag in time between the collection of information and its documentation.
2. *The subjectivity of the information.* The accuracy of public and objective information (birth date, frequency of interviews, and so on) can be verified, but the accuracy of private and subjective information (values, inferences, and so on) cannot. Much of the information most relevant to social work practice is subjective, under personal control, and therefore unverifiable.
3. *The context of information gathering.* There are important differences between the "ground rules" necessary for data collection in research and the "ground rules" of social work practice; these differences may, in turn, affect the suitability of records as the data base for research. For example, the research interview differs considerably from the service interview. To maintain consistency, the research interview is carefully structured, using a pre-established protocol; in contrast, the practice interview evolves in response to what is salient in the client-situation and the service transaction. To minimize the interviewer's influence on the subject's responses, the research interviewer remains attentive but is a disinterested listener; in contrast, the practitioner not only is attentive but also reacts, responds, and contributes. To minimize the personal costs of participation and to maximize the potential for candor, the research interviewee remains anonymous; in contrast, the client (or another interested party) is likely to be deeply affected by the information revealed in the interview. Because of selective focus, interpersonal influence, and personal investment in the service transaction, the service interview may not produce information that is complete and free from bias.
4. *The selectivity of service records.* Social work recording necessarily involves selection. The most complete and detailed records omit some information. Not only do the worker and the information source exercise discretion in information gathering, but the worker also exercises discretion in deciding what to record. A structured record (forms,

checklists, and so on) can guide the selection process and encourage the documentation of needed information. Nevertheless, the recorder makes choices in documentation even in completing a form. Furthermore, it is important to be aware that the criteria for selecting information for a record written to be used in case continuity and supervision may not meet the criteria for selection for the planned research project. The agency's records may not contain the needed information, or the needed information may not appear with sufficient frequency or in adequate detail.

Another consideration in using records in research is consistency. The content of a record may vary from entry to entry; records also may vary from client to client, from program to program, and from one service modality to another. Most importantly, records may vary from worker to worker. Some of these variations will be immediately apparent, as when narrative records take different forms or contain different information. Other variations are less apparent, such as when workers use different definitions for common phenomena or define divergent phenomena using a common term. An agency cannot immediately assume, but should seek evidence to support the assumption, that recorders share meanings for frequently used terms and record similar phenomena in a comparable manner.

A final and often decisive consideration is the accessibility of existing information. Information that is documented in systematic form is ready for use in research, whereas narrative reports usually must be transformed into a more usable form. It is not surprising, then, that management records are more often used in research than are clinical or educational records. However, information that is accessible is not necessarily suitable for research. Although information that can be easily quantified may appear to be appropriate for research, it may actually be neither reliable nor valid. Like other information in records, information that is readily accessed must be checked for accuracy, specificity, completeness, and consistency before it is used as research data.

After examining records for their adherence to these criteria for research data, the agency may conclude that existing records do provide suitable information to answer its research questions, or the agency may decide that its records are an inadequate data source. These findings will assist the agency in deciding whether to proceed with a specific research project and what sources of data to use. The agency may decide to use the available data despite recognized limitations; then, in planning, implementing, interpreting, and reporting the findings of the study, the agency may acknowledge these limitations. The agency may decide to use other sources of information instead of, or in addition to, what is available in existing records; for example, the agency may choose to develop an interview protocol and a special recording form to be used in future information collection, selection, and documentation.

Each of these options has both costs and benefits. The advantages of using existing records are that the data are already available, that no new recording forms or interviewing protocols need to be added to the worker's current responsibilities, and that the existing information represents ongoing practices. The disadvantages of their use are that the data may not be reliable, valid, complete, specific, comparable, or in suitable form. Conversely, prospective use of records in research, incorporating careful preparation of the record and of the practitioners who will collect and document the data, can prevent many of these disadvantages and provide better-quality data for answering some research questions; however, such a plan may be costly.

7 Privacy

Social workers observe the intimate details of their clients' lives. In seeking and receiving service, clients are obliged to share information about themselves, their circumstances, and their relationships with people and social institutions. This information is used in planning and delivering services most appropriate to the client's wishes and needs; in fact, the purpose and process of some therapeutic approaches is the revelation of thoughts, feelings, and experiences which the client usually hides from others. Without this information, individualized social work service would be impossible. Because this information forms the core of many social service transactions, it also forms the core of the social work record.

The client's obligation to share personal information is predicated upon a reciprocal obligation on the part of the social worker and the organization: the obligation not to reveal this information except in specified, socially valued circumstances. The confidential nature of the relationship between client, worker, and organization is a fundamental social right of the client and an ethical and legal responsibility for the worker and the organization. However, the client's right to privacy has, in recent years, been eroded by changes in the way information is handled in all social institutions. Not only have the boundaries of the worker-client-organization relationship been expanded, but new technologies have also raised the potential for access to, and misuse of, client information. In response, the federal government, state governments, and public and private institutions have developed policies and procedures intended to protect the individual's right to privacy by setting parameters on the flow of information about the client into, within, and out of the service relationship. The specific provisions vary by state, by field of practice, by funding source, by service program, by the profession of the service provider, and by the client group. But underlying these various policies and procedures are four basic principles of privacy.

Privacy Principles

The four basic principles of privacy are confidentiality, abridgment, access, and anonymity. **Confidentiality** is the primary means through which social workers protect their clients' privacy. Confidentiality means safeguarding from disclosure personal information that the client reveals in the context of the professional relationship. The responsibility for confidentiality resides with the practitioner but must be supported by the ethics of the profession, by the policies and practices of the organization, by the actions of other service providers and of funding and accrediting agencies, and by law. Standards for professional social workers were established in the NASW Code of Ethics (1979) which states:

> H. Confidentiality and privacy—The social worker should respect the privacy of clients and hold in confidence all information obtained in the course of professional service.
> (1). The social worker should share with others confidences revealed by clients without their consent only for compelling professional reasons.
> (2). The social worker should inform clients fully about the limits of confidentiality in a given situation, the purposes for which information is obtained, and how it may be used.

Social workers reveal personal information only under prescribed circumstances and for socially valued purposes. First, they may reveal information if the client authorizes the disclosure. For example, a client who is moving is being referred for services to an agency in another community. That agency needs information about the client and about the services the client has received. The worker in the referring agency informs the client about what information would be disclosed to the new agency with the client's permission. The client agrees to sign a "release of information" form, authorizing the referring agency to disclose information to the new agency. The agency may disclose the information only to the agency specified in the release, and may not disclose the information if the client fails to sign the release, if the release has expired, or if the client chooses to rescind the authorization to release information.

Secondly, social workers may reveal personal information within the agency when it is necessary for the delivery of service, and they may reveal it to outsiders when such disclosure is required by law or when it is needed to protect the client or others from harm. For example, social workers document personal information in client records and disclose information to other professionals delivering services within the agency, as well as to supervisors and other advisors. These disclosures are intended to facilitate service delivery and enhance the quality of services. Disclosures within the organization afford the client some protection, because other professionals are also bound by the ethics of confidentiality. However, social workers are properly concerned about the potential for inadvertent breaches in confidentiality when personal information is widely known within the agency. In addition, social workers may have a legal duty to report client actions to outside agencies with or without the client's consent. For example, they are required to report instances of suspected child abuse and neglect to state agencies. They may also be compelled to testify about the client's past actions in court, under penalty of contempt. Furthermore, they may be permitted or required to take action to protect the client or others from the client's future actions. For example, they may disclose information to protect a client who is threatening suicide or to warn others who may become the target of the client's violent behavior.

Confidentiality is enhanced when organizations establish and monitor policies that proscribe inappropriate or unnecessary disclosure of information about its clients. For example, an agency can develop procedures that physically safeguard records of both open and closed cases. It can discourage casual discussion of cases and promote an agency climate in which clients and their personal rights are respected. It can prohibit the use or dissemination of social security numbers to third parties, so that information in data banks is less accessible to outsiders. It can limit monitors' access to information in the record to what is vital for maintaining funding or accreditation. Indeed, an organization may even forgo a contract or other funding opportunity if accountability procedures potentiate breaches of client privacy.

Confidentiality is strengthened by granting privileged communication to social work clients. Privilege means that, under specified circumstances, clients may prohibit social workers from testifying in court. States that have statutes granting social worker privilege recognize that the client's need for a confidential relationship with a social worker is more important than the court's need for evidence. However, in practice, there are many exceptions to privilege, and courts tend to define social worker privilege narrowly. Even in situations in which privilege applies, clients may waive this right if they wish their worker to testify.

In general, a social worker's ability to protect a client's privacy through confidentiality is limited. The dual role of social work, to represent simultaneously the interests of the client and society, means that confidentiality in agency-based social work practice is never absolute. Moreover, social work's mission with clients who receive public funds and who are the focus of community concern also undermines confidentiality. However, as social work is accorded full professional status, its ability to protect client privacy through confidentiality will parallel that of other professions working in similar settings. Furthermore, social workers have other mechanisms that they may use to protect their clients' privacy.

Abridgment protects client privacy by limiting the collection, documentation, and retention of personal information. Social workers, guided by privacy laws and agency policies, may limit information in the record to certain sources, to specific content, and to a specified period of time. Records that rely on the client or applicant for service as the primary source of information, are focused only on information needed to establish eligibility and deliver services, and are expunged or abstracted after a period has elapsed following termination all protect client privacy. In contrast, records that include information from many sources, contain personal information that is not directly pertinent to the purpose of service, or are retained indefinitely may unnecessarily intrude upon a client's privacy.

Access to records by clients, their families, or their agents enhances client privacy by allowing the recipient of services to learn what information is being collected and documented, and how information is being interpreted and used by the agency. Although most clients do not see their records, those who do have many different reasons for seeking access. Some are curious about what is being written about them; others are interested in how they are perceived. Some wish to confirm what they have been told, whereas others feel that information is being withheld. Some wish to see their records prior to signing a release of information, whereas others wish to have a copy of their records following termination of services. Some are encouraged to review their records by agency policy or by their social worker; others may initiate a request for access on their own or on the advice of an attorney, physician, or other advisor.

The NASW Code of Ethics sets general standards that encourage client access to records:

> H. (3). The social worker should afford clients reasonable access to any official social work records concerning them.
> (4). When providing clients with access to records, the social worker should take due care to protect the confidences of others contained in those records.

Access to records not only protects client privacy but can empower the client. For example, access permits clients to make informed decisions about the use of information within the organization as well as about the release of information to outside agencies (Reamer, 1987). It can open communication and reinforce trust between worker and client. However, social workers are often wary of the potential for adverse effects if the client or other family members read the record. For example, social workers recognize that clients may not understand or may be upset by what they read. Furthermore, they are concerned about protecting the privacy of others who may have revealed confidential information that is documented in the client's record.

In practice, there is a continuum of policies on access, ranging from those organizations that encourage and allow clients full access to their records to those that would permit access only under court order. Some agencies, including those that operate under the Federal Privacy Act of 1974, have a relatively open policy, permitting the client to see, copy, amend, and challenge the information in the record while service is ongoing. Most agencies, however, place some limitations on access. Some, including many hospitals, permit access only after service has been terminated; if the client makes a request for access to the record, the organization offers to copy the entire record, charging the client for this service. Other organizations permit review while the case is in progress but require that a professional be present when the record is being inspected, to explain and discuss the record's contents. Some organizations inform all clients of their right to see their record, whereas others provide information and access only if a client asks. Finally, some agencies do not ordinarily permit access to their records. Adoption records, which are sealed by the court and usually inaccessible through the agency, are a notable example of a closed-records policy.

Anonymity protects privacy by permitting the use of client information for specific and valued purposes if the client's name and other identifying information are obscured. Indeed, many uses of the record do not require that the client be identified. Information from records can be monitored by oversight agencies, used in education and research, and presented to the public without disclosing the client's identity. Social workers can keep their clients' identity anonymous by blocking out names and other revealing information when records are used in education or research, by pooling anonymous information for presentations inside and outside the organization, by reading from pertinent sections rather than allowing monitors direct access to client records, and by abstracting records for reports to funding and other outside agencies.

The four basic principles of privacy both limit and increase the flow of information about the client-situation. Abridgment limits the flow of information from and about the client into and within the organization. Confidentiality limits the flow of information out of the professional relationship and the organization. Client access increases the flow of information from the professional relationship and the organization to the client and others acting on the client's behalf. Anonymity increases the flow of information within and out of the organization but without divulging the client's identity.

Privacy Provisions and Standards

In preparing their records, social workers are guided by laws, regulations, accreditation standards, and agency guidelines, as well as by the ethical principles of their profession. If they are to comply with their legal obligations and make full use of the protections available to their clients, social workers must understand the federal and state legislation and regulations under which they practice; they should also be familiar with related case law and legal precedent. Because privacy laws and regulations differ by field of practice and organizational setting, social workers need to be familiar with the legal provisions that apply to the organization in which they work. For example, public assistance programs fall under different standards than public schools. Because privacy laws and regulations differ by client group, practitioners need to know that they must follow different procedures—for example, in work with substance abusers than in work with those suspected of child abuse. Because privacy laws differ by state, social workers in similar agencies may follow different procedures. Finally, because some state laws and regulations apply to their profession rather than to their agency or clientele, social workers may need to go beyond established agency procedures to fulfill their legal obligations and maximize their clients' privacy. A notable example of such a provision is testimonial privilege, which usually is attached to legislation licensing or regulating social work practice. Thus, social workers need to study the provisions and standards that apply to their agencies, their clientele, and their profession.

Definition of the Record

In studying relevant laws, social workers need to evaluate how the term *record* is defined. Many laws begin by defining what is and what is not considered part of the official record. Moreover, some guidelines state what information should be included in the record. The definition of the record indicates how the practitioner and the organization are to protect client privacy while meeting accountability standards. When the content of the record is limited to certain information, privacy is protected through abridgment. When the "official record" permits exclusion of sensitive personal information, privacy is protected through confidentiality. When clients and others acting on the client's behalf are permitted to review "the record," privacy is protected through access.

The Federal Privacy Act of 1974, under which federally funded social programs operate, broadly defines *record* as:

> any item, collection, or grouping of information about an individual that is maintained by an agency, including, but not limited to, his [or her] education, financial transactions, medical history, and criminal or employment history and that contains his [or her] name, or the identifying number, symbol, or other identifying particular assigned to the individual.

This act provides clients with the right to see the record and, if the individual disagrees with its content, permission to request that the record be amended or corrected. If permission is denied, the client has the right to have a protest included in the document. The Federal Privacy Act further protects the client by abridging the record's source, contents, and uses. Agencies may keep only relevant and necessary information, and may collect such information "to the greatest extent practicable" from the client if such information may be used to deny the client federal "rights, benefits, or privileges" under federal programs. Of course, the client is liable for giving false or misleading information. These provisions of the Federal Privacy Act, then, protect client privacy through access and abridgment; they also offer the client the right to amend or contest the record's content.

The Federal Family Education and Privacy Rights Act of 1974 (often called the Buckley Amendment), which applies to all public educational institutions, takes a different approach in defining what constitutes the "educational record." This act allows the family to see and challenge the educational record. However, it offers special protection to the student by excluding from its definition of "educational record" and, therefore, from family review

> records . . . in the sole possession of the maker thereof which are not accessible or revealed to any other person . . . [and] records on a student who is eighteen years of age or older, or is attending an institution of postsecondary education, which are made or maintained by a physician, psychiatrist, psychologist, or other recognized professional . . . and are not available to anyone other than persons providing such treatment.

The Buckley Amendment, then, protects privacy by requiring that the educational record, including social work notes, be subject to family access. However, information that is considered especially sensitive is afforded the special protection of confidentiality.

The Illinois Mental Health and Developmental Disabilities Confidentiality Act of 1979 defines the official "record" as

> any record kept by a therapist or by an agency in the course of providing mental health or developmental disabilities service to a recipient concerning the recipient and the services provided.

However, this exemplary state act also states that the

> [r]ecord does not include the therapist's personal notes, if such notes are kept in the therapist's sole possession and are not disclosed to any other person, except the therapist's supervisor, consulting therapist or attorney. If at any time such notes are disclosed, they shall be considered part of the . . . record.

The therapist's personal notes may include

> information disclosed to the therapist in confidence by other persons on condition that such information would never be disclosed to the recipient or other persons; information disclosed to the therapist by the recipient which would be injurious to the recipient's relationship to other persons; and the therapist's speculations, impressions, hunches, and reminders.

Like the Buckley Amendment, the Confidentiality Act of 1979 provides for an official and an unofficial record. In both cases, the unofficial record includes information that is especially sensitive and may have a negative impact if read by clients or family members. However, in the confidentiality act, information revealed to the practitioner is not afforded the special guarantees of confidentiality if the practitioner chooses to place it in the official record. If information is widely available within the organization, it is subject to an alternative protection: access by the client, guardian, or others so authorized.

Although not a legal provision, the accreditation standards of the Joint Commission on Hospital Accreditation (JCAH) in its *Accreditation Manual for Hospitals* (1987) also define the content of the record:

> As appropriate, pertinent information relating to the following is [to be] included in the medical record: Observations and social assessment of the patient and, as relevant, of the patient's family; [t]he proposed plan for providing any required social work services; [a]ny social therapy/rehabilitation provided to the patient and the patient's family; [s]ocial work summaries, including any recommendations for follow-up; and [a]s appropriate . . . home environment evaluations for the attending practitioner, cooperative activities with community agencies, and follow-up reports. (p. 261)

The JCAH guidelines provide for separate storage of "certain portions of the medical record [that] are so confidential that extraordinary means [are] necessary to preserve their privacy, such as in the treatment of some psychiatric disorders" (p. 102). Such information, although still considered part of the medical record and subject to review and quality assurance, is afforded special physical protection. In general, the JCAH guidelines refer to security and consent for disclosure as the primary means for protecting privacy and confidentiality. They neither prescribe nor proscribe client access, although many states have enacted legislation that makes hospital and physician records available to patients.

When they examine the laws, regulations, and other policies under which they and other organizations operate, social workers need to study how the term *record* is defined. Among the most important questions to be asked are:

What information is considered part of the record?

Are specific elements of content to be included in the record?

Are specific types of sensitive information afforded special protection by being excluded from the record? If so, what actions must a worker take in order to guarantee such protection?

What are the implications of the definition of the record for the protection of client privacy? Is privacy to be protected through confidentiality, client access, or abridgment?

Limitations on Disclosure

Laws and regulations clearly distinguish between the use of information within an organization and its release to outside individuals and institutions. In general, practitioners and organizations are given wide latitude in internal use of information; moreover, the definition of what constitutes internal usage is broad, extending to parent and oversight agencies. For example, information transferred from a local branch to the central administration of a large state agency is considered an internal transaction and is not restricted. Use of personal information to obtain funding, in management or financial audits, in program evaluations, or in statistical reports is not considered disclosure and does not require consent. Although special protections may be extended to sensitive information that is handled confidentially within the organizations, privacy provisions do not usually restrain the use of personal information within an organization; instead, they rely upon the ethical judgment and conduct of professional practitioners. However, privacy provisions do strictly limit the transfer of information across agency boundaries.

In most routine situations, disclosure of personal information is prohibited without prior authorization by the client or the client's agent. Although exceptions are sometimes justified, authorizations are to be obtained before information is transferred and, whenever possible, should be written rather than verbal. (For a model release of information authorization form, see Chapter 5.) Although there are penalties for unauthorized routine disclosure, they are seldom applied. The Federal Family Education and Privacy Rights Act of 1974, for example, prescribes withholding of all federal funds from the institution as penalty for disclosure of information from educational records without proper authorization. Other federal privacy laws and state "fair information practices" acts prescribe similar penalties for unauthorized release of personal information.

Privacy policies sometimes require that authorization for disclosure of personal information include an informed-consent procedure. The federal regulations guiding the disclosure of information from alcohol and drug abuse patient records include such a provision. In this case, "informed consent" means that the client's decision to release information is (1) free from coercion, (2) based upon full knowledge of what information is to be disclosed, to whom, and for what purpose, (3) time-limited, and (4) subject to revocation. Because informed-consent procedures empower the client, are ethically sound, and offer the organization and the practitioner legal protection, organizations that are not under mandate may still wish to adopt a similar standard and develop their own procedures for informed consent. As a general rule, clients should be given the opportunity to review relevant portions of the record prior to authorizing a disclosure. They should receive a full explanation of the possible results of their decision, including the potential risks and benefits of choosing to release or not to release the information. If a client is unfit or unable to participate in making this decision, a parent, guardian, or conservator should be given similar information so he or she can authorize disclosure only if it is in the best interests of the client. The purpose of informed-consent procedures is to permit clients to make a fair decision regarding the dissemination of sensitive personal information.

There are a number of nonroutine situations in which personal information may be released without prior consent. A notable example is the requirement in all states that social workers and other professionals report cases of suspected child abuse and neglect. Medical emergencies and threats of violence are examples of other situations in which social workers may choose, but in most jurisdictions are not required, to disclose information without prior consent. Whenever information is disclosed without a signed release from the client, workers are advised to make a notation in the record indicating the date of the disclosure, what information was disclosed, to whom, for what purpose, and under what special conditions and authority. A subsequent notation should document how and when the client was informed of the content and circumstances of the disclosure.

In addition to these specific exemptions in which information may be released without the client's prior consent, there are many situations in which information may be released if the client is not identified directly or indirectly. For example, the Federal Drug Abuse Prevention, Treatment, and Rehabilitation Confidentiality of Patient Records Act of 1977 (FDACA) specifically exempts from the requirement of prior consent information used in scientific research, management audits, financial audits, and program evaluations when patient anonymity is assured. Other laws, regulations, and policies make any release of case information for research, education, and other purposes contingent on ensuring the anonymity of the client.

The disclosure of confidential information in court proceedings is addressed in federal and state confidentiality acts and in state laws regulating the practice of social work. Recognizing that personal information may be released without prior consent under court order, the Federal Privacy Act requires that agencies make a concerted effort to notify clients of such action. The Massachusetts Fair Information Practices Act goes one step further, requiring state and local agencies to "maintain procedures to ensure that no personal data are made available in response to a demand for data made by means of compulsory legal process, unless the data subject has been notified of such demand in reasonable time that he [or she] may seek to have the process quashed." Other states may wish to develop a policy based upon this exemplar, because it both informs clients and gives them an opportunity to respond prior to the release of information.

The disclosure of confidential information from social work records in court involves a two-step process. In the first step, any party in a case may subpoena witnesses or records. Upon receipt of a subpoena *duces tecum,* the worker or organization is required to produce the record in question. Unless the subpoena is quashed (nullified) or an excuse is accepted by the court, failure to produce the record can result in contempt penalties. In the second step of the process, the record is actually introduced as evidence. At this point, the attorney for the client or the agency may assert professional privilege to prevent the record from being entered or the worker from giving testimony.

As of fall 1989, 36 states* plus the District of Columbia, Puerto Rico,

* Arizona, Arkansas, California, Colorado, Delaware, Florida, Georgia, Idaho, Illinois, Iowa, Kansas, Kentucky, Louisiana, Maine, Maryland, Massachusetts, Michigan, Mississippi, Mon-

and the Virgin Islands had statutes in place that confer testimonial privilege upon certain social worker–client communications. Although these laws differ in language, in general they impose a duty on the social worker not to disclose in court, without the client's consent, information revealed in the context of the confidential relationship. Thus, if the client invokes privilege and the court determines that such privilege applies in the case in question, the social worker cannot be compelled to testify, and records that document the substance of the privileged communication cannot be used as evidence.

However, even in jurisdictions in which social worker privilege exists, social workers still may be required to testify or to present their records in court. First, in most states, privilege status is conferred through acts that license or regulate the practice of social work. Thus, privilege applies only to communications with social workers who are registered under that act. Secondly, in some states, privilege applies only to communication that takes place within the context of giving and receiving services. Thus, communication that takes place with those who are not officially clients or who are outside the realm of the social worker's professional employment may not be subject to privilege. Thirdly, privilege is subject to a number of exceptions and waivers. For example, in almost all states, clients may waive privilege if they wish the worker to testify. In addition, because it would be unfair if workers were prohibited from testifying in their own behalf, clients who sue their social workers automatically waive their right to privilege. Furthermore, in many states, communication about contemplating or committing criminal acts is not privileged. In some states, such as Kentucky, this means that the social worker may be compelled to testify in "proceedings in which the commission of such crime is the subject of inquiry" (Ky. Rev. Stat. Sect. 335.170 (3)). In other states, such as Massachusetts, this means that the social worker "shall not be required to treat such information as confidential" (Mass. Gen. Laws, Ch. 112 (135)). In all states, social workers must report all suspected child abuse or neglect. Thus, communication that indicates possible abuse or neglect is assumed to be an exception to privilege. However, in one recent case, social worker–client privilege was upheld in the trial of a man accused of rape and sexual abuse of his daughter, even though the social worker had initially reported the case (*People* v. *Randolf Bass,* Bronx S. Ct., reported in *New York Law Journal,* April 27, 1988).

Privilege extends only to relationships in which communication is presumed to be confidential. Thus, privilege does not apply to situations in which the client is aware that information revealed to the worker may be used in court. Thus, for example, in cases of family violence, marital discord, child custody, mental illness, and antisocial behavior in which social workers gather evidence for the court or provide services as an adjunct to the court, privilege

---

tana, Nebraska, Nevada, New Hampshire, New Mexico, New York, North Carolina, Ohio, Oklahoma, Oregon, South Dakota, Tennessee, Texas, Utah, Virginia, Washington, West Virginia, and Wyoming may not apply. Privilege also may not apply to situations in which a third party is privy to communication. Thus, information revealed in couples, family, and group therapy may not be privileged. Some courts have held that privilege applies in such situations because others who are present are essential to effective treatment (see also *Yaron* v. *Yaron,* NY Sup. Ct., 1975). Other courts have applied the "third person rule," which holds that communication between client and attorney that takes place in front of a "casual" third party is not privileged. Unless a statute explicitly extends privilege to such communication, as Colorado's does to group therapy (Colo. Rev. Stat., 12-63.5-115), social workers should not assume that courts will find that privilege applies.

Although legislatures have recently created social worker privilege in many states, legal scholars believe that courts view any privilege unfavorably because it limits the court's access to information (Savrin, 1985; Knapp, VandeCreek, and Zerkel, 1987; Smith, 1986–1987). It is not surprising, then, that judges interpret privilege narrowly, balancing the need to protect confidential relationships against the court's need for evidence. Social workers are well advised not just to work to extend privilege but to protect existing privilege from encroachments. In interaction with clients and in recordkeeping, they must guard against actions that may lead to a waiver of privilege. If they or their records are subpoenaed, they should seek legal counsel and, if necessary, inform both their own and their client's counsel of their testimonial privilege. With their agency's support, they should invoke privilege and testify only if ordered to do so. As society becomes more litigious, as more aspects of personal life come under the jurisdiction of the court, and as more families come into court to break apart and re-form, privilege becomes increasingly important in protecting client privacy. It is particularly ironic that, despite privilege, social workers cannot always assure clients of confidentiality, which is the essential goal of privilege.

In examining the laws, regulations, and other policies under which social workers, their agencies, and other organizations operate, social workers need to study how personal information revealed in confidence and documented in their records is protected from disclosure. Among the most important questions to be asked are:

What procedures are used in gaining client authorization for release of information? Do the procedures meet the criteria of informed consent?

Under what conditions are social workers required to disclose information about clients without their consent?

Under what conditions are social workers permitted to disclose information about clients without their consent?

How is authorization to disclose information documented?

Are social worker–client communications protected by privileged communication? Under what conditions may privilege be invoked?

Open Records

The Freedom of Information Act of 1966 opened to the public records kept by federal government units. State public records acts perform a similar function, making the records of state agencies available for public inspection. Through these provisions, anyone may scrutinize the activities of such agencies as the FBI, legislative bodies, and public social service agencies. Most of the statutes place limitations on what information may be examined, and most specifically prohibit the release of the names or records of clients. However, some open records laws do permit the release of personal information. According to Schrier (1980), "Many commentators have voiced concerns about the inconsistency between the purposes of the federal and state legislation on privacy and freedom-of-information or open-records acts. Although the open-records acts of most states specifically exclude private information, some, such as Ohio's, clearly allow for access to personal information" (p. 453). Schrier cites a 1978 ruling by the Ohio Supreme Court that allows the disclosure of names and addresses as well as medical information on municipal hospital patients, under the Ohio Public Records Act. In resolving discrepancies between the state's privacy and open-records provisions, the "court held that any doubt about disclosure was to be resolved in favor of public disclosure" (p. 454). Although the intent of open-records statutes was not to undermine privacy but to enhance accountability, in practice these statutes may lead to the publication of personal data. In most states, however, these provisions limit disclosure of personal information and apply primarily to fiscal and management documents. Clients are more likely to gain access to their records through privacy than through open-records provisions.

Guarantees of Access

Privacy laws typically allow the client, or others acting on the client's behalf, to inspect, copy, amend, and challenge the contents of the record without having to seek court intervention. The Federal Privacy Act exemplifies open access by ensuring that a client who seeks or receives services in federally funded programs (except correctional agencies) is:

Informed of what records are being maintained

Informed that he [or she] has access to the record

Informed of how access is obtained

Permitted to see the record

Permitted to bring with him [or her] another person when he [or she] sees the record

Permitted to copy, correct, amend, and challenge the record

There are, however, some limitations on access. The agency is not required to disclose:

The source of information in the record if such information is collected with the promise of anonymity

Information collected before the act went into effect

Information collected in "anticipation of a civil action or proceeding"

Furthermore, correctional agencies do not have to make their records accessible to their clients.

The Federal Family Education and Privacy Rights Act provides students and their parents similar access to records kept by educational institutions. In addition, a few states have omnibus privacy laws that give the client the right of access to and challenge of records kept by state and sometimes local public agencies as well. Like the Federal Privacy Act, these state laws usually exempt correctional agencies from the obligation to make their records available to clients. Several states have enacted laws that grant access to some health and social service records to specific client groups. For example, in Illinois, which does not have omnibus privacy legislation, clients or their agents may have access under separate provisions to mental health, hospital, and physicians' records.

Many organizations, under no legal obligation to make their records accessible to clients, still give access following guidelines suggested by accrediting and professional organizations. In general, these guidelines recommend limited rather than full access to the record, based upon the discretion of the professional or the organization. For example, the Family Service Association of America (FSAA) in the *Position Paper on Privacy and Confidentiality,* published in 1977, suggested that member agencies allow clients to examine their records. Reading the record should be "viewed as part of the counseling process" (p. 12), and therefore either the client's own worker, or another worker if the client desires, should be present. Although the client may bring along another person to examine the record with him or her, some limitations are placed upon access. Records of family or group process are accessible only if others present give consent or if a worker reads aloud the portion of the record that pertains to the client. In addition, a client's record should be accessible to him or her only at six-month intervals. FSAA views access as a right and suggests that clients should be able to amend the record. However, clients should be "discouraged from duplicating case material" (p. 13), although they may make notes to take with them. These guidelines allow the agency some leeway in dealing with clients who may be harmed by reading the record. Such clients should be either refused access or given access only when accompanied by "a duly qualified and credentialed professional in the clinical professions" (p. 13).

Although not directly advocating full client access to records, the 1975 delegate assembly of the National Association of Social Workers (NASW) supported access to information in computerized data banks. NASW recommended a bifurcated privacy policy. One set of principles was applied to governmental, regulatory, and business organizations where automated systems were in use, and another was applied to public and private social welfare agencies. The delegate assembly followed the Department of Health, Education, and Welfare's recommendations on automated personal data systems. Such systems should be acknowledged; information in the system should be accessible to and challengeable by the client; and use of the information should be governed by client consent. In contrast, NASW recommended only that social welfare agencies develop policies governing who has access to case information and under what conditions. Although consent for disclosure is recommended, NASW stopped short of advocating direct client access to social service records.

In a similar way, the American Medical Association (AMA) supports some limited access to the medical record by the patient or those acting on the patient's behalf. In its report to the Privacy Protection Study Commission (1978), the AMA recommended that patients be given the right of access to, and correction of, their medical records. Rather than suggesting the direct right of amendment and access, however, the AMA proposed that modification of the record be undertaken "with the concurrence of the individual health care practitioner who generated the records" and that confidential medical information be reviewed and disclosed to the patient by a physician "as appropriate" (pp. 565–566).

In reviewing policies and standards that confer the procedural right of access upon clients and others acting on their behalf, social workers need to discover not just whether clients have this right but how the process of access is to be handled. Among the most important questions to be asked are:

Does the subject of the record have the primary right of access to the record, or is this right conferred upon a parent or guardian?

Are there procedural guidelines for informing the client or others of their right of access?

Are there procedural guidelines for handling a request for access or the review of the record?

Must the agency comply with specific standards, such as time limits or the availability of personnel or photocopying?

Limitations on Retention

Although access to the record allows the client to know its contents, to challenge it, and to limit its distribution, the control of the information in the record is not entirely returned to the client until the record is destroyed or expunged. Limitations on retention of the record, then, are not just for the benefit of management; these provisions also protect the client's privacy.

A number of state laws and regulations provide for the expungement or destruction of records. For example, in Arkansas and in many other states, the law provides for the expungement of the arrest records of first offenders. In Massachusetts, as in some other states, public assistance records are to be destroyed 10 years after the termination of service to the client. In Illinois and in many other states, regulations provide for the expungement of records of cases in which child abuse or neglect was investigated but not substantiated. In general, the provisions that exist limit the retention of information that is potentially harmful or stigmatizing to the client. The retention of medical records, for example, is not limited, whereas many states provide for the destruction of criminal records. In reviewing laws or other standards on retention or destruction of records, the most important questions to be asked are:

> Do any provisions exist that encourage retention of records beyond the agency's need for the information?
>
> Do any provisions exist that establish guidelines for the destruction of records or portions of their content?

Current provisions for protecting client privacy under law, regulation, and organizational policy are based on the four principles of privacy: confidentiality, client access, abridgment, and anonymity. Used singly or in combination, these provisions are intended to counterbalance encroachments on personal rights that result from society's interest in the client and in the service transaction. Privacy always competes with accountability. However, when the public interest in supporting the worker-client relationship predominates, there is a stronger commitment to the values of personal privacy. These values are reflected in provisions that protect the confidentiality of the worker-client relationship. When the public interest in the client's behavior predominates, accountability supercedes privacy as a goal, and fewer privacy protections are available. Thus, agencies serving clients who have personal problems operate under different privacy standards than organizations serving clients who are considered troublesome or have social problems. Clients who seek help from health, mental health, and substance abuse programs, whose records are seldom abridged, are likely to be protected through confidentiality and access. Those who receive services from public agencies seldom receive the full protection of confidentiality but may see and challenge their records, which are abridged. School records are protected by confidentiality and access; however, until the student reaches 18 or enters a postsecondary institution, the right of consent belongs to the parent or guardian rather than to the student. Finally, those who are suspected of such criminal acts as child abuse have fewer protections; although their communication with attorneys is privileged, communication with other professionals is not. Furthermore, those convicted of criminal acts have no procedural right of access to their records.

Privacy in Practice

Although social workers have an ethical commitment to client privacy, they can seldom assure a client that their relationship will not become known to others or that the content of their communication will be inviolate. Indeed, clients seldom expect absolute confidentiality. They recognize that social work practice involves interprofessional and interorganizational collaboration. They know that professionals keep records and that insurance companies have access to certain information. If clients are aware of some of the necessary intrusions on their privacy, they should also expect social agencies and social work practitioners to minimize unwarranted intrusions on these rights. This means adhering to relevant laws and regulations, implementing additional organizational policies and procedures as necessary, and honoring professional values in personal conduct.

The goal of social work should be to maximize client privacy while meeting the necessary demands of accountability. To meet this goal, managers and practitioners may need to review their agency's formal standards and practices. They may find, for example, that they can enhance client privacy by abridging the contents of the record, developing new procedures for safeguarding information, updating release of information forms and procedures, protecting the identity of clients whose records are used in research or education, and providing clients with access to information in their records. They should also evaluate how information is handled informally. Under the pressure of their work, social workers may inadvertently reveal personal information in public areas or sidestep procedural guidelines in the interest of expediency. They can learn a great deal by asking themselves: "Knowing how personal information is handled in this organization, would I want to be a client here?"

Abridging the Contents of the Record

The primary consideration in determining what information should be entered into the record is accountability. Personal information should be included in the client's file only if it is pertinent to the purpose of service and if it forms the basis for service decisions and actions. Information shared by the client, observed by the worker, or obtained from other sources should be documented only if that information is relevant to the need for service, to decisions about what and how services are delivered, to the provision of services, or to the evaluation of service impact. Information should be documented only if it will be useful to other practitioners who are engaged in delivering services to the client, if the information is necessary for service accounting, or if it provides a rationale for understanding the decisions, behaviors, or attitudes of important actors in the case. Documenting personal information that does not meet these criteria for accountability may subject a client to unnecessary current and future invasions of privacy.

A second consideration is the type of information in question. Personal information may be public or hidden, sensitive or neutral, stable or transient, historical or current, subjective or relatively objective. Information that is hidden, sensitive, transient, historical, or subjective should be handled with special discretion and should be documented only when it is relevant to the purpose or goals of service. For example, certain personal opinions, private behaviors, and political beliefs are quite sensitive. Although these opinions, behaviors, and beliefs may be interesting, revealing them in the record may place the client at some risk. Unless that information can inform decisions and actions taken in the case, workers are well advised to omit them from the record. However, when such information is clearly relevant but highly sensitive, workers face a more difficult choice, weighing accountability against privacy. For example, a client who is pregnant and moderately depressed reveals that she had an earlier abortion without her husband's knowledge. In such a case, some workers would choose to document the information in the record, whereas others would opt to protect the client by omitting it. Some practitioners might choose to document the information using general rather than specific terms, reporting that "the client revealed a painful experience, which she has not discussed with her husband." Only a few workers can make another choice, documenting the information in their own personal notes but not in the official or public record. Handling hidden, sensitive, transient, historical, and subjective information that is relevant to the delivery of services is among the most difficult decisions that workers make. Sometimes they can reach a compromise, but most often they must choose between accountability and privacy.

A third consideration is the quality of information to be recorded. For social work, the quality of information is not determined by its source alone. That is, information is not of higher quality simply because it is reported by an adult rather than by a child, or by a service provider rather than by a service recipient. Moreover, quality is not determined by whether information is objective rather than subjective. That is, information is not of higher quality because it is a fact rather than a feeling. Instead, the quality of information relevant to social work services is determined by its accuracy, its currency, and its specificity to the client-situation and the service transaction. Information that is inaccurate, superficial, or out-of-date jeopardizes the client's privacy by misrepresenting the truth.

When the quality of information is questionable, the worker may choose to treat its documentation in one of two ways. On the one hand, the worker may withhold the information from the record unless and until its accuracy, currency, and appropriateness are substantiated by other sources. On the other hand, the worker may choose to record the information, carefully dating the entry and including a statement regarding its possible inaccuracy. This second option carries with it the obligation to seek verification of the information and to follow up in the record at a later date, by either substantiating or expunging the information. Sometimes workers discover that information already in the record is inaccurate or out-of-date. Such a discovery carries with it a similar obligation: either to expunge the information or to follow it up with a later notation stating that the information recorded earlier was not then or is not now accurate or applicable to the client-situation.

Other social workers have offered more radical solutions to the question of what to include or exclude from the record. In "Ethical Practices in the Computerization of Client Data: Implications for Social Work Practice and Record Keeping" (1971), Gareth Hill suggested that social workers carefully scrutinize the reliability of the information in their records. Hill pointed out that, whereas social work records contain information ranging from public and factual to private and subjective, obtained from a variety of sources under a variety of conditions, all information entered into computerized data systems is treated as equally factual and objective. Deeply concerned about the potential for misuse of diagnostic labels and other information based upon clinical judgment, Hill suggested that all such information be entirely excluded from records of governmental and private agencies that cannot control the confidentiality of their records, where the "upper administrative boundaries of the agency cannot be guaranteed" (p. 19). He further recommended that, in private casework agencies, workers' clinical notes be unofficial, maintained exclusively by the worker, and destroyed when the case is closed. Hill's solution to the problem of quality, then, was to exclude all judgmental information from the official record.

Some workers in complex, multidisciplinary organizations express an opposing point of view. They suggest that their clients' privacy can best be protected if workers record only assessments and diagnostic impressions, excluding facts, descriptions of events, and client statements. They argue that when a client's record is physically accessible to a large work force of non-professionals, as it may be in a general hospital, for example, clients are more likely to be damaged by detailed descriptions of their relationships and circumstances than by assessments written in professional jargon.

Most social workers will find neither of these viewpoints entirely feasible or desirable. To exclude factual information as well as judgmental information would be to leave the practitioner and the agency with records that document only the services that were delivered and not the reasons they were delivered or their impact. Because both factual and evaluative information are critical in planning, implementing, and evaluating services, workers in most settings need to include both descriptions and assessments in their records. However, recognizing the potential for harm to clients inherent in recording any personal information, they should also carefully select and verify relevant factual information and clearly label and substantiate impressions, assessments, diagnoses, and other information based upon professional judgment. In addition, their agencies need to develop, implement, and monitor special procedures for handling personal information that appears in client records.

Safeguarding Client Information Within the Agency

Any document in which the client is identified should be physically safeguarded from unwarranted access. Files should be accessible only to those directly involved in service provision, in supervision or consultation, or in such support activities as typing and filing. Workers should lock up their case records whenever they are not in use. Records should not be left on the worker's desk during interviews or meetings and should be put away at the end of the day. Records should not be written, transcribed, or stored in rooms open to the public. Whenever possible, records of closed cases should be stored in a different location than records of open cases. Agencies should consider destroying records of cases that have been closed for a long period; the benefit of destroying records to maintain privacy, however, must be weighed against the risk of losing information that may have an important future use, either for the agency or for the client. In large organizations in which records are used by a variety of staff members, a central checkout system not only can limit unwarranted access but also can help to locate records of active cases when they are needed. A log of users, kept inside the record, allows service providers, clients, and other interested parties to know who has had access to the record and on what date.

Computerized records require special safeguards. Computer terminals should be placed out of public view. In complex organizations that have comprehensive, decentralized computer systems used by a variety of personnel, protecting client information can be problematic. Lowe and Sugarman (1978) suggested that such organizations limit access to client information either by assigning passwords or by using encoding and decoding devices. They further proposed that, whenever possible, client identification be omitted from computer-generated reports (p. 219). In fact, if properly managed, computerized systems can actually provide internal protections that are not available in manual systems. Through the use of passwords, users may have access to some, but not all, of the information in the record. Only those with authorization could retrieve specific information from the record. This means, for example, that clerical workers in a hospital can make appointments, file reports, and even retrieve some information from a patient's medical record without gaining access to psychiatric or social service reports. As an additional safeguard, the computer can supply a daily log of users of each record; this information can then be used to monitor privacy. In contrast, when manual records are used, hospital personnel who have access to a record may have access to all information stored in the record. Furthermore, a log of users is not automatically generated in manual records.

Procedures can also be initiated to limit access by oversight agencies and other organizations that have a legitimate right to some information in the record. Agencies may, for example, prohibit monitors from actually seeing client records. Workers may act as intermediaries, either abstracting information from the record in response to written questions or reading to the monitor from the record in response to oral questions.

The computerization of personal data by organizations that receive information from agency records calls for special precautions, because privacy abuses often take place after personal data enter large data banks maintained by third parties. Whenever possible, universal identifiers should not appear in the record and should not be used by the agency in its case identification system. Because information in data banks is often processed by social security numbers, any use of these numbers in agency records makes clients particularly vulnerable to invasions of privacy through computer matching. Although the use of social security numbers may be advocated by some governmental agencies as an efficient means of service accounting and of limiting abuses of the social services, the potential for widespread access to personal information in data banks when universal identifiers are used has led the FSAA to state that "the family service movement recognizes the need for monitoring on the part of third parties paying for service and agency accountability to these sources, but until there is assurance of client privacy safeguards . . . we will fight against the use of universal identification systems" (p. 6).

In addition to establishing and monitoring procedures for handling client records, agencies should be prepared to provide education and training of personnel as needed. Clerical staff and volunteers, who assume a large part of the responsibility for handling client records, need to be trained in agency procedures and their rationales when they begin to work for the agency. Social workers as well as other professional personnel often benefit from workshops and in-service training programs that not only teach new policies and procedures but also reinforce ethical principles.

Releasing Client Information

Releasing Information to Outside Agencies and Individuals All agencies should have a policy for handling incoming requests for information. This policy should go beyond simple compliance with legal requirements by seeking to maximize client privacy and decision making. As a rule, information should be released only with prior, informed, written consent of the client or the client's guardian. Furthermore, agencies should seek a separate release of information for each agency or individual who will receive information. Although some agencies still rely on blanket consent forms, often signed by clients at intake and ostensibly covering all requests for information, these forms do not meet the criterion of informed consent. Indeed, the blanket approach is being supplanted. Eighty percent of the organizations participating in the Records II study ask the client to sign a separate release form for each organization or individual who will receive information. Agencies should handle such authorizations individually and should adopt a release procedure that includes the following steps:

1. The client (or the client's guardian) is informed, prior to any release, that a request for information has been received.
2. When appropriate, the potential recipient of information is investigated.
3. The client is given access to the information that has been requested. The client is given an opportunity to amend or correct the record.
4. The client is informed of the possible consequences of releasing or withholding the information.
5. The client decides, without coercion, to release or withhold information or to take other action.
6. The client who chooses to release the information signs a release form. This release specifies what information is to be released, to whom, for what purpose, and the date on which the authorization begins and expires.
7. The worker also signs the release form.
8. The client is informed about when the release authorization will automatically expire and how to revoke the authorization prior to the expiration date.
9. The information is released as specified by the client.
10. The recipient of information is informed that the information may not be released to other organizations or individuals.

A model release form can be found at the end of Chapter 5.

As a general rule, agencies should not release information without prior consent. However, in some instances an agency may need to release information when prior consent cannot be obtained. Whenever this occurs, in an emergency or in response to a court order, the client should be formally notified. In addition, for the protection of the practitioner and the organization, a full report, including documentation of attempts to secure authorization from the client or the client's agent and a rationale for releasing information without prior consent, should appear in the record. Such documentation should specify the date of release, the reason for release without prior consent, and what information was released, to whom, and for what purpose. The report should be cosigned by a supervisor or other executive officer.

In multidisciplinary settings, such as schools, hospitals, and clinics, the release of information from records may be managed centrally. Often the social work department is not informed when information from current or former clients' records is released. Social workers who practice in such settings would be well advised to discover how requests for information are handled and, when appropriate, to advocate within the organization for better policies and procedures.

Releasing Information for Education and Research In addition to policies and procedures for handling requests from outside agencies and individuals, agencies that receive frequent requests may also wish to establish guidelines for the release of personal information for education and research. In all cases, the information should be released only if the clients remain anonymous. To assure careful and appropriate use of client information, agencies may wish to establish the following policies:

Client records should not be taken from the agency.

Use of records in the classroom is permitted only:

With the approval of the student's supervisor

If all identifying information is deleted by recopying the record, substituting blanks or pseudonyms; by covering the information during duplication; or by "whiting out" the information after duplication

Use of records for research is permitted only:

If the purpose and process of the research are approved by an agency review committee

If the researcher is bound by a code of ethics that ensures the confidentiality of client information; if access to the record is provided indirectly, through an agency intermediary who responds to the researcher's questions but does not let the researcher read the record; or if all identifying information in the record is deleted by the agency, as above

Making Records Accessible to Clients and Their Agents

Clients in many social work agencies and departments today have the right to see their records. Prior to the implementation of the Federal Privacy Act of 1974, this was not the case. Most clients could gain access to their records only if they had a court order. The impetus for giving clients the procedural right of access came in part from federal and state mandates, in part from professional and accreditation guidelines, and in part from organizational and professional initiatives. Although there still is considerable diversity within the field, the client who asks to see his or her record today is more likely to be given access than denied it.

However, despite the importance of client access as a vehicle for promoting client privacy, many clients who are aware of this right are not interested in claiming it, and many professionals who approve of client access in principle are clearly ambivalent about it in practice. Abel and Johnson (1978) found that a large proportion of clinical social workers approved of client access.

Yet, the Records I study found that, although most (88 percent) of the agencies studied had a policy on access, only 20 percent routinely gave clients a written statement informing them about the policy and about how they might obtain access. The Records II study produced similar findings, with only 26 percent of the agencies routinely informing their clients of their right of access. With few exceptions, agencies in the public sector inform clients of this right, whereas agencies in the private sector are likely to discuss access only with clients who ask. Agencies that inform their clients of their right to see or copy their records have more such requests. However, even in agencies that have an open-access policy, relatively few clients seek access to their records. Clearly, most clients are not aware of their rights; those who are may lack interest or be discouraged from pursuing their interest. Some clients may be deterred by such organizational barriers to access as paying the cost of copying the record, following a complicated procedure, or appearing to challenge professional authority. Others may feel that they would be unable to read or understand the technical language of the record.

Giving clients access to their records not only protects privacy; it can also promote worker-client communication and trust. Houghkirk (1977) and Freed (1978) have described their experiences using the record as a component of the therapeutic process. They found that, with a worker present to help the client understand and use the information, reading the record can be a successful means of enhancing client self-awareness. There are many situations in which a client might benefit from reading the record. For example, a suspicious client might be reassured by reading the social worker's assessment. A client who finds it difficult to see progress in a given situation might learn a great deal from reading what was written in the record three months earlier. Yalom (1986) describes an approach he uses in communicating with clients through the record. Before each meeting he sends members of his groups a summary of the previous meeting. Here the record reinforces continuity between meetings and offers a source for discussion during meetings. His approach could be adopted by other creative practitioners.

In evaluating their own policies regarding client access to records, agencies who have an option may wish to consider whether their clients are best served by a policy of open or limited access. Exhibit 7.1 compares procedures associated with open access with those associated with limited access. An open-access policy encourages clients to review their records. Clients are informed of this right and are afforded access to all parts of the record while service is in progress. A limited-access policy responds to clients who indicate an interest in reviewing the record but may further restrict access to a specific time, content, or situation.

Clearly, there are costs as well as benefits in an open-access policy. The experience of the schools, where an open-access policy has been in effect since the middle 1970s as a result of the Buckley Amendment, is instructive. Records that are now accessible both to students and to their parents have changed markedly; they have become, in effect, a method of communication between the school and the parents, rather than just a means of communication

EXHIBIT 7.1 Comparison of Open-Access and Limited-Access Policies

Open Access	Limited Access
All clients are informed, in writing, of their right to see their records.	Clients who inquire may see their records.
Clients may see the entire record.	Clients may see only specified portions of the record.
Access is granted while service is in progress.	Access is granted only after services are terminated.
A worker is available to explain the record if the client so requests.	A worker must be present while the record is being reviewed.
Clients may receive a copy of the record and may challenge or seek to amend the record.	Clients may request a copy of the record.

between professionals within the school system. As a result, social service records are less likely to contain confidential information shared by the student with the social worker. It is ironic that in the effort to establish an important privacy safeguard (that is, by allowing parents to know what is in the record and, therefore, what is being communicated within the organization), the confidentiality of the worker-student relationship has been undermined. In sum, client access has both benefits and costs. Access has benefited clients by increasing the flow of information from the organization to the client, but it has been costly because it has caused service providers to limit their use of the record in interprofessional communication.

Any agency that affords family members even limited access to client records may witness a similar effect. Affording access to the subject of the record but not to other family members, however, can have a very positive effect upon the record and the worker-client relationship. Workers who ask, "What would happen to my relationships with clients if they read what I write?" are more apt to describe client-situations fairly and to share their assessments with clients more directly. Workers who know that a client may at some time review the record will select information more carefully and prepare their records with this new audience in mind.

In addition to weighing the costs and benefits of various approaches to access, agencies that allow even limited access may find it useful to develop specific procedures regarding how access will be implemented. Among the questions to be answered are:

Must the client make a written request for access, or is a verbal request sufficient?

How much advance notice (for example, a week) is required?

May the client make copies of the record, or should the agency provide this service?

May the client amend or challenge the record? How will this process be managed?

How frequently may the record be reviewed?

Social workers in multidisciplinary settings need to develop and coordinate their access policies with those of other departments and of the organization as a whole. Only in rare instances in which social work is administered as an independent unit with separate records can social work implement an access policy that is substantially different from those of the rest of the departments in the organization. Furthermore, not only may policy be institution-wide, but access, like release of information, may also be handled by a central records department. In this case, after evaluating current policies and practices, social workers may choose to work within the organization to initiate or to change access policies. In addition to seeking policies that are in compliance with legislative mandates and professional guidelines, and that are fair, equitable, and ethical, such policies and procedures as they apply to social work records:

Should be formulated with the participation of social work personnel

Should inform social work when either current or former clients request access to records that contain social work content

Should allow social workers to be present when their records are being reviewed

Should include the recorder in decisions to amend the record

Advocating for Privacy

Knowledge of the principles of privacy and of the provisions that apply to their organization and to their clients can be used by social workers to improve their adherence to federal, state, and local social policies and to guidelines promulgated by professional organizations; this knowledge can also be used by social workers as a basis for advocacy for the full exercise of client rights in other social institutions. Practitioners and organizations are in violation of ethical and legal principles if they:

Informally share personal information about clients without client consent

Refuse clients mandated access to their records

Are coercive in seeking personal information or in releasing information to outside agencies or individuals

Are lax in physically safeguarding client information

In advocating for privacy, social workers should take the following steps:

1. Seek information regarding the practitioner's or the organization's
   a. legal responsibilities under federal, state, or local mandates
   b. ethical responsibilities under professional codes or accreditation guidelines
   c. customary practices
2. Seek instances in which the practitioner or the organization did not meet legal or ethical responsibilities.
3. Assess whether these instances reflect
   a. inadequate or inappropriate social policy
   b. inadequate or inappropriate standards of practice for the organization or the individual practitioner
   c. specific breaches of appropriate policy or customary practice

Intervention, then, can be directed toward a change in social policy, agency policy, or specific practices.

Conclusions

Like other components of professional practice, protecting client privacy involves much more than simple compliance with accepted procedures. Social workers must also make a series of choices in establishing agency policy and in the day-to-day management of information about each client. Often these choices require weighing the need to document and communicate information to others against the obligation to protect the client from unnecessary intrusions and from misuse of sensitive information. A few agencies have tried to resolve this dilemma by keeping no records or by keeping records that merely identify the client but do not contain information about the purpose, process, or progress of service. Although this choice appears to maximize privacy, it involves real costs in the loss of documentation for a number of purposes and may, inadvertently, limit client rights by not affording access to information about service decisions. Most agencies that cannot or will not choose to forgo systematic service documentation can provide clear and explicit guidelines to help their workers in making decisions about their records. Then, aided by knowledge of social policy and agency procedures and guided by the ethics of the profession, practitioners can better meet their obligation to use personal information in ways that both protect client privacy and facilitate the delivery of appropriate, timely, and individualized services.

8 Computerization of Records

Many social work agencies and departments today use computers for some aspects of their recordkeeping. If an agency is not already using computers for word or data processing, it is probably considering doing so within the next few years. Although automation does not necessarily change the content and function of social work records, it significantly alters the process of documenting, storing, retrieving, reporting, and using information. This chapter presents an overview of the application of information technology to recordkeeping in social work. In contrast to previous chapters, which concentrate primarily on case records, this chapter broadens its focus to include records used in managing the agency. The chapter begins with an overview of the uses of computers in social work and a brief introduction to the technology. A description and evaluation of various approaches to computerization follow. The chapter concludes with a discussion of some of the potential risks and benefits as well as problems and solutions associated with automating social work records.

Word Processing and Data Processing

All computers collect, store, retrieve, and report information. The most important uses of computers in social work are for word processing and data processing. Word processing involves typing, editing, filing, retrieving, and printing forms and documents. For example:

A social worker dictates the rough draft of a social history into a tape recorder. Using a word processing program, her secretary types the social history into the computer, corrects the spelling using a spelling checker, stores the document, and then prints out a copy for the worker to review and edit. After deleting some words, adding a new section, and rearranging some paragraphs, the worker returns the edited printout to the secretary, who retrieves the original document and, with a few keystrokes, makes the requested changes. The secretary then stores the edited version, replacing the earlier draft, and prints out a copy of the revised social history. The edited document remains stored on disk so that it may later be retrieved, reviewed, and updated.

Most agencies and practitioners recognize the potential benefits of word processing for their records and other documents. Word processing makes it possible to print documents without errors or correction marks, and to retrieve, review, and revise records with little effort or cost. In addition, word processors perform other useful functions, such as printing multiple copies of letters, each with a personalized greeting; preparing reports from archival records; quickly locating and retrieving information, even when it is embedded in narrative reports; and storing large amounts of information in a small space.

Data processing uses the computer to classify, select, compile, compare, sort, and perform other forms of analysis on the information in records. Any type of information that can be identified specifically and documented systematically may be used as a variable and analyzed using data processing. For example:

The Borage County Mental Health Clinic uses data processing to support case management. Workers fill out a brief monthly case reporting form on each case. This form includes only nine variables. These are:

Variable A—Client identification (name or case number)
Variable B—Source of referral
Variable C—Problem type
Variable D—Service goals
Variable E—Date of each service contact
Variable F—Name of worker providing service at each service contact
Variable G—Services provided at each service contact
Variable H—Status of goals at three-month intervals
Variable I—Service outcome

Three of these variables (Variables A, E, and F) are documented using a single word or number. The client (Variable A) and the worker (Variable F) may be identified by name (Browne) or number (144). The date of each service contact (Variable E) may be documented by number only (10/18/88) or by a combination of words and numbers (October 18, 1988).

For the remaining six variables, the clinic staff has developed a list of the values (or categories) that each variable can take. As shown in Figure 8.1, these categories may be listed on the form, making the form longer but easier to complete. Alternatively, the categories may be listed in a separate code sheet, as in Figure 8.3. As Figure 8.2 shows, this approach shortens the form. However, when workers refer to a separate document, their recordkeeping becomes more time-consuming, and, when workers rely on their memories rather than consulting the code sheet, their records may be inaccurate.

At the Borage County Mental Health Clinic, data are entered into the computer on a monthly basis. Other organizations may find it more appropriate to develop forms for more frequent data entry—for example, every one or two weeks.

Using just these nine variables, the computer at the Borage Clinic generates a number of useful reports, including:

1. Individual case reports
2. A list of active cases, grouped by problem type, by number of service contacts, by services provided, or by worker
3. A list of service contacts per time period (for example, a month), by worker, problem type, type or number of goals, or outcome
4. A list of cases handled by each worker over the previous year, indicating the number of contacts, type of services provided, service goals, and status of goals or service outcomes
5. A list of cases that received no service in the previous month or that are due for three-month reviews
6. A comparison of outcomes for clients receiving different types of services
7. An analysis of factors influencing client dropout
8. Case information needed for billing, accreditation, peer review, or third-party reimbursement

Table 8.1 presents a sample report. The table lists all cases assigned to one worker that received no services during the previous month. Note that this sample report uses the same variables as the monthly case reporting forms in Figures 8.1 and 8.2.

Although the example of the Borage Clinic is necessarily simple, it suggests that agencies can learn a great deal from computer analysis of information

FIGURE 8.1 Example of a Reporting Form That Includes Categories of Information

Borage County Mental Health Clinic
Monthly Case Reporting Form

Worker: Month of:

Client ID:

Part I (for new cases only)

Source of Referral:
( ) Self
( ) Friend or family
( ) Physician or psychiatrist
( ) School
( ) Mental health agency
( ) Attorney
( ) Crisis line
( ) Other (specify) ______
( ) Unknown

Problem Type*:
( ) Interpersonal conflict
( ) Dissatisfaction in social relations
( ) Problems with formal organizations
( ) Difficulties in role performance
( ) Problems of social transition
( ) Reactive emotional distress
( ) Inadequate resources
( ) Other (specify) ______

Service Goals (up to three):
( ) Teach new skills
( ) Resolve interpersonal conflicts
( ) Link to community agencies
( ) Work through emotional difficulties
( ) Improve or change social environment
( ) Improve or change physical environment
( ) Find job, housing, and/or other resources
( ) Build social support network
( ) Other (specify) ______

*This list is based on the "Target Problem" typology used in task-centered practice. See Reid and Epstein's *Task-Centered Casework* (1972).

they usually include in their records. Almost all of the 73 social work agencies and departments that responded to the Records II survey were either already using computers for some aspects of recordkeeping (56 respondents) or planning to initiate computer use within two years (13 respondents). Forty-three of the agencies already using computers were using them for word processing; 49 were using computers for data processing.

FIGURE 8.1 (continued)

Borage County Mental Health Clinic
Monthly Case Reporting Form

Worker: Month of:

Client ID:

Part II (for all cases)

Date of Each Contact:		Services Provided During the Month:
________	________	( ) Case management
________	________	( ) Crisis intervention
________	________	( ) Behavioral intervention
________	________	( ) Psychosocial casework
________	________	( ) Group work
________	________	( ) Marital counseling
________	________	( ) Family therapy
________	________	( ) Information or referral
________	________	( ) Provision of resources
________	________	( ) Assessment or evaluation
________	________	( ) Other (specify) ________

Status of Each Goal at Last Contact During the Month:

Goal 1	Goal 2	Goal 3
( ) Achieved	( ) Achieved	( ) Achieved
( ) Improved	( ) Improved	( ) Improved
( ) No change	( ) No change	( ) No change
( ) Worsened	( ) Worsened	( ) Worsened
( ) Activity deferred	( ) Activity deferred	( ) Activity deferred

Part III (at closing only)

Service Outcome:
( ) All goals achieved
( ) At least one but not all goals achieved
( ) No goals achieved
( ) Client dropped out
( ) Services terminated by agency
( ) Services no longer needed
( ) Referral successful
( ) Referral unsuccessful
( ) Other (specify) ________

A Brief Introduction to Computer Technology

The most important factors determining what an automated recordkeeping system can do are its software and hardware. **Software** programs are instructions that control the functions of the computer. There are two general types of software programs: those that run the computer and control its resources (operating systems) and those that perform special functions (applications

FIGURE 8.2 Example of a Short Recording Form (Refer to the Code Sheet of Values)

Borage County Mental Health Clinic
Monthly Case Reporting Form

Worker: Month of:

Client ID:

Part I (for new cases only)

Source of Referral: 1—( ) 2—( ) 3—( ) 4—( ) 5—( ) 6—( )

7—( ) 8—( ) (specify) ________________________ 9—( )

Problem Type*: 1—( ) 2—( ) 3—( ) 4—( ) 5—( ) 6—( )

7—( ) 8—( ) (specify) ________________________

Service Goals (up to three): 1—( ) 2—( ) 3—( ) 4—( ) 5—( )

6—( ) 7—( ) 8—( ) (specify) ________________________ 9—( )

Part II (for all cases)

Date of Each Contact: ______ ______ ______ ______ ______

______ ______ ______ ______ ______ ______ ______

______ ______ ______ ______ ______ ______ ______

Services Provided During the Month: 1—( ) 2—( ) 3—( ) 4—( )

5—( ) 6—( ) 7—( ) 8—( ) 9—( ) 10( )

11—( ) (specify) ________________________

Status of Each Goal at Last Contact During the Month:
Goal 1: 1—( ) 2—( ) 3—( ) 4—( ) 5—( )
Goal 2: 1—( ) 2—( ) 3—( ) 4—( ) 5—( )
Goal 3: 1—( ) 2—( ) 3—( ) 4—( ) 5—( )

Part III (at closing only)

Service Outcome: 1—( ) 2—( ) 3—( ) 4—( ) 5—( )

6—( ) 7—( ) 8—( ) (specify) ________________________

* This list is based on the "Target Problem" typology used in task-centered practice. See Reid and Epstein's *Task-Centered Casework* (1972).

FIGURE 8.3 Code Sheet of Values for a Short Recording Form

Borage County Mental Health Clinic
Code Sheet for Monthly Case Reporting Form

Source of Referral:
1—Self
2—Friend or family
3—Physician or psychiatrist
4—School
5—Mental health agency
6—Attorney
7—Crisis line
8—Other
9—Unknown

Problem Type*:
1—Interpersonal conflict
2—Dissatisfaction in social relations
3—Problems with formal organizations
4—Difficulties in role performance
5—Problems of social transition
6—Reactive emotional distress
7—Inadequate resources
8—Other

Service Goals:
1—Teach new skills
2—Resolve interpersonal conflicts
3—Link to community agencies
4—Work through emotional difficulties
5—Improve or change social environment
6—Improve or change physical environment
7—Find job, housing, and/or other resources
8—Build social support network
9—Other

Services Provided During the Month:
1—Case management
2—Crisis intervention
3—Behavioral intervention
4—Psychosocial casework
5—Group work
6—Marital counseling
7—Family therapy
8—Information or referral
9—Provision of resources
10—Assessment or evaluation
11—Other

Status of Each Goal:
1—Achieved
2—Improved
3—No change
4—Worsened
5—Activity deferred

Service Outcome:
1—All goals achieved
2—At least one but not all goals achieved
3—No goals achieved
4—Client dropped out
5—Services terminated by agency
6—Services no longer needed
7—Referral successful
8—Referral unsuccessful

* This list is based on the "Target Problem" typology used in task-centered practice. See Reid and Epstein's *Task-Centered Casework* (1972).

TABLE 8.1 Sample Report Using Variables, A, C, D, E, and F

Open Cases Receiving No Services, October 1989

Worker: Elgin
Total Cases Open: 66
Total Cases No Services: 19

Client #	Problem Type	Goals	Last Recorded Contact
87-033	5	1,3,5	8/89
87-142	4	1,2,8	8/89
87-151	4	1,5,7	7/89
87-158	1	2,5	5/89
88-096	3	2,3	5/89
88-113	7	1,3	6/89
88-132	5	5,6,7	5/89
88-149	4	1,8	8/89
88-176	7	3	3/89
88-209	1	2,8	9/89
88-217	4	3,7	8/89
89-008	4	3,5,8	6/89
89-034	6	2,4,8	7/89
89-074	3	3,7	7/89
89-105	4	3,8	9/89
89-147	4	2,5	8/89
89-153	1	2,4	7/89
89-177	4	1,4	9/89
89-184	3	3,7,8	9/89

programs). Computer users may choose from a dizzying array of ready-made applications packages. Or they may create their own software or hire programmers to develop new software or customize available packages. With so many available options, social service agencies and practitioners need to select applications programs carefully to ensure that the programs suit their particular recordkeeping needs.

Today, most agencies that control their own computer systems purchase standardized packages for word processing, data base management, accounting, and other applications. This approach has many benefits. The purchaser knows how much a software package will cost and can investigate its quality and reliability. Moreover, many vendors provide initial training of staff free of charge. Agencies that choose this approach, however, should be aware of other, less apparent costs. They may need to purchase a software package for each system or a multi-user license. They should also recognize that the time spent in training and in adapting to a new system can also be quite costly. For example, some agencies have found that clerical personnel with experience using one package resist learning and using new packages; some agencies have had high staff turnover during periods when new systems are introduced. Moreover, even when practitioners have no direct access to the computer, their practice may be deeply affected by automation or by new software. They may be asked to alter their recordkeeping practices, learn new forms, and adjust to new procedures. Finally, agencies may discover that the packages they purchased are not immediately useful; they may need outside consultants to configure generic data base and business applications packages for use in their social service agency. Thus, even agencies that are experienced in computer use should be prepared for a potentially difficult transition period for training, developing new recording forms and procedures, and customizing software to accommodate agency needs.

Hardware is the equipment that, along with software, makes up a computer system. In addition to a central processing unit, computers today typically include a keyboard, a display screen, a floppy disk for storage, and a printer. Many computers also include a mouse, a light pen, or a touchpad, all of which, in addition to the keyboard, can be used to enter information; a hard disk or an optical disk for data entry or storage; and a modem for linking one computer with another over telephone lines.

Purchasing a Computer System

For social service organizations, the most important features of hardware are the size of the computer system, the available software, the amount of memory, the cost, and security. These features, and some of the options to consider, are discussed in this section.

Size Computer systems can vary in size from a self-contained portable or stationary unit to a room-size mainframe connected by telephone terminals in distant locations (telecommunications). The size and power of a system influence how many users may be accommodated simultaneously, the speed at which information can be processed, and, to some extent, the functions that the computer can realistically perform.

However, one large computer may not be well suited to all of an agency's recordkeeping needs. Although large, expensive mainframes are an integral part of record management in many statewide agencies and hospitals, they are not efficient for all their computer tasks. Rather, because of their low cost and adaptability, personal computer systems are extremely useful in large as well as small organizations. A personal computer can be used independently for word and data processing and can also be used to transfer information to and from the central mainframe. Moreover, personal computers can be linked together into networks, so that information can be shared between workstations.

Available Software An important criterion for evaluating hardware for purchase is the current availability of suitable applications software. In general, software development lags behind hardware. Agencies need to be wary when hardware salespeople attempt to sell them new systems by telling them that the software they need will be ready "real soon now." Software development is notoriously slow, and software manufacturers lose interest in hardware that does not sell well. As a result, software that is not already available may be delayed or may never be written. In some cases, a used computer or an older model may be a better value than a new model. A system that is one or two years old is still quite new and is likely to be much less expensive than a newer model. Furthermore, the purchaser can investigate whether the hardware is reliable and whether the necessary software is available and suitable.

Memory A computer's memory is its storage capacity. Every computer has main memory (sometimes called random-access memory—RAM—or primary storage), which is the space available for the programs and information in use. The capacity of a computer's main memory determines which software programs it can run and how much information it can process at one time. Every computer also has secondary storage space for programs and information that are not in use. Today, all large computers and many personal computers have built-in hard disks that provide faster access to programs and information in secondary storage. Additional information may be stored outside the computer on removable floppy disks, tape cartridges, or optical disk cartridges, making the external storage capacity of computer systems virtually limitless.

Cost Although many agencies assume that the cost of hardware is the primary expense associated with automation, many additional costs should be considered. Among these costs are software, which may cost from one third to twice as much as hardware; new recording forms and manuals; consultation for training personnel and for programming software; building modification, including new wiring, security for hardware, and antistatic rugs; and service or service maintenance agreements.

Given the high price of automation, agencies usually look for ways to economize. One suitable option is to purchase a used or older system; another is to lease a newer system. However, some other options have proven to be poor economies. Agencies should avoid buying an inexpensive system that does not meet current needs, with the idea of upgrading or expanding it later. Computers have not developed incrementally, and new systems are seldom compatible with older ones. Furthermore, by the time the agency needs more capacity, purchasing or leasing a new system is apt to be a better investment than upgrading an older system that may be out-of-date.

Security The degree to which an agency can protect the confidentiality of client records is, in part, related to the computer system it uses. Just as an interested party can break into a file cabinet in which written records are stored, an interested party with physical or electronic access and computer expertise may be able to break into a computer and gain access to its files. Information in smaller systems can be compromised by bypassing password security and gaining direct access to data files. Information in larger systems or networks is susceptible to security breaches because of wider access to the system from inside as well as from outside the organization through telecommunications.

In general, computer security devices offer some protection by limiting and monitoring access to data. Sign-ons enhance security by providing a list of accessed files by user, thus monitoring and deterring unwarranted access. Passwords limit access to files; they may also be used to permit different levels of access. Depending on one's department and job description, for example, agency personnel may be able to gain access to all or only some files and may be able to perform all or only some functions, such as reading and adding but not deleting information. Data encryption codes information in a data file. Those who might otherwise gain direct access to information in data files would be unable to decipher the coded information.

Approaches to Automation

Social work organizations and departments may choose from a vast array of computer technology to assist them in agency, program, personnel, and case management. An organization might find limited or extensive use for computers depending upon resources, personnel, information needs, service delivery patterns, and accountability structure. The findings of the Records II survey suggest that, in current practice, social service agencies are utilizing computers in four areas of recordkeeping:

1. Business functions and agency management
2. Office management
3. Client tracking, decision support, and caseload management
4. Case records

Indeed, one can understand an agency's use of computers by studying the recordkeeping functions that the computer performs and by learning who controls the system and who has direct access to the system. To understand fully how an agency uses computers, one must study the role that the computer plays in the day-to-day practice of direct-service workers, supervisors, and managers in the agency.

Business Functions and Agency Management

In social service agencies today, the computer is most often used to perform business functions, and to analyze information and report to management about clients, services, and workers. The system is used for billing, budgeting, and accounting; for paying clients, workers, and other agencies; for monitoring service delivery and productivity; for preparing routine forms and reports for oversight and funding agencies; and for preparing special reports, such as those used in accreditation and peer review.

Business and management functions may be performed by outside contractors, by individual units, or by a special department within the organization. For control and efficiency, many large organizations centralize this activity in a management information system (MIS). Although any manual or automated record system used to provide data for management decisions might be called a management information system, the term *MIS* generally refers to the mainframe systems developed for and maintained by large and complex organizations, such as state public welfare departments. An MIS can accommodate large amounts of information and can generate many and diverse reports. It is generally managed by computer experts rather than by social workers or other professionals.

In most agencies today, direct-service workers do not have direct access to computers when the system is used primarily for business and management functions. Typically, workers record information about clients, services, and their own activities on a variety of structured forms. This information is then entered into the computer by clerical workers in the individual unit or in the central office.

In theory, the worker's task in preparing forms for these purposes need not be more cumbersome than with a manual system. In practice, however, this may not be the case. Many agencies, lured by the capacity and potential of the system, have placed extra burdens upon the practitioner. Practitioners are frequently required to collect more information than before, and to complete many and redundant forms. Moreover, despite their efforts, practitioners seldom directly benefit from the reports the computer generates. Most reports focus on managerial issues rather than on those of concern to the practitioner. Furthermore, these reports are too often used as a means of monitoring and controlling direct-service workers' activities rather than in assisting them with their responsibilities. It is not surprising, then, that many workers focus their dissatisfaction on the computer. Although the field has concentrated its attention on system development and data management issues, the practitioner's role has not been made easier, and his or her information needs have not been successfully addressed.

The social work manager is not just the principal user of the information generated by the system. The manager also plays an important role in developing a recording and reporting system that meets the agency's information needs. The manager is also responsible for training staff and for monitoring and improving the recording process, so that the information that enters the system is accurate and complete and staff time is used efficiently. These tasks are often easier to accomplish when information is processed in the manager's own unit rather than centrally. However, even in a centralized system, the social work manager can take an active role in assuring that demands on the worker are fair, and that reports to the department meet its information needs.

Office Management

A large proportion of social work agencies and departments today use computers to perform office management functions alone, or office management in addition to business and agency management functions. Computers are used for such office functions as typing and storing narrative records, preparing single or multiple copies of letters, and tracking client appointments and worker calendars. Clerical workers are usually in control of the system, although direct-service workers and managers may also have access to a personal computer or a workstation.

Agencies that use computers for this purpose are usually very satisfied. Most clerical workers today expect to use a computer, and many are well prepared for the task. Direct-service workers seldom complain. They do not have to change their approach to recordkeeping or fill out more forms for the system. Moreover, they benefit directly when their letters, reports, and records are prepared and edited efficiently and when their appointments and calendars are automated. Managers have a similarly positive response to this use of the computer.

The only difficulties with this approach to automation are associated with networking, which is the linking of computers to share information. Respondents to the Records II survey echo the complaints of other managers who have had hardware and software problems. They complain that interfaces, software, and cabling are very expensive and do not always work well. They describe difficulties loading programs, downloading data, and accessing memory. Some agencies have found computer networks to be less efficient than personal computers used individually or in combination with a mainframe.

It is hard to imagine a social work agency or a social worker in independent practice whose recordkeeping would not benefit from using a computer for word processing and other office management applications. Even in a small office, the cost of a new, used, or leased personal computer is so modest that it can often pay for itself in less than a year by significantly reducing the time it takes to fill out forms and to type error-free letters and reports, and by freeing up storage space.

Client Tracking, Decision Support, and Caseload Management

Computers are increasingly being used to assist direct-service workers in making practice decisions, although the practice is not yet widespread. Workers may receive a monthly computer-prepared profile of each open case, including the client's personal characteristics and service history. They may receive exceptions reports, listing cases due for routine review or closing, or cases in which documentation does not meet quality assurance or reimbursement standards. Such reports can assist workers in making case and caseload management decisions. Workers may also have immediate access by computer to information useful in making mental health diagnoses, locating appropriate community service resources, or finding pertinent research and scholarship. On-line access to such data bases can improve the quality, efficiency, and timeliness of service decisions and actions.

Providing a computer or workstation for each practitioner might improve the quality and timeliness of records and of decision making; however, the high cost of this approach means that it will probably not be feasible for most social service agencies in the next decade. (Recognizing this, some practitioners have purchased their own computers, which they use for recordkeeping.) Nonetheless, practitioners could share a terminal that would give them access to case records or on-line decision-support information; they could also receive computer-generated reports that would be useful in managing their cases and their caseloads.

Case Records

In a few organizations, some or all of the organization's official case records are automated and on-line. This use of computers, found most often in hospitals, would be appropriate in a variety of organizations, especially those in which case information is frequently entered and retrieved. Typically, the organization purchases or leases a mainframe with decentralization terminals that are used interactively. Many users, therefore, have direct access to the case record. Depending on what their access level will permit, users may read, record, or edit material in the record.

Because of its high cost, this model has not been widely adopted or fully implemented. A fully automated system would be "paperless"; each practitioner would have access to a terminal, and all case records would be computerized. In practice, however, this is not usually the case. In some hospitals, for example, the automated record is used for appointments and for identifying information, but it is not used for complete case histories. In some schools, educational records are automated but social service records are not. Thus, automated case records are usually supplemented by other computer- or manually prepared records. In addition, these organizations generally have a centralized system to perform business and management functions, as well as decentralized workstations for data entry and for office functions.

Although automated case records offer real potential for enhancing the timeliness and usefulness of records, this model has not yet appreciably altered the social service record or the social work practitioner's role in recordkeeping. Direct-service workers, who are not yet generally responsible for direct entry of data into the computer, are unlikely to have direct access to a computer. The Records II survey found that practitioners had direct access to terminals in only 17 of the 56 agencies and departments in which computers were being used. Moreover, several of the respondents indicated that practitioners' lack of direct access to terminals was a major problem associated with computerization of records in their agencies. Social workers continue to record manually and to read a written or printed record. Indeed, because this approach to recordkeeping is susceptible to problems of informational privacy, some social work departments have chosen not to participate fully in their organization's automated case records. They are concerned that the confidentiality of personal information in clients' records may be breached.

Benefits and Problems Associated with Computer Use

As the preceding examples have shown, computers can significantly improve an agency's recordkeeping. However, organizations that have automated their records have not found the process easy. Automating records involves not just a major commitment of the agency's resources for purchasing and maintaining the system, upgrading the building, and training personnel. It also involves major changes in the everyday activities of the organization.

For example, computers require maintenance and sometimes break down. When they break down, files may be lost, and, while they are out of order, information cannot be entered, processed, or retrieved. Agencies can be somewhat prepared for these contingencies by purchasing service contracts and by ensuring that information in the system is routinely backed up on floppy disk, streamer tape, or optical disk. However, system "down time" may mean that needed information is inaccessible; this may lead to a backlog of work that is stressful for clerical workers, practitioners, and managers.

In the 1970s and early 1980s, agencies experienced a number of problems associated with selecting systems and implementing the transition to automated recordkeeping. Many organizations purchased hardware that did not meet current needs and could not be upgraded successfully. Others relied on vendors who made false or exaggerated claims about the systems they marketed, and who did not provide adequate training or service. Some organizations did not adequately budget for the indirect costs of computerization. Many encountered difficulty in gaining the coöperation of direct-service workers, who were seldom consulted about their needs and were often required to change their recordkeeping practices. Finally, a number of agencies discovered problems in their use of the reports generated by the system. In some cases, reports were not specifically tailored to management needs. As Poertner and Rapp (1980) suggested, "Any manager who wants to can have a desk or closet full of computer printouts. However, these printouts never seem to contain the information that managers need to make important day-to-day decisions" (p. 114). In other cases, practitioners sensed that the system was being used to monitor their productivity and highlight their errors rather than to support and inform their practice.

Those who responded to the Records II survey in 1987 and 1988 were experiencing many of the benefits of automation but reported some of the same problems. They most often mentioned ready access to information or ease and efficiency of analysis as benefits to their organizations. They found the computer especially helpful in surfacing trends, making rapid budget changes, analyzing statistics, reviewing and updating client information, and compiling resource files. Some indicated that the computer enabled them to undertake tasks that they would have otherwise been unable to perform. Although some agencies had found that computers simplified recordkeeping and yielded more complete and accurate records, many were disappointed that these anticipated benefits had not been achieved. They indicated that automation complicates some tasks, takes up too much worker time, and makes data more difficult to evaluate and errors more difficult to track down. As expected, many indicated that they had resource problems: not enough time, not enough training, or not enough computers or terminals. Others reported hardware and software problems such as incompatible systems within the organization, unreliable hardware, or difficulties locating appropriate software or configuring available systems.

By the late 1980s, social work professionals began to recognize the need to find solutions to problems associated with hardware and software selection and use, information management, and organizational change. Yet, the problems faced by direct-service workers remain poorly understood and largely unresolved. In many agencies that use computers, automation has not simplified the worker's job but rather added demands for paperwork. Certainly the diminished resource base of the social services can in part be blamed for some of the problems associated with automating records. Fewer social workers managing larger caseloads supported by fewer clerical workers are trying to meet increased demands for documentation. Yet, even if the resource base of the social services were to increase, many of the difficulties workers face would remain.

If social service organizations are to achieve the full benefits of automating their records, they will need to achieve three related goals. First, the worker's recordkeeping tasks must be simplified. Working together, practitioners and managers need to develop realistic guidelines that meet the agency's minimum information needs while using the practitioner's time efficiently. Guidelines should include a statement of what information is to be included in the record and when that information is to be documented. Practitioners should not be assigned repetitive or duplicate tasks, such as filling out forms or summarizing monthly activities; these tasks can be more efficiently performed by a clerical worker. For example, the worker's computerized daily calendar can be used in preparing statistical reports, recording service units, and computing monthly productivity data.

Secondly, computers must be used to meet the information needs of direct-service workers. Computers are most likely to benefit practitioners in their day-to-day case and caseload management if practitioners have direct access to computer terminals. However, organizations that adopt other approaches to automation can also meet practitioner needs if the system is used to generate practice-related documents and reports in a timely fashion.

Thirdly, recording guidelines should seek to portray practice realistically. An automated system is ineffective in controlling the practice or in changing worker behavior. Therefore, agencies should not use an automated system for such purposes. Agencies that seek to alter the practice or the practitioner through documentation requirements and procedures find marked discrepancies between practice and the record. If records are to be accurate and meaningful, then, recordkeeping guidelines should reflect the realities of service delivery.

From Planning to Implementation

It is not always possible for social work agencies and departments to select the computer systems they will use; decisions about the system are sometimes made at another level of the organization. Furthermore, it is not always possible to take a long time selecting the right system and planning for the transition to automation; resources may suddenly become available and may need to be spent quickly. However, agencies and departments should always plan thoroughly for automation, involving workers from all levels: administrators, direct-service workers, and clerical personnel. Agencies that involve staff in all phases of planning encourage commitment to the process and use of the system. The commitment of direct-service workers is especially important, for the following reasons:

The success of a system depends in large part on the quality of the reports that are generated.

The quality of the reports generated by the system depends in large part on the accuracy, completeness, and timeliness of the information upon which the reports are based.

The accuracy, completeness, and timeliness of the information in the system depend in large part on the investment of direct-service workers in making the system work.

Selecting an appropriate computer system requires a series of choices that should end, not begin, with the decision about what system to purchase, lease, or use. Instead, the agency should begin by assessing whether a computer could improve its recordkeeping. If the answer to any of the following questions is yes, the use of a computer might help:

1. Does the agency produce a great deal of paperwork? If so, are clerical workers so overloaded that work is backlogged? Are workers doing their own clerical work? Is typewritten work full of errors?
2. Is available information inadequate for use in decisions about clients, services, personnel, and resource utilization?
3. Does the agency have a large information base that is not being used in decision making? Does the agency need to process large amounts of information for use in decision making?
4. Is needed information inaccessible because it is not being recorded at all, because it is not being recorded on time, or because it is being written in a form that makes retrieving information difficult?
5. Are several records, reports, or forms being completed using the same information? Are records being kept for more than one audience?
6. Is the agency funded by a variety of sources that have different reporting requirements? Are funding sources questioning the agency's recordkeeping practices? Is the agency seeking funds from sources that require stricter accountability standards than currently exist?
7. Could services be improved if better case management information were available?

The answers to these questions may provide the agency with a range of automation goals. The next step is to explore the options available to the agency in meeting its goals. This data collection step should involve interviews with diverse vendors as well as visits to other similar agencies and departments that have successfully automated their records. Many agencies profit from the service of a specialized consultant or systems analyst during this and subsequent stages. However, the advice of outside "experts" should not be accepted uncritically. Agency personnel know best how the agency works and what system would work best in the agency.

The next step involves evaluating the various options. Of course, budgetary constraints, current and future, are a critical factor. But feasible costs must also be assessed against automation goals. Would a very costly system (software, hardware, personnel, space) that meets all of the agency's goals be a better investment than a more modest system that meets only some of the current goals? Would it be better to begin by purchasing computer services, leasing a system, or purchasing a small system that is expandable in the future? It is also important to evaluate the extent to which an automation approach would support and enhance the existing information system or would alter radically current recording policies, practices, and procedures. Although even limited automation requires some change in recording practices, a more significant departure from current practices is likely to be more disruptive and to involve greater implementation costs.

Having reviewed their goals, options, and preferences, agencies that choose to initiate computerization of their records must decide next which system to purchase, lease, or use. Then, even before automation begins, the organization must begin its transition. Staff should be introduced to the system itself, and to the way in which recordkeeping practices and procedures will be altered. Some or all of the staff should be trained in computer use. Depending upon the model selected, new recording forms may be developed, tested, modified, and introduced into general use. Although experience with the computer usually leads to further changes, some prior preparation in expectation, skill, and procedure can significantly ease the stress of transition.

The first few months of automation establish whether or not computerization is accepted and incorporated into agency functioning. No matter how carefully the transition has been planned, problems are likely to arise. Some of these problems are obvious. For example, a form may need to be redesigned to accommodate additional information, or available packaged software may need to be adapted to meet agency needs. Further education and training of staff at all levels of the organization may also be necessary.

Other problems, however, may be less apparent. Workers may find their recordkeeping responsibilities more arduous and time-consuming than before. This can lead to significant problems in morale and opposition to the system. Staff morale problems can best be ameliorated through prevention, rather than by waiting for real difficulties to emerge. Morale can be enhanced if workers are involved in planning and implementation, if they are regularly consulted about the strengths and limitations of the new system (and the system is altered to respond to perceived limitations), if recordkeeping is made meaningful, and if workers receive useful information that was not available before. If morale problems arise in spite of such efforts, they should not be dismissed as resistance and interpreted as individual problems requiring individual solutions. Rather, such problems should be credited and interpreted as organizational problems requiring organizational solutions.

Automated recordkeeping, like other approaches to documentation, is a means to a valued end, not an end in itself. It is useful so long as it enhances the quality of social work services and facilitates accountability to the community, the profession, and the client.

References

Abel, C., & Johnson, W. (1978). Clients' access to records: Policy and attitudes. *Social Work, 23*(1), 42–46.

Addison, L. (1985, November). Mental health information: Shrinking plaintiffs' privilege. *Texas Bar Journal,* 1222–1224.

Alexander, M., Siegel, C., & Murtaugh, C. (1985). Automating the psychiatric record for care review purposes: A feasibility analysis. *Computers in Human Services, 1*(4), 1–16.

American Hospital Association. (1978). *A reporting system for hospital social work.* Chicago: Author.

American Medical Association. (1978, March 23). Statement presented to Hon. Herman E. Talmadge, re Privacy Protection Study Commission and recommendations thereon of the Department of Health, Education and Welfare. Washington, DC.

American Psychiatric Association. (1987). *Diagnostic and statistical manual of mental disorders* (3rd ed., rev.). Washington, DC: Author.

Applying computers in social service and mental health agencies: A guide to selecting equipment, procedures, and strategies. (1981 [Special issue]). *Administration in Social Work, 5*(3/4).

Aptekar, H. (1960). Record writing for the purposes of supervision. *Child Welfare, 39*(2), 16–21.

Barker, R. (1986). Spelling out the rules and goals: The written worker-client contract. *Journal of Independent Social Work, 1*(2), 43–49.

Barker, R. (1987). To record or not to record: That is the question. *Journal of Independent Social Work, 2*(2), 1–5.

Beinecke, R. (1984, November). PORK, SOAP, STRAP, and SAP. *Social Casework,* pp. 554–558.

Bell, C. (1978). *Accessibility of adoption records: Influences on agency policy.* Ann Arbor, MI: University Microfilms.

Bernstein, B. E. (1977). Privileged communications to the social worker. *Social Work, 22*(4), 264–268.

Bloom, M., & Fischer, J. (1982). *Evaluating practice: Guidelines for the accounting professional.* Englewood Cliffs, NJ: Prentice-Hall.

Blount, A. (1985). Mental health center approach. In D. Campbell & R. Draper (Eds.), *Applications of systemic family therapy.* Orlando: Grune & Stratton.

Bonney, N., & Streicher, L. (1970). Time-cost data in agency administration. *Social Work, 15*(4), 23–31.

Bork, K. (1953). A staff examination of recording skill (Parts 1 & 2). *Child Welfare, 32*(2), 3–8; (3), 11–14.

Boyd, L., & Hylton, J. (1978). Computers in social work practice: A review. *Social Work, 23*(5), 368–371.

Bristol, M. C. (1936). *Handbook on social case recording.* Chicago: University of Chicago Press.

Brodsky, S. (1972). Shared results and open files with the client. *Professional Psychology, 3*(4), 362–364.

Bunston, T. (1985, April). Mapping practice: Problem solving in clinical social work. *Social Casework,* pp. 225–236.

Burgess, E. W. (1928). What social case records should contain to be useful for sociological interpretation. *Social Forces, 6*(4), 524–532.

Camenga, M. (1974). *A guide to record keeping and social services: A system for child development programs.* Atlanta: Humanics Press.

Campbell, D., & Stanley, J. (1963). *Experimental and quasi-experimental designs for research.* Chicago: Rand McNally.

Cerveny, K., & Kent, M. (1983–1984). Evidence law: The psychotherapist-patient privilege in federal courts. *Notre Dame Law Review, 59,* 791–816.

Christian, W., & Hannah, G. (1983). *Effective management in human services.* Englewood Cliffs, NJ: Prentice-Hall.

Commonwealth v. Collette, 387 Massachusetts 424, 439 N.E. 2d 1223 (1982).

Confidentiality of health and social service records: Where law, ethics, and clinical issues meet. (1976, December). *Proceedings of the Second Midwest Regional Conference.* Chicago: University of Illinois at Chicago Circle.

Delgado, R. (1973). Underprivileged communications: Extension of the psychotherapist-patient privilege to patients of psychiatric social workers. *California Law Review, 61,* 1050–1071.

Demlo, L., Campbell, P., & Brown, S. (1978). Reliability of information abstracted from patients' medical records. *Medical Care, 16*(12), 995–1005.

Dwyer, M., & Urbanowski, M. (1965). Student process recording: A plea for structure. *Social Casework, 46*(5), 283–286.

Edwards, R., & Reid, W. (1989, January). Structured case recording in child welfare: An assessment of social workers' reactions. *Social Work,* pp. 49–52.

Eliot, T. (1928). Objectivity and subjectivity in the case record. *Social Forces, 6*(4), 539–544.

Family Service Association of America Task Force on Privacy and Confidentiality. (1977). *Position paper on privacy and confidentiality.* New York: Family Service Association of America.

Fanshel, D. (1975). Parental visiting of foster children: A computerized study. *Social Work Research and Abstracts, 13*(3), 2–10.

Fein, E. (1975). A data system for an agency. *Social Work, 20*(1), 21–24.

Feinstein, A. (1973). The problems of the problem-oriented medical record. *Annals of Internal Medicine, 78*, 751–762.

Fisher, C. (1972). Paradigm changes which allow sharing of results. *Professional Psychology, 3*(4), 364–369.

Foster, L. (1980). State confidentiality laws: The Illinois act as model for new legislation in other states. *American Journal of Orthopsychiatry, 50*(4), 659–775.

Freed, A. (1978). Clients' rights and casework records. *Social Casework, 59*(8), 458–464.

Frings, J., Kratovil, R., & Polemis, B. (1958). *An assessment of social case recording.* New York: Family Service Association of America.

Gansheroff, N., Boszormenyi-Nagy, I., & Matrulla, J. (1980). Clinical and legal issues in the family therapy record. In J. Howells (Ed.), *Advances in Family Psychiatry.* New York: International Universities Press.

Garfield, G., & Irizarry, C. (1971). The record of service. In W. Schwartz & S. Zalba (Eds.), *The practice of group work.* New York: Columbia University Press.

Garfinkel, H. (1968). *Studies in ethnomethodology.* (pp. 186–207). Englewood Cliffs, NJ: Prentice-Hall.

Garvin, C. (1981). *Contemporary group work.* (pp. 202–205). Englewood Cliffs, NJ: Prentice-Hall.

Giglio, R., Spears, B., Rumpf, D., & Eddy, N. (1978). Encouraging behavior changes by use of the client-held record. *Medical Care, 16*(9), 757–764.

Gingerich, W. (1985). Three software programs from applied innovations for the human services clinician. *Computers in Human Service, 1*(3), 83–91.

Gobert, J. (1976, January). Accommodating patient rights and computerized mental health systems. *North Carolina Law Review, 54*, 153–187.

Godwin, P. (1988, August). Could your medical records wreck your life? *Better Homes and Gardens*, pp. 40–42.

Goldman, M. (1964, July). An agency conducts a time and cost study. *Social Casework, 45*(7), 393–397.

Hamilton, G. (1936, 1938). *Social case recording.* New York: Columbia University Press.

Hamilton, G. (1946). *Principles of social case recording.* New York: Columbia University Press.

Hartman, A. (1978). Diagrammatic assessment of family relationships. *Social Casework, 59*(8), 465–476.

Hartman, B., & Wickey, J. (1978). The person-oriented record in treatment. *Social Work, 23*(4), 296–299.

Haselkorn, F. (1978). Accountability in clinical practice. *Social Casework, 59*(6), 330–336.

Hedlund, J., Vieweg, B., & Cho, D. (1985). Mental health computing in the 1980s. *Computers in Human Services, 1*(1), 3–33; *1*(2), 1–31.

Helms, D. J. (1975). A guide to the new federal rules governing the confidentiality of alcohol and drug abuse patient records. *Contemporary Drug Problems, 4*(3), 259–283.

Henry, D., DeChristopher, J., Dowling, P., & Lapham, E. V. (1981). Using the social history to assess handicapping conditions. *Social Work in Education, 3*(1), 7–19.

Henry, S. (1981). *Group skills in social work*. Itasca, IL: Peacock Publishers.

Herzlinger, R. (1977). Why data systems in nonprofit organizations fail. *Harvard Business Review, 55*(1), 81–86.

Hill, G. (1971). Ethical practices in the computerization of client data: Implications for social work practice and record keeping. Washington, DC: National Association of Social Workers.

Hill, J., & Ormsby, R. (1953, October). The Philadelphia cost study. *Social Work Journal, 34*, 165–178.

Hochwold, H. (1952). The use of case records in research. *Social Casework, 33*(2), 71–76.

Hodge, M. H. (1977). *Medical information systems: A resource for hospitals*. Germantown, MD: Aspen Systems Corporation.

Holbrook, T. (1983, December). Case records: Fact or fiction? *Social Service Review*, 645–658.

Hollis, F. (1967). Explorations in the development of a typology of casework treatment. *Social Casework, 48*(6) 335–341.

Hollis, F., & Wood, M. (1981). *Casework: A psychosocial therapy* (3rd ed.). New York: Columbia University Press.

Hoshino, G., & McDonald, T. (1975). Agencies in the computer age. *Social Work, 20*(1), 10–14.

Houghkirk, E. (1977). Everything you've always wanted your clients to know but have been afraid to tell them. *Journal of Marriage and Family Counseling, 3*(2), 27–33.

Hudson, W. (1982). *The clinical measurement package*. Homewood, IL: Dorsey Press.

Hurley, M. (1985). Duties in conflict: Must psychotherapists report child abuse inflicted by clients and confided in therapy? *San Diego Law Review, 22*, 645–668.

In re Clear, 58 Misc. 2d 703, 296 New York S. 2d 188, Family Court (1969).

In re Koretta W., 118 Misc. 2d 660, 461 New York S. 2d 205, Family Court (1983).

Itzin, F. (1960). The use of tape recordings in field work. *Social Casework, 41*(4), 197–202.

Ives, K. (1978). Revising an agency's service information system. *Administration in Social Work, 2*(1), 111–115.

Ivey, A. (1987). *Intentional interviewing and counseling.* North Amherst, MA: Microtraining Associates.

Jackson, J. (1987, May/June). Clinical social work and peer review: A professional leap ahead. *Social Work,* pp. 213–220.

Jayaratne, S., & Levy, R. (1979). *Empirical clinical practice.* New York: Columbia University Press.

Johnson, H. (1978). Integrating the problem-oriented record with a systems approach to case assessment. *Journal of Education for Social Work, 14*(3), 71–77.

Joint Commission on Accreditation of Hospitals. *Accreditation manual for hospitals.* Chicago: Author.

Kadushin, A. (1963). Diagnosis and evaluation for (almost) all occasions. *Social Work, 8*(1), 12–19.

Kagle, J. D. (1982a). Social work records in health and mental health organizations: A status report. *Social Work in Health Care, 8*(1) 37–46.

Kagle, J. D. (1982b). Using single subject measures in practice decisions: Systematic documentation or distortion? *Arete,* 7(2), 1–9.

Kagle, J. D. (1983). The contemporary social work record. *Social Work, 28*(2), 149–153.

Kagle, J. D. (1984). Restoring the clinical record. *Social Work, 29*(1), 46–50.

Kagle, J. D. (1987a). Preventing clients from dropping out of treatment. *Journal of Independent Social Work, 1*(3) 31–43.

Kagle, J. D. (1987b). Recording in direct practice. *Encyclopedia of Social Work* (18th ed., pp. 463–467). Washington, DC: National Association of Social Workers.

Kagle, J. D. (1988). *How to overcome worker resistance and improve your agency's records.* Paper presented at the National Association of Social Workers' Meeting of the Profession, Philadelphia, PA.

Kagle, J. D. (1989). *Privileged communication: A client right and a professional principle.* Paper presented at the annual program meeting of the Council of Social Work Education, Chicago, IL.

Kaiser, B. (1975). Patients' rights of access to their own medical records: The need for a new law. *Buffalo Law Review, 24*(2), 317–330.

Kane, R. (1974). Look to the record. *Social Work, 19*(4), 412–419.

Karls, J., & Wandrei, K. (in press). P-I-E: A new language for social work.

Kelley, V., & Weston, H. (1974). Civil liberties in mental health facilities. *Social Work, 19*(1), 48–54.

Kelley, V., & Weston, H. (1975). Computers, costs, and civil liberties. *Social Work, 20*(1), 15–19.

Kiresuk, T., & Garwick, G. (1979). Basic goal attainment procedures. In B. Compton & B. Galaway (Eds.), *Social work processes* (2nd ed.). Homewood, IL: Dorsey Press.

Kiresuk, T., & Sherman, R. (1968). Goal attainment scaling: A general method for evaluating comprehensive mental health programs. *Community Mental Health Journal, 4*, 443–453.

Knapp, S., VandeCreek, L., & Zirkel, P. (1987). Privileged communications for psychotherapists in Pennsylvania: A time for statutory reform. *Temple Law Quarterly, 60*(2), 267–292.

Knox, F. (1965). *The Knox standard guide to design and control of business forms.* New York: McGraw-Hill.

Knox, F. (1981). *Managing paperwork: A key to productivity.* New York: Thomond Press.

Kraemer, K. L., Dutton, W., & Northrop. A. (1980). *The management of information systems.* New York: Columbia University Press.

Kreuger, L. (1987). Microcomputer software for independent social work practice. *Journal of Independent Social Work, 1*(3), 45–58.

Kreuger, L., & Ruckdeschel, R. (1985, May/June). Microcomputers in social service settings: Research applications. *Social Work,* pp. 219–224.

Kucic, A. R., Sorensen, J., & Hanbery, G. (1983). Computer selection for human service organizations. *Administration in Social Work, 7*(1), 63–75.

Laska, E., & Bank, R. (Eds.). (1975). *Safeguarding psychiatric privacy: Computer systems and their uses.* New York: John Wiley & Sons.

Levi, J. (1981). The log as a tool for research and therapy. *Social Work, 26*(4), 333.

Levine, R. (1976). Child protection records: Issues of confidentiality. *Social Work, 21*(4), 323–324.

Levitan, K., Willis, E., & Vogelgesang, J. (1985). Microcomputers and the individual practitioner: A review of the literature in psychology and psychiatry. *Computers in Human Services, 1*(2), 65–84.

Levy, C. (1979a). Code of ethics. *NASW News, 24*(2), 6–7.

Levy, C. (1979b). NASW ethics task force. *NASW News, 24*(1), 9.

Lindenthal, J., Jordan, T., Lentz, J., & Thomas, C. (1988, March/April). Social workers' management of confidentiality. *Social Work,* pp. 157–158.

Lindsay, A. (1952). *Group work recording.* New York: Association Press.

Little, R. (1949). Diagnostic recording. *Journal of Social Casework, 30*(1), 15–19.

Lorents, A. (1982). Small computers: The directions of the future in mental health. *Administration in Social Work, 6*, 57–68.

Lowe, B., & Sugarman, B. (1978). Design considerations for community mental health management information systems. *Community Mental Health Journal, 14*(3), 216–223.

Lusby, S., & Rudney, B. (1973). One agency's solution to the recording problem. *Social Casework, 54*(10), 586–590.

Lutheran Social Services of Wisconsin & Upper Michigan. (1987). *Eval-U-Treat: A unified approach to program evaluation and direct service delivery.* Milwaukee, WI: Lutheran Social Service.

Mair, W. C. (1977). Computer abuse in hospitals. *Hospital Progress, 58*(3), 61–63.

McCormick, M. (1978). Privacy: A new American dilemma. *Social Casework, 59*(4), 211–220.

McCullough, L., Farrell, A., & Longabaugh, R. (1986). The development of a microcomputer-based mental health information system: A potential tool for bridging the scientist-practitioner gap. *American Psychologist, 41*(2), 207–214.

McKane, M. (1975). Case-record writing with reader empathy. *Child Welfare, 54*(8), 593–597.

Meldman, M., McFarland, G., & Johnson, E. (1976). *The problem-oriented psychiatric index and treatment plans.* St. Louis: Mosby Company.

Meyer, R., & Smith, S. (1977). A crisis in group therapy. *American Psychologist, 32*, 638–643.

Miller, D., & Thelen, M. (1986). Knowledge and beliefs about confidentiality in psychotherapy. *Professional Psychology: Research and Practice, 17*(1), 15–19.

Mitchell, R. (1984). *The client record: A tool for optimizing quality mental health service and malpractice prevention.* Paper presented at the annual meeting of the National Council of Community Mental Health Centers, New Orleans, LA.

Mutschler, E. (1987). Computer utilization. *Encyclopedia of Social Work* (18th ed., pp. 316–326). Washington, DC: National Association of Social Workers.

Mutschler, E., & Cnann, R. (1985). Success and failure of computerized information systems: Two case studies in human service agencies. *Administration in Social Work, 9*(1), 67–79.

Mutschler, E., & Hasenfeld, Y. (1986, September/October). Integrated information systems for social work practice. *Social Work*, pp. 345–349.

National Association of Social Workers. (1973). *Legal regulation of social work practice.* Washington, DC: Author.

National Association of Social Workers. (1975). *Policy on information utilization and confidentiality* (pp. 214–219). Washington, DC: Author.

National Association of Social Workers. (1979). NASW code of ethics. *NASW News, 25*, 24–25.

Nelson, J. (1981, Summer). Issues in single-subject research for non-behaviorists. *Social Work Research and Abstracts, 17*, 31–37.

Newkham, J., & Bawcom, L. (1982). Computerizing an integrated clinical and financial record system in a CMHC. *Administration in Social Work, 6*, 97–111.

Newman, F. L., & Sorensen, J. E. (1981). *The program director's guidebook for the design and management of client-oriented systems.* Belmont, CA: Wadsworth.

Noble, J. (1971). Protecting the public's privacy in computerized health and welfare information systems. *Social Work, 16*(1), 35–41.

Northern, H. (1969). *Social work with groups.* New York: Columbia University Press.

Nurius, P., & Mutschler, E. (1984). Use of computer-assisted information processing in social work practice. *Journal of Education for Social Work, 20*(1), 83–94.

O'Brien, J. (1983). *Computers and information processing in business.* Homewood, IL: Richard D. Irwin.

Pannor, R., & Peterson, M. (1963). Current trends in case recording. *Child Welfare, 42*(5), 230–234.

Pardeck, J. (1986). Microcomputers in clinical social work practice: Current and future uses. *Family Therapy, 13*(1), 15–21.

Pardeck, J., Umfress, K., & Murphy, J. (1987). The use and perception of computers by professional social workers. *Family Therapy, 14*(1), 1–8.

Pawlak, E., & LeCroy, C. (1981). Critical incident recording for supervision. *Social Work with Groups, 4*, 181–191.

Payne, M. (1978). Social work records. *Social Work Today, 9*(32, 33).

People v. Randolf Bass, Bronx State Supreme Court. Reported in *New York Law Journal,* June 17, 1988.

Perlman, G. (1988, September/October). Mastering the law of privileged communication: A guide for social workers. *Social Work,* pp. 425–429.

Phillips, B., Dimsdale, B., & Taft, E. (1982). *Administration in Social Work, 6*, 129–143.

Pinkus, H. (1977). Recording in social work. *Encyclopedia of Social Work.* Washington, DC: National Association of Social Workers.

Poertner, J., & Rapp, C. (1980). Information system design in foster care. *Social Work, 25*(2), 114–121.

Popiel, D. (1980). Confidentiality in the context of court referrals to mental health professionals. *American Journal of Orthopsychiatry, 50*(4), 678–685.

Privacy Protection Study Commission. (1977a). *Personal privacy in an information society.* Washington, DC: U.S. Government Printing Office.

Privacy Protection Study Commission. (1977b). *Privacy law in the states.* Washington, DC: U.S. Government Printing Office.

Prochaska, J. (1977). Confidentiality and records. *Social Casework,* (58), 371–372.

Promislo, E. (1979). Confidentiality and privileged communication. *Social Work, 24*(1), 10–13.

Rapp, C. (1987). Information utilization for management decision making. *Encyclopedia of Social Work* (18th ed., pp. 937–944). Washington, DC: National Association of Social Workers.

Rawley, C. (1938–1939). A functional examination of recording. *The Family, 19*, 298–305.

Reamer, F. (1986, November/December). The use of modern technology in social work: Ethical dilemmas. *Social Work,* pp. 469–472.

Reamer, F. (1987, September/October). Informed consent in social work. *Social Work,* pp. 425–429.

Reid, W. J., & Epstein, L. (1972). *Task-centered casework*. New York: Columbia University Press.

Reynolds, M. (1976). Threats to confidentiality. *Social Work, 21*(2), 108–113.

Reynolds, M. (1977). Privacy and privilege: Patients', professionals', and the public's rights. *Clinical Social Work Journal, 5*(1), 29–42.

Richmond, M. (1917). *Social diagnosis*. New York: Russell Sage Foundation.

Richmond, M. (1925). Why case records? *Family, 6*, 214–216.

Robinson, E., Bronson, D. & Blythe, B. (1988, June). An analysis of the implementation of single-case evaluation by practitioners. *Social Service Review*, 285–301.

Rubin, E. (1976). The implementation of an effective computer system. *Social Casework, 57*(7), 438–444.

Russell Sage Foundation. (1970). *Guidelines for collection, maintenance, and dissemination of pupil records*. New York: Author.

Sackheim, G. (1949). Suggestions on recording techniques. *Journal of Social Casework, 30*(1), 20–25.

Sacks, H. (1975). Title XX—A major threat to privacy and a setback for informed consent. *Connecticut Medicine, 39*(12), 785–787.

Sacks, H. (1976). Strategies and remedies for confidentiality deficits in title XX and title IV D legislation. *Connecticut Medicine, 40*(2), 471–473.

Sauer, A. (1978). *Procedures for operating a service delivery information system*. New York: Family Service Association of America.

Savrin, P. (1985). The social worker–client privilege statutes: Underlying justifications and practical operations. *Probate Law Journal, 6*, 243–276.

Schoech, D. (1979). A microcomputer-based human service information system. *Administration in Social Work, 3*(4), 423–440.

Schoech, D. (1987). Information systems: Agency. *Encyclopedia of Social Work* (18th ed., pp. 920–931). Washington, DC: National Association of Social Workers.

Schoech, D., & Aranglo, T. (1979). Computers in the human services. *Social Work, 24*(2), 96–103.

Schoech, D., & Schkade, L. (1980). Computers helping caseworkers: Decision support system. *Child Welfare, 59*(9), 556–575.

Schrier, C. (1980). Guidelines for recordkeeping under privacy and open-access laws. *Social Work, 25*(6), 452–457.

Schwartz, G. (1989, May). Confidentiality revisited. *Social Work*, pp. 112–226.

Seaberg, J. (1965). Case recording by code. *Social Work, 10*(5), 92–98.

Seaberg, J. (1970). Systematized recording—A follow-up. *Social Work, 15*(3), 32–41.

Shaw, D. R. (1981). *Your small computer: Evaluating, selecting, financing, and operating the hardware and software that fits*. New York: Van Nostrand Reinhold.

Sheffield, A. E. (1920). *The social case history: Its construction and content*. New York: Russell Sage Foundation.

Shuman, D., & Weiner, M. (1982). The privilege study: An empirical examination of the psychotherapist-patient privilege. *North Carolina Law Review, 60*, 893–942.

Siegel, C., & Fischer, S. K. (1981). *Psychiatric records in mental health care.* New York: Brunner/Mazel.

Simmons, J. (1978). A reporting system for hospital social service departments. *Health and Social Work, 3*(4), 102–112.

Sircar, S., Schkade, L., & Schoech, D. (1983). The data base management system alternative for computing in human services. *Administration in Social Work, 7*(1), 51–62.

Smith, S. (1986–1987). Medical and psychotherapy privileges and confidentiality: On giving with one hand and removing with the other. *Kentucky Law Journal, 75*, 473–555.

Smith, S. R. (1986–1987). Privileges and confidentiality. *Kentucky Law Journal, 75*, 475–557.

Sorosky, A., Baran, A., & Pannor, R. (1978). *The adoption triangle: The effects of the sealed record on adoptees, birth parents, and adoptive parents.* Garden City, NY: Anchor Press.

Sosin, M. (1986, September). Administrative issues in substitute care. *Social Service Review,* pp. 360–375.

Southard, E. E., & Jarrett, M. (1922). *Kingdom of evils.* New York: Macmillan.

Spano, R., Kiresuk, T., & Lund, S. (1977). An operational model to achieve accountability for social work in health care. *Social Work in Health Care, 3*(2), 33–42.

Spevack, M., & Gilman, S. (1980). A system for evaluative research in behavior therapy. *Psychotherapy: Theory, Research and Practice, 17*(1), 37–43.

State v. Martin, 274 N.W. 2d 893, South Dakota (1979).

Statutes.

Arkansas Statutes Ann., § 43-1231, *et seq.* (Arrest Expungement).

Child Abuse Prevention and Treatment Act of 1974 (PL 93-247) and Amendments of 1978 (PL 95-266) and 1984 (PL 98-457).

Colorado Revised Statutes, § 12:63.5-115 (Privileged Communication).

Family Educational Rights and Privacy, 20 U.S.C. § 1232g (Buckley Amendment PL 93-568).

Federal Drug Abuse Prevention, Treatment, and Rehabilitation Confidentiality of Patient Records, 21 U.S.C. § 1175 (Drug Abuse), 42 U.S.C. § 4582 (Alcohol Abuse).

Federal Privacy, 5 U.S.C. § 552a (PL 93-579).

Freedom of Information, 5 U.S.C. § 552 (PL 89-554).

Illinois Revised Statutes.

§ 4.4 (1989).

§ 23-2050, *et seq.* (Abuse & Neglect).

§ 51-71, *et seq.* (Hospital, Physician Records).

§ 91-801, *et seq.* (Mental Health).
§ 111-4.4, *et seq.* (Privileged Communication).

Kentucky Rev. Statutes, § 335: 170, *et seq.* (Privileged Communication).

Massachusetts Code Ann.
§§ 66A-1-3 (Fair Information Practices).
§ 66-17A (Public Welfare Records).
§ 112: 135 (Privacy).

Ohio Revised Code Ann.
§ 149.40, *et seq.* (Freedom of Information).
§ 1347.01, *et seq.* (Privacy).

Oklahoma Statutes, Title 59, § 1272: 1.2, *et seq.* (Privileged Communication).

Streat, Y. (1987, November). Case recording in children's protective services. *Social Casework*, pp. 553–560.

Sussman, A. (1971). The confidentiality of family court records. *Social Service Review, 45*(4), 455–481.

Swan, P. (1976). Privacy and recordkeeping remedies for the misuse of accurate information. *North Carolina Law Review, 54*, 585–621.

Swift, L. (1928). Can the sociologist and social worker agree on the content of case records? *Social Forces, 6*(4), 535–538.

Sytz, F. (1949). Teaching recording. *Journal of Social Casework, 30*(10), 399–405.

Tarasoff v. Regents of the University of California, 17 California 3d 425, 551 P. 2d 334 (1976).

Tatara, T. (1987). Information systems: Client data. *Encyclopedia of Social Work* (18th ed., pp. 931–937). Washington, DC: National Association of Social Workers.

Taylor, A. (1953). Case recording: An administrative responsibility. *Social Casework, 34*(6), 240–246.

Templeton, M. (1986). The psychotherapist-patient privilege: Are patients victims in the investigation of medical fraud? *Indiana Law Review, 19*, 831–851.

Thomas, E. J. (1978, Winter). Research and service in single-case experimentation: Conflicts and choices. *Social Work Research and Abstracts, 14*, 20–31.

Timms, N. (1972). *Recording in social work*. Boston: Routledge & Kegan Paul.

Tomm, K., & Wright, L. (1982). Multilevel training. In R. Whiffen & J. Byng-Hall (Eds.), *Family therapy supervision: Recent developments in practice*. Orlando: Academic Press.

Toseland, R. (1987). Treatment discontinuance: Grounds for optimism. *Social Casework, 68*(4), 195–204.

Toseland, R., & Rivas, R. (1984). *An introduction to group work practice*. New York: Macmillan.

Towle, C. (1941). *Social case records from psychiatric clinics*. Chicago: University of Chicago Press.

Turner, J. (1987). Confidences of malpractice plaintiffs: Should their secrets be revealed? *South Texas Law Review, 28*, 71–91.

Tuzil, T. (1978). Writing: A problem-solving process. *Social Work, 23*(1), 67–70.

Urbanowski, M. (1974). Recording to measure effectiveness. *Social Casework, 55*(9), 546–553.

Urdang, E. (1979, November). In defense of process recording. *Studies in Social Work,* pp. 1–15.

Vogel, L. (1985). Decision support systems in the human services: Discovering limits to a promising technology. *Computers in Human Services, 1*(1), 67–80.

Volland, P. (1976, Spring). Social work information and accountability systems in a hospital setting. *Social Work in Health Care, 1,* 277–286.

Watkins, S. (1989, March). Confidentiality and privileged communications: Legal dilemma for family therapists. *Social Work,* pp. 133–136.

Weed, L. (1968). Medical records that guide and teach. *New England Journal of Medicine, 278,* 593–600.

Weed, L. (1969). *Medical records, medical evaluation, and patient care.* Cleveland: Case Western Reserve University Press.

Weisberg, R. (1986). Child abuse and neglect: The high cost of confidentiality. *Stanford Lawyer, 24*(3), 24–25, 74.

Weissman, J., & Berns, B. (1976). Patient confidentiality and the criminal justice system: A critical examination of the new federal confidentiality regulations. *Contemporary Drug Problems, 5*(4), 531–552.

Westin, A. F., & Baker, M. (1972). *Data banks in a free society: Computers, recordkeeping, and privacy.* New York: Quadrangle.

Wheeler, S. (Ed.). (1976). *On record: Files and dossiers in American life.* New Brunswick, NJ: Transaction.

Whiting, L. (1988). *State comparison of laws regulating social work.* Silver Springs, MD: National Association of Social Workers.

Wigmore, J. (1961). *Evidence 8* (3rd ed.). Boston: Little, Brown.

Wigmore, S. J. (1961). *Evidence in trials at common law* (rev. ed., J. McNaughton, Ed.). Boston: Little, Brown.

Wilcznski, B. (1981). New life for recording: Involving the client. *Social Work, 26*(4), 313–317.

Wilke, C. (1963). A study of distortions in recording interviews. *Social Work, 8*(3), 31–36.

Wilson, D. (1974). Computerization of welfare recipients: Implications for the individual and the right to privacy. *Rutgers Journal of Computers and Law, 4*(1), 163–208.

Wilson, G., & Ryland, G. (1949). *Social group work practice* (pp. 70–77). Boston: Houghton Mifflin.

Wilson, S. (1978). *Confidentiality in social work: Issues and principles.* New York: Free Press.

Wilson, S. (1980). *Recording—Guidelines for social workers.* New York: Free Press.

Wodarski, J. (1986). The application of computer technology to enhance the effectiveness of family therapy. *Family Therapy, 13*(1), 5–13.

Yalom, I. (1986). *Psychotherapy with groups*. Paper presented at the National Conference on Clinical Social Work in San Francisco, CA.

Yaron v. Yaron, 83 Misc. 2d 276, 372 New York S 2d 518 (1975).

Young, D. (1974a). Computerized information systems in child care: Techniques for comparison. *Child Welfare, 53*(7), 453–463.

Young, D. (1974b). MIS in child care. *Child Welfare, 53*(2), 102–110.

Zuboff, S. (1983). New worlds of computer-mediated work: Paying heed to staff resistance can help managers. *Public Welfare, 41*(1), 36–44.

Index